THE POWER OF SILENCE

Robert Cardinal Sarah
with Nicolas Diat

The Power of Silence
Against the Dictatorship of Noise

With an Afterword by
Pope Emeritus Benedict XVI

Translated by Michael J. Miller

IGNATIUS PRESS   SAN FRANCISCO

Original French edition:
La force du silence: Contre la dictature du bruit
© 2016 by Librairie Arthème Fayard, Paris, France

Front cover photograph:
The Pantheon, Rome
© iStock photo/Barcin

Cover design by Roxanne Mei Lum

For Benedict XVI, great friend of God,
master of silence and prayer.

For Raymond-Marie Tchidimbo,
former Archbishop of Conakry,
prisoner and victim of a bloody dictatorship.

For all the unknown Carthusians who have been seeking God
for almost a thousand years.

What is it then that this desire and this inability proclaim to us, but that there was once in man a true happiness of which there now remain to him only the mark and empty trace, which he in vain tries to fill from all his surroundings, seeking from things absent the help he does not obtain in things present? But these are all inadequate, because the infinite abyss can only be filled by an infinite and immutable object, that is to say, only by God Himself.

—Blaise Pascal, *Pensées*

O dialect of my interior village,
Sweet speech of my imaginary lands,
Riverside jargon of my invisible stream,
Language of my country, of my spiritual fatherland,
O word more dear to me than French itself,
O my silence! I speak you and recite you.
I sing you a thousand times for my soul's delight
And I hear you resound like triumphant organs.

—Jean Mogin, *Pâtures du silence*
[Pastures of silence]

CONTENTS

INTRODUCTION

Why did Robert Cardinal Sarah decide to devote a book to silence? We spoke for the first time about this beautiful subject in April 2015. We were returning to Rome after spending several days in the Abbey in Lagrasse.

At that magnificent monastery, located between Carcassonne and Narbonne, the cardinal paid a visit to his friend, Brother Vincent. Shattered by multiple sclerosis, the young religious knew that he was reaching the end of his life. In the prime of life, he found himself paralyzed, confined to his bed in the infirmary, condemned to merciless medical protocols. The smallest breath was an immense effort for him. On this earth, Brother Vincent-Marie of the Resurrection was already living in the Great Silence of heaven.

Their first meeting had taken place on October 25, 2014. That day left a deep impression on Cardinal Sarah. Right away he recognized an ardent soul, a hidden saint, a great friend of God. How could anyone forget Brother Vincent's spiritual strength, his silence, the beauty of his smile, the cardinal's emotion, the tears, the modesty, the colliding sentiments? Brother Vincent was incapable of uttering a simple sentence because the sickness deprived him of the use of speech. He could only lift his gaze toward the cardinal. He could only contemplate him, steadily, tenderly, lovingly. Brother Vincent's bloodshot eyes already had the brightness of eternity.

That sunny autumn day, as we left the little room where the monks and the nurses ceaselessly took over from one another with extraordinary devotion, the Abbot of Lagrasse, Father Emmanuel-Marie, brought us into the monastery gardens, near the church. It was necessary to get some air in order to accept God's silent will, this hidden plan that was inexorably carrying off a young, good religious toward unknown shores, while his body lay tormented.

The cardinal returned several times to pray with his friend, Brother Vincent. The patient's condition kept worsening, but the quality of the silence that sealed the dialogue of a great prelate and a little monk grew in an increasingly spiritual way. When he was in Rome, the cardinal often called the Brother. The one spoke gently, and the other remained silent. Cardinal Sarah spoke again to Brother Vincent a few days before his death. He was able to hear his breathing, husky and discordant, the attacks of pain, the last efforts of his heart, and to give him his blessing.

On Sunday, April 10, 2016, when Cardinal Sarah had come to Argenteuil for the conclusion of the exhibition of the Holy Tunic of Christ, Brother Vincent gave up his soul to God, surrounded by Father Emmanuel-Marie and his family. How can the mystery of Brother Vincent be understood? After so many trials, the end of his journey was peaceful. The rays from paradise passed noiselessly through the windows of his room.

During the last months of his life, the little patient prayed a lot for the cardinal. The monks who cared for the Brother at every moment are certain that he remained alive for a few additional months so as to protect Robert Sarah better. Brother Vincent knew that the wolves were lying in wait, that his friend needed him, that he was counting on him.

This friendship was born in silence, it grew in silence, and it continues to exist in silence.

The meetings with Brother Vincent were a fragment of eternity. We never doubted the importance of each of the minutes spent with him. Silence made it possible to raise every sentiment toward the most perfect state. When it was necessary to leave the abbey, we knew that Vincent's silence would make us stronger to confront the world's noises.

On that Sunday in spring when Brother Vincent joined the angels of heaven, the cardinal wished to come to Lagrasse. A great calm reigned over the whole monastery. The Brother's silence had descended upon the places that he had known. Of course it was not easy to walk past the deserted infirmary.

In the choir of the church, where the Brother's body reposed for several days, the prayer of the monks was beautiful.

An African cardinal came to bury the young religious with whom he was never able to have a discussion. The son of the Guinean bush spoke in silence with a little French saint; this friendship is unique and indestructible.

The Power of Silence could never have existed without Brother Vincent. He showed us that the silence into which illness had plunged him allowed him to enter ever more deeply into the truth of things. God's reasons are often mysterious. Why did he decide to try so severely a joyful young man who was asking for nothing? Why such a cruel, violent, and painful sickness? Why this sublime meeting between a cardinal who had arrived at the summit of the Church and a sick person confined to his room? Silence was the salt that seasoned this story. Silence had the last word. Silence was the elevator to heaven.

Who was looking for Brother Vincent? Who came to take him without a word? God.

For Brother Vincent-Marie of the Resurrection, the program was simple. It fit into three words: God or nothing.

Another stage marks this spiritual friendship. Without Brother Vincent, without Father Emmanuel-Marie, we would never have gone to the Grande Chartreuse.

When the idea germinated of asking the Father General of the Carthusian Order to take part in this book, we scarcely thought that such a project was possible. The cardinal did not want to disturb the silence of the principal monastery of the Order, and it is extremely rare for the Father General to speak.

Nevertheless, on Wednesday, February 3, 2016, in the early afternoon, our train stopped at the station in Chambéry ...

The gray sky was suspended over the mountains that surround the town. The sadness of winter seemed to set the landscape and the people in a sticky glue. As we approached the Chartreuse mountain range, a snowstorm started and covered the valley with a perfect white. After coming through St. Laurent du Pont on the famous way of Saint Bruno, the road became almost impassable.

Driving along by the high walls of the monastery, we came across the novice master, Father Seraphico, and several young monks who were returning from their walk. They turned around as the cardinal's automobile passed, greeting him discreetly. Then the car stopped in front of a long, solemn, austere building: we had arrived at the Grande Chartreuse. Thick clumps of snowflakes fell, the wind rushed into the fir trees, but the silence already enveloped our hearts. We slowly crossed the main courtyard, then were directed to the large priors' house, built by Dom Innocent le Masson in the seventeenth century, which opens onto the imposing officers' cloister.

The seventy-fourth Father General of the Carthusian Order, Dom Dysmas de Lassus, welcomed the cardinal with an especially touching simplicity.

At the heart of this mystical geography, Saint Bruno's dream of solitude and silence has taken shape since the year 1084. In the historical anthology *La Grande Chartreuse, au-delà du silence*, Nathalie Nabert speaks about an incomparable blend: "Carthusian spirituality was born of the encounter of a soul and a place, from the coincidence between a desire for a quiet life in God and a landscape, *Cartusie solitudinem*, as the ancient documents describe it, the isolation and wild beauty of which attracts souls to even greater solitude, far from the 'fugitive shadows of the world', allowing men to pass 'from the storm of this world to the tranquil, sure repose of the port'. That is how Bruno of Cologne would refer to it in the evening of his life in the letter that he writes to his friend Raoul le Verd to attract him to the desert."

Quickly, after a conversation that lasted no more than five minutes, we arrived at our cells. From the window of the room where I was settled, I could contemplate the monastery, clothed in its white mantle, nestled against the overwhelming slope of the Grand Som, more beautiful than any of the images that have built up the immutable myth of the Grande Chartreuse. The long, solemn series of separate buildings lined up in a row, then, down below, the buildings housing the "obediences" or workshops of the lay Brothers.

Very rarely can an outsider pass through the doors of the citadel. In this inspired place, the long tradition of the eremitic Orders, the tragedies of history, and the beauty of creation cross paths. But that is nothing compared with the depth of the spiritual realities; the Grande Chartreuse is a world where souls have abandoned themselves in God and for God.

At half past five, Vespers (Evening Prayer) gathered the Carthusians in the narrow, dark conventual church. In order to get there, it was necessary to walk through endless cold, austere corridors, where I kept thinking about the generations of Carthusians who had hastened their steps in order to participate in the Divine Office. The Grande Chartreuse is the house of the centuries, the voiceless house, the holy house.

I thought again also about the hateful, disturbing eviction of the religious on April 29, 1903, following the passage of Émile Combes' law on the expulsion of the religious congregations, which was reminiscent of the dark hours of the French Revolution and the forced departure of the Carthusians in 1792. It is necessary to reflect on that profanation and the arrival in the ancient monastery of an infantry battalion after it had smashed the heavy entrance gates, then of two squadrons of dragoons and hundreds of demolitions specialists. The magistrates and the soldiers made their way into the church, and the Fathers were brought out of their choir stalls one by one and led outdoors. The enemies of God's silence triumphed in shame. On the one side were the fierce supporters of a world liberated from its Creator, and on the other—the faithful, poor Carthusians, whose only wealth was the beautiful silence of heaven.

On that February evening in 2016, from the first gallery, I saw the white, hooded shadows who were taking possession of the stalls. The Fathers quickly opened the large antiphonaries that allowed them to follow the musical scores of the Vesper texts. The light diminished little by little, the chanting of the psalms followed; the cardinal, who had taken his place beside Dom Dysmas, cautiously turned the pages of the ancient books to follow the prayer. Behind him, the rood screen that separated the stalls of the Fathers in choir from those of the lay Brothers sketched in the half-light a large cross that seemed to lend still greater dignity to this striking darkness.

Carthusian plain chant imparts a slowness, a depth, and a piety that is sweet and at the same time rough. At the end of Vespers, the monks intoned the solemn *Salve Regina*. Since the twelfth century, every day, the Carthusians have intoned this antiphon to the Virgin Mary. Today there are hardly any monasteries where these notes still resound.

Outside, night had fallen, and the faint lights of the monastery finally stopped time. The only thing that broke the silence was the rumbling of the packs of snow that fell from the roofs. A fog seemed to climb from the depths of the narrow valley, and the black mountain slopes provided grandiose, gloomy scenery.

The monks went back to the cells. After walking through the immense corridors of the cemetery cloister, each one returned to the *cubiculum* where he passed such a significant part of his earthly existence. The silence of the Grande Chartreuse reasserted its inalienable rights. While walking through the gallery of maps, where depictions of the Charterhouses from all over Europe decorated the walls, it was easy to see how far Saint Bruno's Order had been able to spread so as to satisfy the thirst of so many religious who wanted to find heaven, far from the noises of the world.

While the earth is sleeping, or trying to forget, the nocturnal Divine Office is the burning heart of Carthusian life. On the first page of the antiphonary that Dom Dysmas had prepared before I arrived, I could read this notice: "*Antiphonarium nocturnum, ad usum sacri ordinis cartusiensis.*" It was quarter past midnight, and the monks were extinguishing the few vigil lights that were still lit in the church. Perfect darkness covered the whole sanctuary when the Carthusians intoned the first prayers. The night made it possible to observe more clearly than ever the glowing point of light marking the presence of the Blessed Sacrament. The sound of the wood in the old walnut stalls seemed to blend with the voices of the monks. The psalms followed one after the other to the slow rhythm of a Gregorian chant tone; those who regularly attend the Divine Office at Benedictine abbeys might regret the lack of purity in the style. But Night Prayer does not lend itself well to merely esthetic considerations. The liturgy unfolds in a half-light that seeks God. There are the voices of the Carthusians, and a perfect silence.

Toward half past two in the morning, the bells rang for the Angelus. The monks left the church one by one. Is the nocturnal Divine Office madness or a miracle? In all the Charterhouses in the world, night prepares for day, and day prepares for night. We must never forget the sweet, powerful statement of Saint Bruno in his letter to Raoul le Verd: "Here God gives his athletes, in return for the labor of the combat, the desired reward: a peace that the world does not know and joy in the Holy Spirit."

The Prefect of the Congregation for Divine Worship and the Discipline of the Sacraments was profoundly touched by the two nocturnal services that marked his stay. He shares with Isaac the Syrian this beautiful thought from the *Ascetical Homilies*:

> Prayer offered up at night possesses a great power, more than the prayer of the day-time. Therefore all the righteous prayed during the night, while combatting the heaviness of the body and the sweetness of sleep and repelling corporeal nature.... There is nothing that even Satan fears so much as prayer that is offered during the vigilance at night.... For this reason the devil smites them with violent warfare, in order to hinder them, if possible, from this work [as was the case with Anthony the Great, Blessed Paul, Arsenius, and other Desert Fathers].... But those who have resisted his wicked stratagems even a little, who have tasted the gifts of God that are granted during vigil, and who have experienced in themselves the magnitude of God's help that is always nigh to them, utterly disdain him and all his devices.... Which of the solitaries, though possessing all the virtues together, could neglect this work, and not be reckoned to be idle without it? For night vigil is the light of the thinking, and by it the understanding is exalted, the thought is collected, and the mind takes flight and gazes at spiritual things and by prayer it is rejuvenated and shines brilliantly.

For the Cardinal, night warms a man's heart. The one who keeps vigil at night goes out of himself, the better to find God. The silence of night is the most capable of crushing all the dictatorships of noise. When darkness descends upon the earth, the asceticism of silence can acquire more luminous dimensions. The words of the Psalmist are final: "In the night ... I think of God, and I moan; I meditate, and my spirit faints. You keep my eyelids from closing; I am so troubled that I cannot speak. I consider the days of old, I remember the years long ago. I commune with my heart in the night; I meditate and search my spirit" (Ps 77:2–6).

Before we departed, the cardinal wanted to have a moment of recollection in the cemetery. We walked through the monastery, those long, magnificent galleries, like labyrinths carved out by prayer. The large cloister measures 709 feet from north to south, 75 feet from east to west, or a quadrilateral with a perimeter of 1,568 feet. The foundations of this Gothic complex go back to the twelfth century; since then, permanent silence has reigned. In the Carthusian deserts, the cemetery is located at the center of the cloister.

The graves bore no names, dates, or mementos. On the one side, there were stone crosses, for the generals of the Order, and on the other—wooden crosses for the Fathers and the lay Brothers. The Carthusians are buried in the ground without a coffin, without a tombstone; no distinctive mark recalls their individual lives. I asked Dom Dysmas de Lassus the location of the crosses of the monks who had been his contemporaries and whose deaths he had witnessed. Dom Dysmas no longer knew. "The gusts of wind and the mosses have already done their work", he declared. He could find only the grave of Dom André Poisson, one of his predecessors, who died in April 2005. The former general died at night, alone, in his cell; he departed to join all the sons of Saint Bruno, and the vast troop of hermits, in heaven.

Since 1084, Carthusians have not wanted to leave any trace. God alone matters. *Stat Crux dum volvitur orbis*—the world turns and the Cross remains.

Before leaving, in the sunshine beneath an immaculate blue sky, the cardinal blessed the tombs.

A few moments later, we left the Grande Chartreuse. The Benedictine monk who had come to pick us up declared: "You are leaving paradise ..."

In the *Dialogues of the Carmelites*, Georges Bernanos wrote: "When wise men reach the end of their wisdom, it is advisable to listen to the children." The Carthusians are wise men and children together.

During this year of work, a phrase from the *Diary of a Country Priest* by Bernanos was the reliable compass of our reflection:

> My inner quiet—blessed by God—has never really isolated me. I feel all human-kind can enter and I receive them thus only at the threshold of my home.... Alas, mine is but a very precarious shelter. But I imagine the quiet of some souls is like a vast refuge. Sinners at the end of their tether can creep in and rest, and leave comforted, forgetting the great invisible temple where they lay down their burden for a while.

Similarly, in *Le Silence comme introduction à la métaphysique* [Silence as an introduction to metaphysics], the philosopher Joseph Rassam asserted that "silence is within us the wordless language of the finite being that, by its own weight, seeks and carries our movement toward the infinite Being. This is to say that thought does not arrive at the affirmation of God on its own power, but through its docility to the prevenient light of being that is received and welcomed as a gift. The act of silence that defines this reception bears within it prayer, in other words, the movement by which the soul raises itself to God." For Joseph Rassam, as for Robert Cardinal Sarah, "although speech characterizes man, silence is what defines him, because speech acquires sense only in terms of this silence." This is the beautiful and important message of *The Power of Silence*.

On April 16, 2013, a few weeks after his election, Pope Francis recalled: "The prophets, 'you killed them', and then venerated them. [They build monuments for them, but after killing them.] That is a manifestation of resistance to the Holy Spirit." In this world, the man who speaks about silence can experience the same ups and downs. Admiration, rejection, and condemnation follow one another and disappear.

The words of the silent are often true prophecies but also lights that people seek to extinguish.

In this book, Robert Cardinal Sarah had only one aim, which is summed up in this thought: "Silence is difficult, but it makes man able to allow himself to be led by God. Silence is born of silence. Through God the silent one, we can gain access to silence. And man is unceasingly surprised by the light that bursts forth then. Silence is more important than any other human work. For it expresses God. The true revolution comes from silence; it leads us toward God and others so as to place ourselves humbly and generously at their service" (Thought 68, *The Power of Silence*).

What virtue does Cardinal Sarah expect from the reading of this book? Humility. From this perspective, he can adopt as his own the step taken by Rafael Cardinal Merry del Val. Having retired from the public business of the Church, the former Secretary of State of Saint Pius X had composed a beautiful "Litany of Humility", which he recited every day after celebrating Mass:

> O Jesus, meek and humble of heart,
> Make my heart like yours.
> From self-will, deliver me, O Lord.

From the desire of being esteemed, deliver me, O Lord.
From the desire of being loved, deliver me, O Lord.
From the desire of being extolled, deliver me, O Lord.
From the desire of being honored, deliver me, O Lord.
From the desire of being praised, deliver me, O Lord.
From the desire of being preferred to others, deliver me,
    O Lord.
From the desire of being consulted, deliver me, O Lord.
From the desire of being approved, deliver me, O Lord.
From the desire to be understood, deliver me, O Lord.
From the desire to be visited, deliver me, O Lord.
From the fear of being humiliated, deliver me, O Lord.
From the fear of being despised, deliver me, O Lord.
From the fear of suffering rebukes, deliver me, O Lord.
From the fear of being calumniated, deliver me, O Lord.
From the fear of being forgotten, deliver me, O Lord.
From the fear of being ridiculed, deliver me, O Lord.
From the fear of being suspected, deliver me, O Lord.
From the fear of being wronged, deliver me, O Lord.
From the fear of being abandoned, deliver me, O Lord.
From the fear of being refused, deliver me, O Lord.
That others may be loved more than I,
Lord, grant me the grace to desire it.
That others may be esteemed more than I,
Lord, grant me the grace to desire it.
That, in the opinion of the world, others may increase
    and I may decrease,
Lord, grant me the grace to desire it.
That others may be chosen and I set aside,
Lord, grant me the grace to desire it.
That others may be praised and I go unnoticed,
Lord, grant me the grace to desire it.
That others may be preferred to me in everything,
Lord, grant me the grace to desire it.
That others may become holier than I,
provided that I may become as holy as I should,
Lord, grant me the grace to desire it.
At being unknown and poor,

Lord, I want to rejoice.
At being deprived of the natural perfections of body and
    mind,
Lord, I want to rejoice.
When people do not think of me,
Lord, I want to rejoice.
When they assign to me the meanest tasks,
Lord, I want to rejoice.
When they do not even deign to make use of me,
Lord, I want to rejoice.
When they never ask my opinion,
Lord, I want to rejoice.
When they leave me at the lowest place,
Lord, I want to rejoice.
When they never compliment me,
Lord, I want to rejoice.
When they blame me in season and out of season,
Lord, I want to rejoice.
Blessed are those who suffer persecution for justice' sake,
For theirs is the kingdom of heaven.

Nicolas Diat
Rome, September 2, 2016

I

SILENCE VERSUS THE WORLD'S NOISE

*The greatest things are accomplished in silence—not in the clamor and dis-
play of superficial eventfulness, but in the deep clarity of inner vision; in the
almost imperceptible start of decision, in quiet overcoming and hidden sacrifice.
Spiritual conception happens when the heart is quickened by love, and the free
will stirs to action. The silent forces are the strong forces. Let us turn now to
the stillest event of all, stillest because it came from the remoteness beyond the
noise of any possible intrusion—from God.*

—Romano Guardini, *The Lord*

NICOLAS DIAT: *In the anthology* Voix cartusienne, *the Carthusian Dom
Augustin Guillerand correctly writes that "solitude and silence are guests of
the soul. The soul that possesses them carries them with it everywhere. The
one that lacks them finds them nowhere. In order to re-enter silence, it is
not enough to stop the movement of one's lips and the movement of one's
thoughts. That is only being quiet. Being quiet is a condition for silence, but
it is not silence. Silence is a word, silence is a thought. It is a word and a
thought in which all words and all thoughts are concentrated." How are we to
understand this beautiful idea?*

ROBERT CARDINAL SARAH:
1. There is one great question: how can man really be in the image
of God? He must enter into silence.

When he drapes himself in silence, as God himself dwells in a great
silence, man is close to heaven, or, rather, he allows God to manifest
himself in him.

We encounter God only in the eternal silence in which he abides.
Have you ever heard the voice of God as you hear mine?

God's voice is silent. Indeed, man, too, must seek to become silence. In speaking about Adam in paradise, Saint Augustine wrote: "Vivebat fruens Deo, ex quo bono erat bonus" (He lived in the joy of God, and, by virtue of this good, he himself was good.) By living with the silent God, and in him, we ourselves become silent. In his book *I Want to See God*, Father Marie-Eugène de l'Enfant Jésus writes:

> God speaks in silence, and silence alone seems able to express Him. For the spiritual person who has known the touch of God, silence and God seem to be identified. And so, to find God again, where would he go, if not to the most silent depths of his soul, into those regions that are so hidden that nothing can any longer disturb them?
>
> When he has reached there, he preserves with jealous care the silence that gives him God. He defends it against any agitation, even that of his own powers.

2. At the heart of man there is an innate silence, for God abides in the innermost part of every person. God is silence, and this divine silence dwells in man. In God we are inseparably bound up with silence. The Church can affirm that mankind is the daughter of a silent God; for men are the sons of silence.

3. God carries us, and we live with him at every moment by keeping silence. Nothing will make us discover God better than his silence inscribed in the center of our being. If we do not cultivate this silence, how can we find God? Man likes to travel, create, make great discoveries. But he remains outside of himself, far from God, who is silently in his soul. I want to recall how important it is to cultivate silence in order to be truly with God. Saint Paul, drawing on the Book of Deuteronomy, explains that we will not encounter God by crossing the seas, because he is in our heart:

> Do not say in your heart, "Who will ascend into heaven?" (that is, to bring Christ down) or "Who will descend into the abyss?" (that is, to bring Christ up from the dead). But what does [the law] say? The word is near you, on your lips and in your heart (that is, the word of faith which we preach); because, if you confess with your lips that

Jesus is Lord and believe in your heart that God raised him from the
dead, you will be saved. (Rom 10:6–9; Deut 30:12–14, 16)

4. Through Sacred Scripture, when it is listened to and meditated
upon in silence, divine graces are poured out on man. It is in faith,
and not by traveling in distant lands or by crossing seas and continents,
that we can find and contemplate God. Actually, it is through long
hours of poring over Sacred Scripture, after resisting all the attacks of
the Prince of this world, that we will reach God.

Dom Augustin Guillerand is on the right track: what men possess in themselves, they find nowhere else. Unless silence dwells in
man, and unless solitude is a state in which he allows himself to be
shaped, the creature is deprived of God. There is no place on earth
where God is more present than in the human heart. This heart truly
is God's abode, the temple of silence.

5. No prophet ever encountered God without withdrawing into solitude and silence. Moses, Elijah, and John the Baptist encountered
God in the great silence of the desert. Today, too, monks seek God
in solitude and silence. I am speaking, not just about a geographical
solitude or movement, but about an interior state. It is not enough to
be quiet, either. It is necessary to become silence.

For, even before the desert, the solitude, and the silence, God is
already in man. The true desert is within us, in our soul.

Strengthened with this knowledge, we can understand how silence
is indispensable if we are to find God. The Father waits for his children in their own hearts.

6. It is necessary to leave our interior turmoil in order to find God.
Despite the agitations, the busyness, the easy pleasures, God remains
silently present. He is in us like a thought, a word, and a presence
whose secret sources are buried in God himself, inaccessible to
human inspection.

Solitude is the best state in which to hear God's silence. For someone who wants to find silence, solitude is the mountain that he must
climb. If a person isolates himself by going away to a monastery, he
comes first to seek silence. And yet, the goal of his search is within
him. God's silent presence already dwells in his heart. The silence

that we pursue confusedly is found in our own hearts and reveals God to us.

Alas, the worldly powers that seek to shape modern man systematically do away with silence.

I am not afraid to assert that the false priests of modernity, who declare a sort of war on silence, have lost the battle. For we can remain silent in the midst of the biggest messes and most despicable commotion, in the midst of the racket and howling of those infernal machines that draw us into functionalism and activism by snatching us away from any transcendent dimension and from any interior life.

For many mystics, the fruitfulness of silence and solitude is similar to that of the word pronounced at the creation of the world. How do you explain this great mystery?

7. The word is not just a sound; it is a person and a presence. God is the eternal Word, the *Logos*. This is what Saint John of the Cross declares in his *Spiritual Maxims* when he writes: "The Father spoke one Word, which was His Son, and this Word He always speaks in eternal silence, and in silence must It be heard by the soul." The Book of Wisdom already pointed out this same interpretation in regard to the way in which God intervened to deliver his chosen people from their captivity in Egypt. This unforgettable act took place during the night: "While gentle silence enveloped all things, and night in its swift course was now half gone, your all-powerful word leaped from heaven, from the royal throne" (Wis 18:14–15). Later on, this verse would be understood by the Christian liturgical tradition as a prefiguration of the silent Incarnation of the Word in the crib in Bethlehem. The [contemporary French] hymn for the feast of the Presentation of the Lord in the Temple also sings about this Coming: "Who among us can understand what begins here noiselessly, the offering of the grain as the first-fruits?" Saint John Chrysostom, in his *Homilies on the Gospel of Saint Matthew*, does not hesitate to add: "Therefore [the fact] that He was of us, and of our substance, and of the Virgin's womb, is manifest from these things, and from others beside; but how, is not also manifest. Do not either thou then inquire; but receive what is revealed, and be not curious about what is kept secret." Let us accept it in silence and faith.

8. God achieves everything, acts in all circumstances, and brings about all our interior transformations. But he does it when we wait for him in recollection and silence.

In silence, not in the turmoil and noise, God enters into the innermost depths of our being. Father Marie-Eugène de l'Enfant-Jésus was right when he wrote in I Want to See God: "This divine law surprises us. It goes so much against our experience of the natural laws of the world. Here below, any profound transformation, any great external change produces a certain agitation and noise. The great river, for example, reaches the ocean only by the sounding onward rush of its water." If we observe the great works, the most powerful acts, the most extraordinary and striking interior transformations that God carries out in man, we are forced to admit that he works in silence. Baptism brings about a marvelous creation in the soul of the infant or the adult who receives this sacrament in the name of the Father, of the Son, and of the Holy Spirit. The newly baptized person is immersed in the name of the Trinity; he is inserted into the Triune God. A new life is given to him, enabling him to perform the godly acts of the children of God. We heard the words of the priest: "I baptize you ... "; we saw the water flow on the infant's forehead. Yet we perceived nothing of this immersion into the inner life of the Trinity, grace, and creation which requires nothing less than the personal, almighty action of God. God has uttered his Word in the soul in silence. In that same silent darkness, the subsequent developments of grace generally come.

9. In June 2012, in a luminous lectio divina at the Basilica of Saint John Lateran, Benedict XVI explained the reality and the deep meaning of baptism:

> We have already heard that the Lord's last words to his disciples on this earth were: "Go therefore and make disciples of all nations, baptizing them in the name of the Father and of the Son and of the Holy Spirit" (cf. Mt 28:19). Make disciples and baptize them.... Why is it necessary to be baptized?... A first door opens if we read these words of the Lord carefully. The choice of the word "in the name of the Father" in the Greek text is very important: the Lord says "eis" and not "en", that is, not "in the name" of the Trinity—as when we say that a vice-prefect speaks "on behalf" of the prefect, an ambassador

speaks "on behalf" of the government: no. It says: "*eis to onoma*", that is, an immersion into the name of the Trinity, a being inserted in the name of the Trinity [that is, a silent, invisible but real and life-giving] interpenetration of being in God and of our being, a being immersed in God the Trinity, Father, Son and Holy Spirit; just as it is in marriage, for example. Two people become one flesh, they become a new and unique reality with a new and unique name.... Consequently, being baptized means being united to God; in a unique, new existence we belong to God, we are immersed in God himself.

It is the same with priestly ordination. In silence, through the sacrament of Holy Orders, a man becomes not only an *alter Christus*, another Christ, but much more: he is *ipse Christus*, Christ himself. At that moment nothing appears externally, but in the silence, in the depths of his being, there is a true and real identification with Christ. Saint Ambrose, in his treatise *On the Mysteries*, exhorts us, saying: "You saw there the deacon, you saw the priest, you saw the chief priest [i.e., the bishop]. Consider not the bodily forms, but the grace of the Mysteries." Externally, as priests, we remain sinners, but in reality we are as though "transubstantiated" and configured to Christ himself. In the act of transubstantiation, the priest takes the role of Christ.

10. The transubstantiation of bread and wine into the Body and Blood of Christ, the most extraordinary, the most momentous transformation, occurs in the utmost sacred silence. We hear the priest pronounce the words of the consecration, but the miracle of transubstantiation comes about imperceptibly, like all the greatest works of God. Silence is the law of the divine plans.

11. God's being has always been present in us in an absolute silence. And a human being's own silence allows him to enter into a relationship with the Word that is at the bottom of his heart. Thus, in the desert, we do not speak. We listen in silence; man enters into a silence that is God.

How can we define silence in its simplest meaning, in other words, the silence of everyday life? According to the Petit Robert *[a French dictionary], silence is "the attitude of someone who refrains from speaking". It refers to "the absence*

of noise or agitation, the state of a place where no sound can be heard".
Can silence be defined in no other way than by negation? Is the absence of
speech, noise, or sound always silence? Similarly, is it not paradoxical to try
to "speak" about silence in everyday life?

12. Silence is not an absence. On the contrary, it is the manifestation of a presence, the most intense of all presences. In modern society, silence has come into disrepute; this is the symptom of a serious, worrisome illness. The real questions of life are posed in silence. Our blood flows through our veins without making any noise, and we can hear our heartbeats only in silence.

13. On July 4, 2010, in a homily for the eighth centenary of the birth of Pope Celestine V, Benedict XVI gravely insisted on the fact that "we live in a society in which it seems that every space, every moment must be 'filled' with projects, activities and noise; there is often no time even to listen or to converse. Dear brothers and sisters, let us not fear to create silence, within and outside ourselves, if we wish to be able not only to become aware of God's voice but also to make out the voice of the person beside us, the voices of others." Benedict XVI and John Paul II often conferred a positive dimension on silence. Indeed, although it is associated with solitude and the desert, silence is by no means self-absorption or muteness, just as true speech is not garrulousness but, rather, a condition for being present to God, to neighbor, and to oneself.

What is the correct understanding of exterior silence? "God is the friend of silence. See how nature—trees, flowers, grass—grows in silence; see the stars, the moon, and the sun, how they move in silence", Saint Teresa of Calcutta said poetically [in her book *A Gift for God*].

14. The episode of Jesus' visit to the home of Martha and Mary, related by Saint Luke (Lk 10:38–42), eloquently illustrates the priceless character of silence in everyday life: "Martha, Martha, you are anxious and troubled about many things" (Lk 10:41). Jesus rebukes Martha, not for being busy in the kitchen—after all, she did have to prepare the meal—but for her inattentive interior attitude, betrayed by her annoyance with her sister. Since the days of Origen, some

commentators have tended to heighten the contrast between the two women, to the point of seeing in them respectively the example of an active life that is too scattered and the model of the contemplative life that is lived out in silence, listening, and interior prayer. In reality, Jesus seems to sketch the outlines of a spiritual pedagogy: we should always make sure to be Mary before becoming Martha. Otherwise, we run the risk of becoming literally bogged down in activism and agitation, the unpleasant consequences of which emerge in the Gospel account: panic, fear of working without help, an inattentive interior attitude, annoyance like Martha's toward her sister, the feeling that God is leaving us alone without intervening effectively. Thus, in speaking to Martha, Jesus says: "Mary has chosen the good portion" (Lk 10:42). He reminds her of the importance of "calming and quieting the soul" (see Ps 131:2) so as to listen to one's heart. Christ tenderly invites her to stop so as to return to her heart, the place of true welcome and the dwelling place of God's silent tenderness, from which she had been led away by the activity to which she was devoting herself so noisily. All activity must be preceded by an intense life of prayer, contemplation, seeking and listening to God's will. In his Apostolic Letter *Novo millennio ineunte*, John Paul II writes: "It is important however that what we propose, with the help of God, should be profoundly rooted in contemplation and prayer. Ours is a time of continual movement which often leads to restlessness, with the risk of 'doing for the sake of doing'. We must resist this temptation by trying 'to be' before trying 'to do'." This is the innermost, unchangeable desire of a monk. But it happens also to be the deepest aspiration of every person who seeks the Eternal One. For man can encounter God in truth only in silence and solitude, both interior and exterior.

15. The more we are clothed in glory and honors, the more we are raised in dignity, the more we are invested with public responsibilities, prestige, and temporal offices, whether as laymen, priests, or bishops, the more we need to advance in humility and to cultivate carefully the sacred dimension of our interior life by constantly seeking to see the face of God in prayer, meditation, contemplation, and asceticism. It can happen that a good, pious priest, once he is raised to the episcopal dignity, quickly falls into mediocrity and a concern for

worldly success. Overwhelmed by the weight of the duties that are incumbent on him, worried about his power, his authority, and the material needs of his office, he gradually runs out of steam. He manifests in his being and in his works a desire for promotion, a longing for prestige, and a spiritual degradation. He is harmful to himself and to the flock over which the Holy Spirit set him as guardian to feed the Church of God, which God acquired for himself by the blood of his own Son. We all run the danger of being preoccupied with worldly business and concerns if we neglect the interior life, prayer, the daily face-to-face encounter with God, the ascetical practices necessary for every contemplative and every person who wants to see the Eternal One and to live with him.

16. Recall what Saint Gregory the Great wrote in a letter to Theoctista, the sister of the Byzantine Emperor Flavius Mauricius Tiberius, which is found in the collection *Registrum Epistolarum*. Faced with a tension between monastic life and his papal office, with all the social and political responsibilities that the latter involved, he bitterly spelled out in these terms his difficulties in harmonizing contemplation and action:

> I have lost the profound joys of my peace and quiet, and I seem to have risen externally, while falling internally. Wherefore, I deplore my expulsion far from the face of my Creator. For I was trying every day to move outside the world, outside the flesh, to drive all corporeal images from my mind's eye and to regard the joys of Heaven.... "You cast them down while they were being raised up" [Ps 72(73):18]. For he did not say "You cast them down after they had been raised up," but "while they were being raised up," because the wicked and those who seem to rise up from outside, while propped up by a temporal office, collapse on the inside. And so their being raised up is itself their ruin.... Indeed there are many who know how to control external successes in such a way that they in no way collapse internally because of them. So it is written: "God does not despise the powerful; since he is powerful also [Job 36:5]."

Saint Gregory underscores the conflict that he is experiencing; he wants to harmonize the contemplative life and the active life, symbolized by Mary and Martha. A deep tension between silence and monastic peace and his new temporal duties could be resolved only by intensifying his interior life and an intimate relationship with God.

17. Similarly, in a letter to Raoul le Verd, Saint Bruno writes with his characteristic tact, commenting on Saint Luke:

> In any case, what benefits and divine exaltation the silence and solitude of the desert hold in store for those who love it, only those who have experienced it can know. For here men of strong will can enter into themselves and remain there as much as they like, diligently cultivating the seeds of virtue and eating the fruits of paradise with joy. Here they can acquire the eye that wounds the Bridegroom with love, by the limpidity of its gaze, and whose purity allows them to see God himself. Here they can observe a busy leisure and rest in quiet activity. Here also God crowns his athletes for their stern struggle with the hoped-for reward: a peace unknown to the world and joy in the Holy Spirit.... This life is the best part chosen by Mary, never to be taken away from her.... I could only wish, brother, that you too, had such ... divine love. If only a love like this would take possession of you! Immediately, all the glory in the world would seem like so much dirt to you, whatever the smooth words and false attractions it offered to deceive you. Wealth and its concomitant anxieties you would cast off without a thought, as a burden to the freedom of the spirit....
>
> For what could be more perverted, more reckless and contrary to nature and right order, than to love the creature more than the Creator, what passes away more than what lasts forever, or to seek rather the goods of earth than those of heaven?... It is rather divine love which proves itself the more useful, precisely to the extent that it is more in accord with right reason. For what could be [so] beneficial and right, so fitting and connatural to human nature as to love the good? Yet what other good can compare with God? Indeed, what other good is there besides God? [Hence] the soul that has attained some degree of holiness and has experienced in some small measure the incomparable loveliness, beauty and splendour of this good, is set on fire with love and cries out: "My soul is thirsting for God, the God of my life; when shall I enter and see the face of God?" (Ps 42[41]:2)

The desire to see God is what urges us to love solitude and silence. For silence is where God dwells. He drapes himself in silence.

In every era, this experience of an interior life and an intimate, loving relationship with God has remained indispensable for those who seek true happiness.

18. Every day it is important to be silent so as to determine the outlines of one's future action. The contemplative life is not the only state in which man must make the effort to leave his heart in silence.

In everyday life, whether secular, civil, or religious, exterior silence is necessary. Thomas Merton wrote in *The Sign of Jonas*:

> Exterior Silence—its special necessity in our world in which there is so much noise and inane speech. As *protest* and *reparation* against the "sin" of noise.
> ... Silence not a virtue, noise not a sin. True. But the turmoil and confusion and constant noise of modern society are the expression of the *ambiance* of its greatest sins—its godlessness, its despair. A world of propaganda, of endless argument, vituperation, criticism, or simply of chatter, is a world without anything to live for....
> Catholics who associate themselves with that kind of noise, who enter into the Babel of tongues, become to some extent exiles from the city of God. (Mass becomes racket and confusion. Tension—babble. All prayer becomes exterior and interior noise—soulless and hasty repetition of rosary ...).

The Divine Office recited without recollection, without enthusiasm or fervor, or irregularly and sporadically, makes the heart lukewarm and kills the virginity of our love for God. Gradually our priestly ministry can become like the work of a well-digger who drills wells of stagnant water. By living in a world of noise and superficiality, we provoke God's disappointment, and we cannot fail to hear the sadness and complaints of his heart. Thus says Yahweh: "I remember the devotion of your youth, your love as a bride, how you followed me in the wilderness.... My people have committed two evils: they have forsaken me, the fountain of living waters, and hewed out cisterns for themselves, broken cisterns, that can hold no water" (Jer 2:2, 13).

Thomas Merton continues:

> Though it is true that we must know how to bear with noise, to have interior life, *by exception* here and there in midst of confusion ..., yet

to resign oneself to a situation in which a community is *constantly* overwhelmed with activity, noise of machines, etc., is an abuse.

What to do? Those who love God should attempt to preserve or create an atmosphere in which He can be found. Christians should have quiet homes. Throw out television, if necessary—not everybody, but those who take this sort of thing seriously....

Let those who can stand a little silence find other people who like silence, and create silence and peace for one another. Bring up their kids not to yell so much. Children are naturally quiet—if they are left alone and not given the needle [i.e., teased] from the cradle upward, in order that they may develop into citizens of a state in which everybody yells and is yelled at.

Provide people with places where they can go to be *quiet*—relax minds and hearts in the presence of God—chapels in the country, or in town also. Reading rooms, hermitages. Retreat houses without a constant ballyhoo of noisy "exercises"—they even yell the stations of the Cross, and not too far from [the Abbey of] Gethsemani either.

The Trappist then concludes: "For many it would mean great renunciation and discipline to give up these sources of noise: but they know that is what they need. Afraid to do it because their neighbors would think they were bats."

Modern society can no longer do without the dictatorship of noise. It lulls us in an illusion of cheap democracy while snatching our freedom away with the subtle violence of the devil, that father of lies. But Jesus repeatedly tells us: "If you continue in my word, you are truly my disciples, and you will know the truth, and the truth will make you free" (Jn 8:31–32).

19. Interior silence is the end of judgments, passions, and desires. Once we have acquired interior silence, we can transport it with us into the world and pray everywhere. But just as interior asceticism cannot be obtained without concrete mortifications, it is absurd to speak about interior silence without exterior silence.

Within silence there is a demand made on each one of us. Man controls his hours of activity if he knows how to enter into silence. The life of silence must be able to precede the active life.

20. The silence of everyday life is an indispensable condition for living with others. Without the capacity for silence, man is incapable of

hearing, loving, and understanding the people around him. Charity is born of silence. It proceeds from a silent heart that is able to hear, to listen, and to welcome. Silence is a condition for otherness and a necessity if one is to understand himself. Without silence, there is neither rest nor serenity nor interior life. Silence is friendship and love, interior harmony and peace. Silence and peace have one and the same heartbeat.

In the noise of everyday life there is always a certain agitation that is stirred up in man. Noise is never serene, and it is not conducive to understanding another person. How right Pascal was when he wrote in his *Pensées*: "All the unhappiness of men arises from one single fact, that they cannot stay quietly in their own chamber."

On the merely physical level, man can find rest only in silence. The most beautiful things in life take place in silence. We can read or write when we have silence at our disposal.

How is even one moment of prayer life imaginable apart from silence?

21. Today, in a highly technological, busy world, how can we find silence? Noise wearies us, and we get the feeling that silence has become an unreachable oasis. How many people are obliged to work in a chaos that distresses and dehumanizes them? Cities have become noisy furnaces in which even nights are not spared the assault of noise.

Without noise, postmodern man falls into a dull, insistent uneasiness. He is accustomed to permanent background noise, which sickens yet reassures him.

Without noise, man is feverish, lost. Noise gives him security, like a drug on which he has become dependent. With its festive appearance, noise is a whirlwind that avoids facing itself. Agitation becomes a tranquilizer, a sedative, a morphine pump, a sort of reverie, an incoherent dream-world. But this noise is a dangerous, deceptive medicine, a diabolic lie that helps man avoid confronting himself in his interior emptiness. The awakening will necessarily be brutal.

22. In *I Want to See God*, Father Marie-Eugène wrote:

We live in a fever of movement and activity. The evil is not simply in the organization of modern life, in the haste that it imposes on what we do, the rapidity and facility that it affords our changing of place.

A more profound evil is in the feverish nervousness of temperaments. People no longer know how to wait and be silent. And yet, they appear to be seeking silence and solitude; they leave familiar circles for new horizons, another atmosphere. Most often, however, this is only so as to divert themselves with fresh impressions.

Whatever changes time may bring, God remains the same, *Tu autem idem Ipse es*; and it is always in silence that He utters His Word and that the soul must receive it. The law of silence is imposed on us as on Teresa. The high-strung excitability of the modern temperament makes it more urgently important, and exacts of us a more resolute effort to respect and to submit to it.

Sounds and emotions detach us from ourselves, whereas silence always forces man to reflect upon his own life.

23. Mankind must join a sort of resistance movement. What will become of our world if it does not look for intervals of silence? Interior rest and harmony can flow only from silence. Without it, life does not exist. The greatest mysteries of the world are born and unfold in silence. How does nature develop? In the greatest silence. A tree grows in silence, and springs of water flow at first in the silence of the ground. The sun that rises over the earth in its splendor and grandeur warms us in silence. What is extraordinary is always silent.

In his mother's womb, an infant grows in silence. When a newborn is sleeping in his crib, his parents love to gaze at him in silence, so as not to awaken him; this spectacle can be contemplated only in silence, in wonder at the mystery of man in his original purity.

24. The wonders of creation are silent, and we can admire them only in silence. Art, too, is the fruit of silence. How else but in silence can we contemplate a painting or a sculpture, the beauty of a color and the correctness of a form? Great music is listened to in silence. Wonder, admiration, and silence function in tandem. Popular, tasteless music is performed in an uproar, a pandemonium of shouting, a diabolical, exhausting commotion. It is not something one can listen to; it deafens man and makes him drunk with emptiness, confusion, and despair.

We do not experience the same feelings, the same purity, the same elegance, the same elevation of mind and soul that we experience when we listen silently to Mozart, Berlioz, Beethoven, or Gregorian chant. Man enters then into a sacred dimension, into a celestial liturgy, at the threshold of purity itself. Here music, by its expressive character, by its ability to convert souls, causes the human heart to vibrate in unison with God's heart. Here music rediscovers its sacredness and divine origin.

According to Dom Mocquereau, a Benedictine monk of the Abbey of Solesmes:

> Plato has given us an excellent definition of music. "It is", he says, "art so ordering sound as to reach the soul, inspiring a love of virtue." He would have the best music to be that which most perfectly expresses the soul's good qualities. "It is to serve no idle pleasures," he says in another place, "that the Muses have given us harmony, whose movements accord with those of the soul, but rather to enable us thereby to order the ill-regulated motions of the soul, even as rhythm is given us to reform our manners, which in most men are so wanting in balance and in grace." This was the high ideal which the Greeks had of music.

25. The sentiments that emerge from a silent heart are expressed in harmony and silence. The great things in human life are experienced in silence, under God's watchful eye.

Silence is man's greatest freedom. No dictatorship, no war, no barbarism can take this divine treasure away from him.

In listening to you, we understand that although silence may be the absence of speech, it is above all the attitude of someone who listens. To listen is to welcome the other into one's heart. Does Solomon not say, in the First Book of Kings (see 3:5–15), "Give me, Lord, a heart that listens"? He does not ask for riches or the life of his enemies or power, but a silent heart so as to listen to God.

26. King Solomon asks God to make him a silent man, in other words, a true child of God. He wants neither riches nor glory nor victory over the enemy, but a heart that listens. In a contrary movement, the modern world transforms the person who listens into an inferior human being. With fatal arrogance, modernity exalts the man who is drunk with images and noisy slogans, while killing the interior man.

27. The *Carmelite Rule* prescribes: "Be careful not to indulge in a great deal of talk, for ... sin will not be wanting where there is much talk." Indeed, Saint James the Apostle shows how important it is to mortify the tongue:

> If any one makes no mistakes in what he says he is a perfect man, able to bridle the whole body also. If we put bits into the mouths of horses that they may obey us, we guide their whole bodies. Look at the ships also; though they are so great and are driven by strong winds, they are guided by a very small rudder wherever the will of the pilot directs. So the tongue is a little member and boasts of great things. How great a forest is set ablaze by a small fire!
>
> And the tongue is a fire. The tongue is an unrighteous world among our members, staining the whole body, setting on fire the cycle of nature, and set on fire by hell. For every kind of beast and bird, of reptile and sea creature, can be tamed and has been tamed by mankind, but no human being can tame the tongue—a restless evil, full of deadly poison. With it we bless the Lord and Father, and with it we curse men, who are made in the likeness of God. From the same mouth come blessing and cursing. My brethren, this ought not to be so. (Jas 3:2–10)

Saint James compares the tongue to the rudder of a boat. It is a little piece of wood that allows the whole ship to be steered. The man who holds his tongue controls his life, as the sailor directs the ship. Conversely, the man who talks too much is a ship adrift. Indeed, garrulousness, that unhealthy tendency to externalize all the treasures of the soul by displaying them in season and out of season, is supremely harmful to the spiritual life. It sets out in the direction opposite to that of the spiritual life, which ceaselessly becomes more interior and deeper so as to draw near to God. Carried away toward the outside by a need to say everything, the talkative person is far from God and from all profound activity. His life is spent entirely on his lips and spills out in floods of words that carry off the increasingly meager fruits of his thought and of his soul. For he no longer has the time or the inclination to recollect himself, to think, to live profoundly. Through the agitation that he creates around him, he interferes with the fruitful work and recollection of others. Superficial and vain, the talkative person is a dangerous being. The now widespread habit of testifying in public to the divine graces granted in the innermost depths of a man's soul exposes him to the dangers of superficiality, the self-betrayal of his interior friendship with God, and vanity.

28. We must learn, Thomas Merton says, that "the inviolability of one's spiritual sanctuary, the center of the soul, depends on secrecy. Secrecy is the intellectual complement of a pure intention.... Keep all good things secret even from yourself. If we would find God in the depths of our souls, we have to leave everybody else outside, including ourselves." It is disastrous, if we want to find God in our souls and to remain there with him, to try to communicate him to others as we see him. We could do so later with the grace that he gives us in silence and by the influence and transparency of our life.

True witness is expressed by the silent, pure, radiant example of the sanctity of our life.

29. Nowadays facile speech and the popularized image are the teachers of many lives. I have the sense that modern man does not know how to stop the uninterrupted flood of sententious, falsely moralizing speech and the bulimic need for corrupt icons.

Silent lips seem impossible for people in the West. But the media also tempt African and Asian societies by driving them to lose themselves in a superabundant jungle of words, images, and noises. The glowing screens need a gargantuan diet in order to distract mankind and destroy consciences. Keeping quiet has the appearance of being a weakness, a sort of ignorance or lack of will. In the modern system, the silent person becomes someone who does not know how to defend himself. He is subhuman. Conversely, the so-called strong man is a man of words. He crushes and drowns the other in the floods of his speeches.

30. The silent man is no longer a sign of contradiction; he is just one man too many. Someone who speaks has importance and value, whereas another who keeps quiet gets little consideration. The silent man is reduced to nothingness. The simple act of speaking imparts value. Do the words make no sense? It makes no difference. Noise has acquired the nobility that silence once possessed.

The man who speaks is celebrated, and the silent man is a poor beggar in whose presence there is no need even to raise one's eyes.

31. I will never stop thanking the good, holy priests who generously give their whole lives for the kingdom of God. But I will untiringly denounce those who are unfaithful to the promises of their ordination. In order to make themselves known or to impose their personal views, both on the theological and the pastoral level, they speak again and again. These clerics repeat the same banal things. I could not affirm that God dwells within them. Who can think their sheer outpourings to be a spring coming from the divine depths? But they talk, and the media love to listen to them in order to reecho their ineptitudes, particularly if they declare themselves in favor of the new posthumanist ideologies, in the realm of sexuality, the family, and marriage. These clerics consider God's thinking about conjugal life to be an "evangelical ideal". Marriage is no longer a requirement willed by God, modeled and manifested in the nuptial bond between Christ and the Church. Some theologians in their presumptuousness and arrogance go so far as to assert personal opinions that are difficult to reconcile with revelation, tradition, the centuries-old Magisterium of the Church, and the teaching of Christ. Thus, highly amplified by the blaring media, they go so far as to dispute God's design.

Have we not arrived at the fulfillment of the prophetic words of Paul VI, quoted by Jean Guitton in his book *Paul VI secret*:

> There is great turmoil at this time in the world and in the Church, and what is in dispute is the faith.... What strikes me, when I look at the Catholic world, is that within Catholicism a sort of non-Catholic thought seems to predominate sometimes, and it may happen tomorrow that this non-Catholic thought will become the strongest within Catholicism. But it will never represent the mind of the Church. A tiny little flock has to continue in existence, however small it may be.

It is urgent to listen again to the voice of Saint Paul in his Second Letter to the Corinthians:

> For we are not, like so many, peddlers of God's word; but as men of sincerity, as commissioned by God, in the sight of God we speak in Christ. (2 Cor 2:17)

Therefore, having this ministry by the mercy of God, we do not lose heart.... We refuse to practice cunning or to tamper with God's word, but by the open statement of the truth we would commend ourselves to every man's conscience in the sight of God. (2 Cor 4:1–2)

Saint Ignatius of Antioch called on priests to "exhort [Christians] to live in harmony with the mind of God. Surely, Jesus Christ, our inseparable life, for His part is the mind of the Father, just as the bishops too, though appointed throughout the vast, wide earth, represent for their part the mind of Jesus Christ." It is a serious responsibility for every bishop to be and to represent the mind of Christ. Bishops who scatter the sheep that Jesus has entrusted to them will be judged mercilessly and severely by God.

32. In his *Epistle to the Ephesians*, Saint Ignatius gives the impression of severity when he discusses silence and fidelity to doctrine:

It is better to keep silence and be something than to talk and be nothing. Teaching is an excellent thing, provided the speaker practices what he teaches. Now, there is one Teacher who spoke and it was done. But even what He did silently is worthy of the Father. He who has made the words of Jesus really his own is able also to hear His silence. Thus he will be perfect: he will act through his speech and be understood through his silence. Nothing is hidden from the Lord; no, even our secrets reach Him. Let us, then, do all things in the conviction that He dwells in us. Thus we shall be His temples and He will be our God within us. And this is the truth, and it will be made manifest before our eyes. Let us, then, love Him as He deserves. Do not be deceived, my brethren. Those who ruin homes will not inherit the kingdom of God. Now, if those who do this to gratify the flesh are liable to death, how much more a man who by evil doctrine ruins the faith in God, for which Jesus Christ was crucified! Such a filthy creature will go into the unquenchable fire, as will anyone that listens to him.

33. Today many people are drunk on speaking, always agitated, incapable of silence or respect for others. They have lost their calm and dignity. Ben Sirach the Sage often recommends sobriety, prudence, and good manners when we are in society. If we are to avoid harming our soul and the souls of others and to prevent anything from

causing us to have a serious fall in our conduct and in our words, moderation and reticence are necessary. In particular, he worries about our attitude when we are at table: "Wine drunk in season and temperately is rejoicing of heart and gladness of soul. Wine drunk to excess is bitterness of soul, with provocation and stumbling. Drunkenness increases the anger of a fool to his injury, reducing his strength and adding wounds" (Sir 31:28–30). As for Saint Albert of Jerusalem, the author of the *Carmelite Rule*, his response is simple. In order to avoid a fall, it is necessary to keep silent and to trust in the wisdom, the inspirations, and the silent action of God. One must not "offend the Spirit of grace". The conquest of silence has the bitter taste of ascetical battles, but God willed this combat, which is within the reach of human effort.

34. Without the silence that precedes it, speech runs the great risk of being useless chattering instead: "In quietness and in trust shall be your strength", Isaiah said (Is 30:15). The prophet rebukes the people of Israel for their idolatrous activism, their turbulent political passions, made up of alliances based on interests or military strategy, sometimes with Egypt, sometimes with Assyria. The people of Israel no longer place their trust in God. Isaiah calls them to conversion, calm, and serenity. Thus silence has a role connected with faith in God. Setting aside agitation and subterfuges, we must throw ourselves silently into God's arms. Man's hope and strength lie in his silent wager on God. But the people in ancient times did not listen to Isaiah. They put their trust in the Egyptian chariots, horses, and military power so as to flee to Egypt. This was raving madness that led to chaos. Instead, the chosen people ought to have commended their lives into the hands of God alone and remained in silence. Our future is in God's hands and not in the noisy agitation of human negotiations, even if they may appear useful. Even today, our pastoral strategies without any demands, without an appeal to conversion, without a radical return to God, are paths that lead nowhere. They are politically correct games that cannot lead us to the crucified God, our true Liberator.

Modern man is capable of all sorts of noise, all sorts of wars, and so many solemn false statements, in an infernal chaos, because he has excluded God from his life, from his battles, and from his gargantuan ambition to transform the world for his selfish benefit alone.

35. Those who are unknown and remain silent are the real men. I am certain that great men rarely resort to facile speeches. They mark out a path by the eloquence of their silences and the austerity of their life, which is inseparably connected with the "mind of Jesus Christ". Likewise, it is magnificent to be noted for one's silence.

At the dawn of this new millennium, the silent ones are the persons most useful to society, because—creatures of silence and interiority— they live out the authentic dimension of man. The human soul does not express itself by words alone.

36. In our consumer society, man incessantly struts like a peacock but takes no care of his soul. He displays a façade and splendid clothes that wear out and are good for the moths.

37. Without underestimating the work of the missionaries and the merit of their sacrifices, we can say that the monks and nuns are the greatest spiritual force in the Church. Contemplatives are the greatest evangelizing and missionary force, the most important and most precious organ that transmits life and maintains the essential energy throughout the body. God chooses persons to whom he en-trusts the mission of dedicating their life to prayer, adoration, pen-ance, suffering, and daily sacrifices, accepted on behalf of their brethren for the glory of God, so as to fill up in their flesh what is lacking in the sufferings of Christ for his Body, which is the Church. These persons are creatures of silence. They are constantly in the presence of God. Night and day they sing the praises of his name, for the Church and for humanity. We do not hear them because they contemplate the Invisible and carry on the work of God.

38. The men and women who pray in silence, in the night, and in solitude are the supporting pillars of Christ's Church. In these con-fused times, contemplatives are the ones who really spend themselves in the generous offering of their lives for an existence that is more faithful to the promises of the Son of God. The true missionary, Saint John Paul II used to say, is the contemplative in action.

39. Since his resignation, Benedict XVI has been like a monk, with-drawn in the silence of a monastery in the Vatican gardens. Like

contemplatives, he is at the service of the Church by dedicating his final efforts, and the love of his heart, to prayer, contemplation, and adoration of God. The Pope Emeritus stands before the Lord for the salvation of souls and for the glory of God alone.

40. And yet, for two millennia, what a surprising paradox it has been to see so many garrulous theologians, so many noisy popes, so many successors of the Apostles who are pretentious and infatuated with their own arguments. But the Church is unshakable, set firmly on Peter "the Rock" and the rock of Golgotha.

41. Christ lived for thirty years in silence. Then, during his public life, he withdrew to the desert to listen to and speak with his Father. The world vitally needs those who go off into the desert. Because God speaks in silence.

42. Keeping quiet by mastering one's lips and tongue is a difficult, blazing, and arid work. But we must delve ever deeper into the interior realities that can shape the world usefully. Man must stand silently before God and tell him: God, since you gave me knowledge and the desire for perfection, lead me continually toward the absolute of love. Make me love more and more, because you are the wise artisan who leaves no work unfinished, as long as the clay of the creature does not oppose you with obstacles and refusals. I surrender wordlessly to you, O Lord. I want to be docile and malleable like clay in your hands, for you are a skillful, benevolent potter.

How do you describe what we could call the silence of the eyes?

43. For some years now there has been a constant onslaught of images, lights, and colors that blind man. His interior dwelling is violated by the unhealthy, provocative images of pornography, bestial violence, and all sorts of worldly obscenities that assault purity of heart and infiltrate through the door of sight.

44. The faculty of sight, which ought to see and contemplate the essential things, is turned aside to what is artificial. Our eyes confuse day and night because our whole lives are immersed in a permanent

light. In the cities that shine with a thousand lights, our eyes no longer find restful areas of darkness, and consciences no longer recognize sin. To a large extent, humanity has lost an awareness of the seriousness of sin and of the disorder that its presence has introduced into personal, ecclesial, and social life. More than fifty years ago, in his homily on September 20, 1964, Blessed Paul VI stated this tragedy in these terms:

> In the language of respectable people today, in their books, in the things that they say about man, you will not find that dreadful word which, however, is very frequent in the religious world—our world—especially in close relation to God: the word is "sin". In today's way of thinking, people are no longer regarded as sinners. They are categorized as being healthy, sick, good, strong, weak, rich, poor, wise, ignorant; but one never encounters the word sin. The human intellect having thus been detached from divine wisdom, this word "sin" does not recur because we have lost the concept of sin. One of the most penetrating and grave words of Pope Pius XII, of venerable memory, was, "the modern world has lost the sense of sin." What is this if not the rupture of our relationship with God, caused precisely by "sin".

Saint John Paul II echoes this to a great extent in his Post-Synodal Apostolic Exhortation *Reconciliatio et Paenitentia* dated December 2, 1984 (no. 18).

45. Far from God and from the lights that spring from the true Light, man can no longer see the stars, cities have become such flashlights that dazzle our eyes. Modern life does not allow us to look calmly at things. Our eyelids remain open incessantly, and our eyes are forced to look at a sort of ongoing spectacle. The dictatorship of the image, which plunges our attention into a perpetual whirlpool, detests silence. Man feels obliged to seek ever new realities that give him an appetite to own things; but his eyes are red, haggard, and sick. The artificial spectacles and the screens glowing uninterruptedly try to bewitch the mind and the soul. In the brightly lit prisons of the modern world, man is separated from himself and from God. He is riveted to ephemeral things, farther and farther away from what is essential.

46. The silence of the eyes consists of being able to close one's eyes in order to contemplate God who is in us, in the interior depths of our personal abyss. Images are drugs that we can no longer do without, because they are present everywhere and at every moment. Our eyes are sick, intoxicated, they can no longer close. It is necessary to stop one's ears, too, because there are sonic images that assault and violate our sense of hearing, our intellect, and our imagination. It is difficult for us not to hear this world that is constantly gesticulating, seeking to stun and daze us so as to abandon us like ships wrecked on the reefs or common, useless scraps cast up on the shore.

47. The tyranny of the image forces man to renounce the silence of the eyes. Humanity itself has returned to the sad prophecy of Isaiah, which was repeated by Jesus: "Seeing they do not see, and hearing they do not hear, nor do they understand.... For this people's heart has grown dull, and their ears are heavy of hearing, and their eyes they have closed, lest they should perceive with their eyes, and hear with their ears, and understand with their heart, and turn for me to heal them" (Mt 13:13, 15).

Is the silence of the heart similarly endangered?

48. The silence of the heart is the most mysterious thing, because although we can decide not to talk by keeping quiet, although we can likewise close our eyes so as to see nothing, we have less control over our heart. In it there is a fire that burns, in which passions, anger, resentments, and violence are difficult to control. It is difficult to conform human love to God's love. Uncontrollable rivers flow through the heart, and it is all man can do to find interior silence. He balks and does not allow himself to be singed by the burning bush of the love of God that blazes incessantly inside of him, in the depths of his heart, without forcing his free will and consent.

49. If man succeeds in "grafting" his heart onto the heart of God, by welcoming the divine powers, he will advance toward silence.

50. How did Saint John manage to place his heart against the heart of Jesus? He just leaned toward Jesus while lying near him, like a faithful

dog who takes his place at his master's feet. This physical proximity is much more than bodily; we are talking about a spiritual graft and an intimate communion that allows Saint John to experience the same sentiments that Jesus does. The one whom Christ "loved" is the Apostle who best described the unfathomable depths of the heart of the Son of God.

51. The journey toward silence of the heart is itself made in silence. Here is the great mystery: silence is attained in silence and grows in silence.

52. Silence of the heart consists of quieting little by little our miserable human sentiments so as to become capable of having the same sentiments as those of Jesus. Silence of the heart is the silence of the passions. It is necessary to die to self in order to join the Son of God in silence. Saint Paul says: "Let each of you look not only to his own interests, but also to the interests of others. Have this mind among yourselves, which was in Christ Jesus" (Phil 2:4–5).

In No Greater Love, *Mother Teresa wrote: "Jesus taught us how to pray, and He also told us to learn from Him to be meek and humble of heart. Neither of these can we do unless we know what silence is. Both humility and prayer grow from an ear, mind, and tongue that have lived in silence with God, for in the silence of the heart God speaks." By differentiating between exterior silence and interior silence, we see that although exterior silence promotes interior silence, silence of speech, gesture, or activity finds its full meaning in the search for God. This search is truly possible only in a silent heart.*

53. Mother Teresa had an intimate knowledge of silence. She had had the hard experience of God's silence, like Saint Teresa of Avila, Saint John of the Cross, and Saint Thérèse of Lisieux. She was a woman of silence because she was a woman of prayer, constantly with God. She wanted to remain in the silence of God. This nun did not like to speak and fled the storms of worldly noise. Mother Teresa enjoyed incredible esteem all over the world, and yet she preserved a childlike spirit. She imitated Christ in his silence, humility, poverty, meekness, and charity. She loved to remain in silence for hours at a time before Jesus present in the Eucharist. For her, to pray was to love with

all her heart, with all her soul, and with all her strength; it was to give
her whole being and all her time to the Lord. The most beautiful
offering that she wanted to make of herself, and of all her activities on
behalf of the poor, was to devote long intervals in her day to a heart-
to-heart conversation with God, so that those moments of intimacy
might allow her heart to swell with an unconditional love. Like Jesus,
her heart always thirsted for love. Jesus' cry "I thirst" is inscribed in
all the sisters' chapels of the Missionaries of Charity.

54. For my part, I know that all the great moments of my day are
found in the incomparable hours that I spend on my knees in darkness before the Most Blessed Sacrament of the Body and Blood of
our Lord Jesus Christ. I am, so to speak, swallowed up in God and
surrounded on all sides by his presence. I would like to belong now
to God alone and to plunge into the purity of his love. And yet, I
can tell how poor I am, how far from loving the Lord as he loved
me to the point of giving himself up for me.

55. I remember the strong, distressing words of Mother Teresa to a
young priest, Angelo Comastri, who today is a cardinal archpriest of
Saint Peter's Basilica in Rome. In his book *Dio scrive dritto*, there are
magnificent passages. Here is his account of that upsetting encounter
with the saint, which I relate here with great emotion:

> I telephoned the general house of the Missionaries of Charity so as to
> be able to meet Mother Teresa of Calcutta, but their answer was cat-
> egorical: "It is not possible to meet Mother; her engagements do not
> allow it." I went there anyway. The Sister who came to open the door
> for me very politely asked me, "What do you want?" "I would just
> like to meet Mother Teresa for a few moments." Surprised, the Sister
> replied, "I am sorry! That is not possible!" I did not budge and thus
> made the Sister understand that I would not leave without having met
> Mother Teresa. The Sister went away for a few moments and came
> back in the company of Mother Teresa. . . .
> I was startled and speechless. Mother had me sit down in a little
> room near the chapel. Meanwhile I had recovered a bit and managed
> to say: "Mother, I am a very young priest: I'm taking my first steps! I
> came to ask you to accompany me with your prayers." Mother looked
> tenderly and kindly at me, then, smiling, she replied: "I always pray
> for priests. I will pray for you also." Then she gave me a Miraculous

Medal, put it in my hand, and asked me, "For how much time do you pray each day?" I was astonished and a little embarrassed. Then, gathering my thoughts, I replied, "Mother, I celebrate Holy Mass each day, I pray the Breviary each day; you know that these days that is a proof of heroism [this was in 1969, before the Divine Office was simplified]! I pray the rosary each day also and very gladly, because I learned it from my mother." Mother Teresa, with her rough hands, clasped the rosary that she always had with her. Then she fixed on me her eyes, which were filled with light and love, and said: "That is not enough, my son! That is not enough, because love cannot be reduced to the indispensable minimum; love demands the maximum!" I did not understand Mother Teresa's words right away, and, as though to justify myself, I replied, "Mother, I expected from you instead this question: What acts of charity do you do?" Suddenly Mother Teresa's face became very serious again, and she said in a stern tone of voice: "Do you think that I could practice charity if I did not ask Jesus every day to fill my heart with his love? Do you think that I could go through the streets looking for the poor if Jesus did not communicate the fire of his charity to my heart?" I then felt very small. . . .

I looked at Mother Teresa with profound admiration and the sincere desire to enter into the mystery of her soul, which was so filled with the presence of God. Enunciating each word, she added: "Read the Gospel attentively, and you will see that Jesus sacrificed even charity for prayer. And do you know why? To teach us that, without God, we are too poor to help the poor!" At that time we saw so many priests and religious abandoning prayer in order to immerse themselves—as they said—in social work. Mother Teresa's words seemed to me like a ray of sunshine, and I repeated slowly in my heart of hearts: "Without God, we are too poor to be able to help the poor!"

56. Let us devote a lot of time to God, to prayer and adoration. Let us allow ourselves to be nourished abundantly and ceaselessly by the Word of God. We know the hardness of our heart, and it takes a lot of time for it to soften and to be humbled at the contact of the Host and to be imbued with the love of God.

57. There is nothing littler, meeker, or more silent than Christ present in the Host. This little piece of bread embodies the humility and perfect silence of God, his tenderness and his love for us. If we want to grow and to be filled with the love of God, it is necessary to plant our life firmly on three great realities: the Cross, the Host, and the

Virgin: *crux, hostia, et virgo*.... These are three mysteries that God gave to the world in order to structure, fructify, and sanctify our interior life and to lead us to Jesus. These three mysteries are to be contemplated in silence.

58. There are external situations that should promote interior silence. It is necessary to provide ourselves with the means of the best possible environment for finding within us the silence that allows us to be in intimate communion with God. Christ very clearly recommends this search for intimacy: "When you pray, go into your room and shut the door and pray to your Father who is in secret; and your Father who sees in secret will reward you" (Mt 6:6). But our real room is precisely ourselves. Man is invited to enter into himself so as to remain alone with God.

Jesus never stops setting the example: "In these days he went out to the hills to pray; and all night he continued in prayer to God" (Lk 6:12). Thus he teaches us the circumstances that are conducive to silent prayer.

In the presence of God, in silence, we become meek and humble of heart. God's meekness and humility penetrate us, and we enter into a real conversation with him. Humility is a condition and a result of silence. Silence needs meekness and humility, and it also opens for us the way to these two qualities. The humblest, meekest, and most silent of all beings is God. Silence is the only means by which to enter into this great mystery of God.

I am certain that silence is a divine liberation that unifies man and places him at the center of himself, in the depths of God's mysteries. In silence, man is absorbed by the divine and the world's movements no longer have any hold on his soul. In silence, we set out from God and we arrive at God.

The external conditions that foster silence depend on the individual and may vary according to the circumstances of one's life. But what should we do in order to enter "inside ourselves"?

59. In the life of prayer, some support is necessary, because we always run the risk of going far from ourselves when we are invaded by noises, dreams, and memories.

Reading the Bible silently and diligently is the best method. The Gospels place the reader in front of Christ, his life and his mind. They help us to contemplate and to meditate on the life of Jesus, from his birth in the crib in Bethlehem to his death and Resurrection. That is how we will feel involved in his life. In this silence that confronts us with his Word, God is close to us. He does not leave us. We perceive him, and he perceives us. This face-to-face inundates us with his light and imbues us with his presence. We stand facing each other, and we welcome each other reciprocally in interior silence.

60. The Gospel explains how important it is to mistrust sterile enthusiasms, intense passions, and ideological or political slogans. When Jesus went down from Bethany to Jerusalem on Palm Sunday, he was given a grand, solemn reception. The people spread coats and branches beneath his feet and acclaimed him as the Son of David. They all cried: "Hosanna! Blessed is he who comes in the name of the Lord, even the King of Israel!" (Jn 12:13). They all gave testimony to the resurrection of Lazarus, who had already been buried in the tomb. For this reason, the crowd welcomed Jesus with great pomp. At the sound of this triumphant entry and this exceptionally festive reception, all Jerusalem was in turmoil. Everyone wondered: "Who is this?" (Mt 21:10). As was his custom, Jesus went into the Temple and healed the lame and the blind who were there (Mt 21:14). These miracles provoked the indignation of the high priests and the scribes. But Jesus was happy to hear the innocent hearts of the little children acclaim him, because it was written that out of their mouths should come the praise of God (Mt 21:16). When the festivities were over and it was late, oddly enough, seeing no one to offer him hospitality or to give him something to eat, Jesus left the city and went back to spend the night in Bethany with his disciples.

The Son of God was welcomed triumphantly but found no one to open his door to him. Similarly, in our age, how often our welcome, our love, and our praises are superficial, without substance, merely a coat of religious varnish.

Today we content ourselves with performing rituals that have no effect on our everyday lives because they are lived without recollection, without interiority, and without truth. The inhabitants of Jerusalem did not understand the profound significance of the visit from the Son of God; the people, indulging in their passions and their political ambitions, were demonstrative, superficial, and noisy.

Prey to all sorts of worldly disturbances, they could not understand the mystery of the visit from the King-Messiah, the King who brings peace to the nations, as the prophet Zechariah had announced:

> Rejoice greatly, O daughter of Zion!
> Shout aloud, O daughter of Jerusalem!
> Behold, your king comes to you;
> triumphant and victorious is he,
> humble and riding on a donkey,
> on a colt the foal of a donkey.
> I will cut off the chariot from Ephraim
> and the war horse from Jerusalem;
> and the battle bow shall be cut off,
> and he shall command peace to the nations;
> his dominion shall be from sea to sea,
> and from the River to the ends of the earth. (Zech 9:9–10)

The inhabitants of Jerusalem wanted a messianic leader, without seeking to comprehend the silent grandeur of Jesus' message. The people did not welcome Christ in their souls; they indulged in a mere demonstration of colorful and excessive force. The most difficult thing is to love Jesus in spirit and in truth, so as to welcome him into one's heart and into the depths of one's being.

True welcome is silent. It is not diplomatic, theatrical, or sentimental.

61. Nowadays, in a similar way, when we acclaim Christ during the major liturgical feasts, we must insistently make sure that our joy is not merely artificial. Often we do not give the Son of God the opportunity to dwell in our hearts.

In *The Imitation of Christ*, we find these extraordinary lines:

> Up with you, then, faithful soul, get your heart ready for the coming of this true Lover, or he will never consent to come and make his dwelling in you; that is his own way of putting it, *If a man has any love for me, he will be true to my word; and we will come to him, and make our abode with him* [John 14:23]. You must make room for Christ, then....

If Christ is yours, then wealth is yours; he satisfies all your wants. He will look after you, manage all your affairs for you most dutifully; you will need no human support to rely on....

Put all your trust in God, centre in him all your fear and all your love; he will make himself responsible for you, and all will go well as he sees best....

Nothing will ever bring you rest, except being closely united to Jesus....

All your thoughts must be at home with God, all your prayer make its way up to Christ continually.

Ah, but it is above your reach (you complain), such high contemplation of heavenly things. Why then, let your mind come to rest in Christ's Passion, and find in his sacred wounds the home it longs for....

You must hold out with him, and for love of him, before you can share his kingdom.

If you'd ever really got inside the mind of Jesus, ever had a single taste of his burning love, considerations of your own loss or gain would mean nothing to you; you would be glad to have insults heaped on you—the love of Jesus fills us with self-contempt.

After our first efforts, however, we may also notice that silence does not entirely belong to us. For once we have passed through the door of prayer, we discover an agitated crowd of thoughts, feelings, and aversions that we have great difficulty in quieting.

These noisy, stubborn multitudes bog down our soul. We can decide to pray and realize that it is impossible to remain concentrated on our interior life. We are distracted by a thousand disturbing things. The interior racket makes all silence impossible. The slightest of passions that has troubled our heart before a prayer can ruin that moment of silence. Noise triumphs, and silence flees....

62. How can we come to master our own interior silence? The only answer lies in asceticism, self-renunciation, and humility. If man does not mortify himself, if he stays as he is, he remains outside of God.

63. When they want to look at God, Oriental peoples kneel down and prostrate themselves, with their face to the ground, as a sign of voluntary humiliation and respectful reverence. Without a strong

desire to be rid of oneself, to make oneself small in the presence of the Eternal, no conversation with God is possible. Similarly, without mastery of one's own silence, no encounter with the other person is possible. If we remain ourselves, we are full of noise, conceit, and anger.

64. Reading should help us to pray by concentrating our attention. Let us not forget the vital connection between prayer and the Word of God. How can we "imagine the Lord at our side" if we do not seek him where he reveals himself? Meditation consists of imagining in silence the earthly, everyday life of Jesus. It is not necessary to recall a historical event; rather, we must seek to bring the Son of God silently into our heart.

Thus it is important to stay in the presence of the Lord so that he can find us available and introduce us into the great silence within that enables him to become incarnate in us, to transform us into himself. And in this silence, which is not emptiness but is filled with the Holy Spirit, the soul will be able to hear rising from his heart, like a murmur: "Abba! Father!" (Rom 8:15). Prayer is successfully being quiet, listening to God, and being able to hear the ineffable moaning of the Holy Spirit, who dwells in us and cries out silently.

65. Our contemporaries have the feeling that prayer consists of saying things to God, shouting and fidgeting in his presence, but prayer is simpler than that. It consists of listening to God speak silently within us. But why, then, do we not watch Jesus pray? Why do we not, like the Apostles, ask him, beg him: "Lord, teach us to pray, as John [the Baptist] taught his disciples" (Lk 11:1)? Why do we seek elsewhere models and examples of prayer, trying to convince ourselves that excitement, noise, and disorder are signs of effusiveness and of the presence of the Spirit of Jesus? Christ is the one Master who can teach us to pray, and to pray is to love and to stay with Jesus in silence and interior solitude.

66. In his *Ascetical Homilies*, Isaac the Syrian wrote:

> Love silence above all things, because it brings you near to fruit that the tongue cannot express. First let us force ourselves to be silent,

and then from out of this silence something is born that leads us into silence itself.... If you begin with this discipline, I know not how much light will dawn on you from it.... Great is the man who by the patience of his members achieves wondrous habits in his soul! When you put all the works of this discipline on one side and silence on the other, you will find the latter to be greater in weight.

In silence, man conquers his nobility and his grandeur only if he is on his knees in order to hear and adore God. It is in the silence of humiliation and self-mortification, by quieting the turmoil of the flesh, by successfully taming the noisy images, by keeping at a distance the dreams, imaginations, and roaring of a world that is always in a whirl, in order to purify himself of all that ruins the soul and separates it from contemplation, that man makes himself capable of looking at God and loving him. Plotinus already wrote in his *Enneads* about how a soul can ascend to the contemplation of the "universal soul": "a soul [must] become worthy to look, emancipate[d] from the lure, from all that binds its fellows in bewitchment, holding itself in quietude. Let not merely the enveloping body be at peace, body's turmoil stilled, but all that lies around, earth at peace, and sea at peace, and air and the very heavens."

67. In *Un autre regard sur l'homme* [Another look at man], Maurice Zundel seems to develop Plotinus' thought in greater depth when he writes:

Our whole life is comprised in this alternative: either I am in myself or I am in God. There is no middle way. When I stop encountering myself, that is when God is really present. When I lose sight of myself, that is when I look at him. When I no longer hear myself, that is when I listen to him, and God, at all levels, consists precisely in losing myself in him. The program is simple, but implementing it is difficult, because we cannot decree an encounter or set the hour in which love will spring forth. There is no path that infallibly ends with an exchange of intimacies. Nothing is freer, more unforeseen, or more gratuitous. All you can do is to remove the obstacles that make such an exchange impossible, and they are all summed up in the noise that one makes with oneself and around oneself. The only chance we have of leaving ourselves is to neutralize our attention, peacefully to withdraw our attention from this whole confused mix of appetites and claims, and to shut off the psychological current that feeds this turmoil; in this recollection, the emptiness that makes us available grows ever wider and deeper. When total silence is established, it is already an announcement of the Presence who fills up the space resulting from the retreat of myself.

68. Silence is difficult, but it enables man to let himself be led by God. From silence is born silence. Through God the silent, we can attain silence. And man is unceasingly surprised by the light that pours forth then.

Silence is more important than any other human work. Because it expresses God. The true revolution comes from silence; it leads us toward God and others so as to place us humbly and generously at their service.

In his Écrits monastiques *[Monastic writings], Father Jérôme wrote: "Silence makes you think of a great wave on the ocean that, after pushing the skiff toward an unknown land, leaves it on a shore that is still feared, where the presence of the Infinite would reign alone." How do you describe contemplative silence?*

69. Contemplative silence can frighten us. It is like a big wave that carries us, without being able to drown us, and causes us to end up on fearsome shores. For man then finds himself facing the terrifying immensity of the mystery. I do not think it is possible to approach God's majesty without trembling in dread and astonishment. Our ancestors were often physically moved by a great fear that simultaneously expressed admiration, respect, and a religious fear of the blazing furnace of God's transcendence.

70. God's silence is a consuming fire for the man who approaches him. Through this divine silence, man becomes a bit estranged from this world. He is separated from the earth and from himself. Silence impels us toward an unknown land that is God. And this land becomes our true homeland. Through silence, we return to our heavenly origin, where there is nothing but calm, peace, repose, silent contemplation, and adoration of the radiant face of God.

71. All the great saints were familiar with this incomparable experience. When their prayers led them to the threshold of the Eternal One's silence, they sensed how close and immense God became. They remained wordlessly in the presence of the Father. The more they ascended toward God, the more silent they became. Saint Philip Neri and Saint Thérèse of Lisieux were confronted with a reality they could not comprehend, but they saw with their own eyes the Infinite and the splendor of love. This immensity came to draw them into a grand silence of adoration and interior peace.

72. Contemplative silence is silence with God. This silence is clinging to God, appearing before God, and placing oneself in his presence, offering oneself to him, mortifying oneself in him, adoring, loving, and hearing him, listening to him and resting in him. This is the silence of eternity, the union of the soul with God.

73. In one of his sermons, John Tauler, a theologian, mystic, and disciple of Master Eckhart, wrote:

> Mary lived retired, and so must the soul espoused to God be in retirement, if it will experience the interior regeneration. But not [only] from those wanderings after temporal things which appear to be faulty, but even from the sensible devotion attached to the practice of virtue, must the soul refrain. It must establish rest and stillness as an enclosure in which to dwell, hiding from and cutting off nature and the senses, guarding quiet and interior peace, rest and repose. It is of this state of the soul that we shall sing next Sunday in the introit of the Mass: "While all things were in quiet silence, and the night was in the midst of her course, Thine Almighty Word, O Lord, came down from Heaven, out of Thy royal throne" (Wisdom xviii, 14–15). That was the Eternal Word going forth from the Father's heart. It is amid this silence, when all things are hushed in even eternal silence, that in very truth we hear this Word; for when God would speak thou must be silent.

Christ often recommends that we withdraw if we want to pray. It may be a remote place, in solitude, so as to be alone with the Alone. But the question of the external setting cannot avoid the problem of interiority. It is important to create the interior room where man finds God in a genuine face-to-face encounter. This spiritual work demands effort in order to avoid all distraction, which presupposes interior asceticism. The search for interior silence is a path to perfection that demands repeated attempts. So often, we have a hazardous kind of excitement and imagination inside us. It is necessary to hide in the Spirit in order to divert and escape the senses. The Holy Spirit is the first condition for silence.

74. Our world no longer hears God because it is constantly speaking, at a devastating speed and volume, in order to say nothing. Modern civilization does not know how to be quiet. It holds forth in an unending monologue. Postmodern society rejects the past and looks at the present as a cheap consumer object; it pictures the future in terms of an almost obsessive progress. Its dream, which has become a sad reality, will have been to lock silence away in a damp, dark dungeon. Thus there is a dictatorship of speech, a dictatorship of verbal emphasis. In this theater of shadows, nothing is left but a purulent wound of mechanical words, without perspective, without truth, and without foundation. Quite often "truth" is nothing more than the pure and misleading creation of the media, corroborated by fabricated images and testimonies.

When that happens, the word of God fades away, inaccessible and inaudible. Postmodernity is an ongoing offense and aggression against the divine silence. From morning to evening, from evening to morning, silence no longer has any place at all; the noise tries to prevent God himself from speaking. In this hell of noise, man disintegrates and is lost; he is broken up into countless worries, fantasies, and fears. In order to get out of these depressing tunnels, he desperately awaits noise so that it will bring him a few consolations. Noise is a deceptive, addictive, and false tranquilizer. The tragedy of our world is never better summed up than in the fury of senseless noise that stubbornly hates silence. This age detests the things that silence brings us to: encounter, wonder, and kneeling before God.

75. Even in the schools, silence has disappeared. And yet how can anyone study in the midst of noise? How can you read in noise? How can you train your intellect in noise? How can you structure your thought and the contours of your interior being in noise? How can

you be open to the mystery of God, to spiritual values, and to our human greatness in continual turmoil?

Contemplative silence is a fragile little flame in the middle of a raging ocean. The fire of silence is weak because it is bothersome to a busy world.

76. Too few Christians today are willing to go back inside themselves so as to look at themselves and to let God look at them. I insist: too few are willing to confront God in silence, by coming to be burned in that great face-to-face encounter.

In killing silence, man assassinates God. But who will help man to be quiet? His mobile phone is continually ringing; his fingers and mind are always busy sending messages.... Developing a taste for prayer is probably the first and foremost battle of our age. Stationed in garrisons of the most pitiful noises, is man prepared to return to silence? The death of silence is apparent. God will always help us to rediscover it.

Saint John of the Cross, in his Spiritual Canticle, *speaks to us about the* musica callada, *the "silent music" produced by the Beloved in the soul that is united to him. How can we attempt to describe the sound of silence?*

77. How can we express in concrete words a "silent music"? This musical phenomenon is necessarily a faint, humble sound heard by God alone. It consists of the notes produced by the harp of our heart when it is consumed with love.

78. It is important to let the Holy Spirit penetrate the innermost regions of the soul. For in that secret space God lives and acts. He works so as to achieve our union with him. As long as man has not come to recognize the great silence of God in the depths of his heart and to understand this mysterious place of the Eternal in his flesh, he cannot get to a true spiritual and human transformation. The true sound of silence is here: we cannot hear the Word if we have not. been previously transformed by God's silence.

79. The soul must listen to the voice of silence. It must agree to be united with silence so as to allow God to enter into it. How do we let God enter into us? That is the question and the true grace of silence.

80. In silence there is collaboration between man and God. The depth of the human soul is God's house. We will be able to let God act by keeping the most perfect interior silence. And it is possible for us to find this silence by being attentive to the voice of silence. Even in a hostile environment, we can find God in ourselves if we seek to listen to the silence that he impresses on our soul.

81. A heart in silence is a melody for the heart of God. The lamp is consumed noiselessly before the tabernacle, and incense ascends in silence to the throne of God: such is the sound of the silence of love.

82. The sound of the silence in God allows us to learn the first note of this canticle which is the song of the heavens. "The language [God] best hears is silent love", John of the Cross says magnificently in his *Maxims on Love*.

83. Silent love, which burns without being consumed and says nothing, is the greatest love. If we remain noiseless while seeking him, God is pleased to hear this availability. What is the silence that God wants to hear? What are the voice and the music that please God? It is silent love that says nothing and consents. It is like the offering and the smoke of the incense that rise before God, together with the prayers of the saints (Rev 8:1–4).

84. The concrete life of monks is a silent love, a self-giving love, a love that is consumed. God receives this silent burnt offering. A burnt offering makes no noise. It burns silently for a long time before the divine majesty, and its fragrance gladdens the heart of God.
    God hears nothing else but this silent, humble, meek love.

85. In the school of the Holy Spirit, we learn to listen to God, in the silence that is the language of true love, which he alone can hear: "For even though that music is silent to the natural senses and faculties, it is sounding solitude for the spiritual faculties. When these spiritual faculties are alone and empty of all natural forms and apprehensions, they can receive in a most sonorous way the spiritual sound of the excellence of God, in Himself and in His creatures", John of the Cross writes in his *Spiritual Canticle*.

86. In his sermon on the birth of Saint John the Baptist, which is dedicated to the voice and the Word, echoing his humble, self-effacing attitude: "He must increase and I must decrease", Saint Augustine does not hesitate to declare: "All voices must decrease in the measure that one advances in the knowledge of Christ. The more wisdom reveals itself to us, the less we need the voice: the voice in the depths, the voice in the Apostles, the voice in the psalms, the voice in the Gospel. Let him come, the Word who was at the beginning! This Word who was God! Thus let the voice gradually cease to perform its function, as the soul progresses toward Christ. For God has a secret language, in many people he addresses the heart, and it is a mighty murmur in the great silence of the heart when he says: I am your salvation."

87. The more man advances in the mystery of God, the more he loses speech. Man is enveloped in a power of love, and he becomes mute from astonishment and wonder. Before God, we disappear, snapped up by the greatest silence.

88. The wisdom of God has generated in every person a great love that nourishes the little silence of the human heart. Astonishment at the divine silence closes our mouth, like a celebrant who, performing his priestly duties before God, burns incense before the divine presence and adores in silence. Nothing in the world is more important than the silence of God. No human noises, even the very sweet sound of the Gospel, can express the magnificent silence of God.

89. In the presence of God, in the presence of his silence, everything disappears; the Apostles, even the evangelists are nothing compared to the silence of heaven. The Gospel is the most beautiful sound on earth, but it remains a mere sound, however sublime and important it may be, when contrasted with the great silence of the Eternal One.

90. In his Incarnation, Christ assumed human limitations. Face to face with God's silence, we are confronted with absolute love. And this great silence also explains the freedom left to man. God's only power is to love silently. He is incapable of any oppressive force. God is

love, and love cannot compel, force, or oppress in order to be loved
in return.

Saint Augustine and Saint John of the Cross went through the desert experience, whether physical or interior. They touched one little
part of the great silence of God, and they were as though absorbed,
engulfed in the divine silence and the furnace of his love.

91. In the manuscripts of Saint Thérèse of the Child Jesus we find
this reflection: "If fire and iron had the use of reason, and if the latter
said to the other, 'Draw me,' would it not prove that it desires to
be identified with the fire in such a way that the fire penetrate and
drink it up with its burning substance and seem to become one with
it?" It is the same for someone who approaches the silence of God.
He himself becomes silence.

92. Great spiritual men are often speechless and spend their days in
silence. They live in the revelation of the mystery. They live in what
takes them out of themselves so as to make them enter into the mystery of God.

There is also what we could call the asceticism of silence. In his Ascetical
Homilies, *Isaac the Syrian wrote: "After a time, a certain sweetness is born
in the heart from the practice of this labor [the asceticism of silence], and it
leads the body by force to persevere in stillness. A multitude of tears is born to
us in this discipline through a wonderful divine vision of something that the
heart distinctly perceives, sometimes with pain, sometimes with amazement.
For the heart humbles itself and becomes like a tiny babe, and as soon as she
begins to pray, tears flow forth in advance of her prayer."*

93. The asceticism of silence reaches its most perfect degree in the
life of those who have tasted this encounter with God through
the contemplation of his face. This is a form of nakedness and poverty. But one gains access to true glory only at this price. The asceticism of silence allows a person to enter into the mystery of God by
becoming little, like a child.

In divine silence there are no words but tears, because man is
touched at the deepest part of his soul, in the region of his being
where God is seated; his silence is an immensity that demands an initially painful asceticism involving a Paschal aspect, an aspect of "Good

Friday". It causes tears to run down our faces. But very quickly we experience the fact that the simplicity of asceticism generates purity, delight, and the joy of contemplation.

94. Silence strips man and makes him like a child: pure but frail, innocent, and without provisions. Silence shapes us as the blacksmith works metal.

95. Silence, man's effort, runs alongside hope, the theological virtue. In reality, the divine power of the theological virtue lifts and directs the human and ascetical impact of silence. Then a second moral virtue appears: fortitude. Its function is to remove the obstacle that prevents the will from obeying reason. Fortitude is active and takes the offensive. The thing is to apply oneself to cultivating this virtue, which drives back all that could prevent man from living in dependence on God. Silence and hope are two conditions allowing fortitude to find its nourishment.

Through this asceticism of silence, how can we not understand and appreciate better the lights offered by these different Bible verses? "When words are many, transgression is not lacking" (Prov 10:19). "He who guards his mouth preserves his life; he who opens wide his lips comes to ruin" (Prov 13:3). "Whoever uses too many words will be loathed" (Sir 20:8). "I tell you, on the day of judgment men will render account for every careless word they utter" (Mt 12:36). "Make balances and scales for your words, and make a door and a bolt for your mouth. Beware lest you err with your tongue, lest you fall before him who lies in wait" (Sir 28:25–26).

96. The asceticism of silence is a necessary medicine: one that is sometimes painful but effective. Through silence, we leave evil behind in exchange for good. Noise has no moderation, like a ship without a captain on a raging sea, whereas silence is a paradise, like a limitless ocean. Silence is also a great rudder that can lead to a safe port. To choose silence is to choose what is extraordinary. The man who loves silence has the opportunity to conduct his life wisely and effectively.

97. In his book *Silence cartusien*, Dom Augustin Guillerand writes: "The suffering of silence can also be God's hallmark on a soul." Silence is a sweet, violent seizure by God. The absence of speech,

austerity, poverty: this is the asceticism of silence, the one that brings us back to the purity of the just.

Bernard Toustrate wrote in the Forum Catholique, *summarizing one degree of Sister Marie-Aimée's "twelve degrees of silence"* [Les Douze degrés du silence]: *"If the tongue is mute, if the senses are calm, if the imagination, memory and creatures keep quiet and form a solitude, if not throughout the soul, then at least in the innermost part of it, then the heart will make only a few noises. Silence of one's likes and dislikes, silence of desires insofar as they are too intense, silence of zeal insofar as it is indiscreet; silence of fervor insofar as it is exaggerated; silence to the point of sighing. . . . Silence of love insofar as it is fanatical. The silence of love is love in silence. . . . It is silence in the presence of God, beauty, goodness, perfection! A silence that has nothing constrained or forced; nor does this silence harm tenderness, the vigor of this love, any more than the admission of faults harms the silence of humility or the beating of an angel's wings that the prophet speaks about harms the silence of his obedience, or the fiat harms the silence of Gethsemane, or the eternal Sanctus harms the silence of the seraphim." How, then, can we define the silence of love?*

98. Silence is the prerequisite for love, and it leads to love. Love is expressed fully only by renouncing speech, noise, excitement, and exaltation. Its highest expression occurs in a death that is silent and totally offered up, for there is no greater proof of love than to give your life for those whom you love (Jn 15:13). The silence of love is the outcome and point of arrival of someone who has given priority to silence in his life. It comes like a beautiful reward when man has managed to silence the dislikes, passions, and furors of his heart.

99. The love that says nothing and asks for nothing leads to the greatest love, the silent love of God. The silence of love is the perfect silence in the presence of God that sums up all goodness, all beauty, and all perfection.

100. Silent love can grow only in humility. There is a fundamental connection between humility and silent love. This agreement is significant and can be seen in God. The Father in whom we believe is infinitely humble, silent, devoid of all concern about prestige. Saint Paul writes—does he not?—to the Philippians: "Have this mind

among yourselves, which was in Christ Jesus, who, though he was in the form of God, did not count equality with God a thing to be grasped, but emptied himself, taking the form of a servant, being born in the likeness of men. And being found in human form he humbled himself and became obedient unto death, even death on a cross" (Phil 2:5–8). On the Cross, God was "like a sheep that before its shearers is silent, so he opened not his mouth" (Is 53:7). Love is always humble, silent, contemplative, and on its knees before the beloved. Jesus illustrates this reality when we see him, on Holy Thursday, on his knees, washing the feet of his Apostles. The washing of their feet is a revelation, an unveiling of what God is. He is love: humble, priestly, sacrificial love; and God's humility is the very depth of God.

101. The silence of love resembles the sounds of the angels' wings when they carry out God's commands. This silence is a love that obeys God's own silence. The silence of love corresponds to a completion: the meeting of two silences, the human silence and the silence of God, that are walking along together. Gethsemane and Christ's Calvary represent the most beautiful union of these two silences.

102. In Ecclesiastes we find some extraordinary verses:

> For everything there is a season, and a time for every
>   matter under heaven:
> a time to be born, and a time to die;
> a time to plant, and a time to pluck up what is planted;
> a time to kill, and a time to heal;
> a time to break down, and a time to build up;
> a time to weep, and a time to laugh;
> a time to mourn, and a time to dance;
> a time to cast away stones, and a time to gather stones
>   together;
> a time to embrace, and a time to refrain from embracing;
> a time to seek, and a time to lose;
> a time to keep, and a time to cast away;
> a time to tear, and a time to sew;
> a time to keep silence, and a time to speak;
> a time to love, and a time to hate;
> a time for war, and a time for peace. (Eccles 3:1–8)

The silence of love comes from the silence that has been able to surpass all these stages so as to render an account to the silence of God.

In a letter to his friend Raoul le Verd, provost of the cathedral chapter in Rheims, Saint Bruno declared: "What benefits and divine exaltation the silence and solitude of the desert hold in store for those who love it, only those who have experienced it can know." What is the real connection between solitude and the silence of the desert?

103. In my thirst to see God and to hear him, I often happened to experience the solitude and the silence of the desert. When I was Archbishop of Conakry, I often isolated myself in a desert place, bathing in solitude and silence. Of course there was vegetation all around me. I heard the birds chirping. But I had created for myself an interior desert, without water or food. There was no human presence. I lived in fasting and prayer, nourished only by the Eucharist and the Word of God.

The desert is the place of hunger, thirst, and the spiritual combat. It is vitally important to withdraw to the desert in order to combat the dictatorship of a world filled with idols that gorge themselves on technology and material goods, a world dominated and manipulated by the media, a world that flees God by taking refuge in noise. It is necessary to help this modern world to have the experience of the desert. There, we get some distance from everyday events. We can flee the noise and the superficiality. The desert is the place of the Absolute, the place of freedom. It is no accident that the desert is the place where monotheism was born. The desert is monotheistic; it preserves us from the multiplicity of idols that men make for themselves. In this sense, the desert is the domain of grace. Far from his preoccupations, man encounters there his Creator and his God.

104. Great things begin in the desert, in silence, in poverty, in abandonment. Look at Moses, Elijah, John the Baptist, and Jesus himself. The desert is where God leads us in order to speak to us in a heart-to-heart conversation (cf. Hos 2:16–23). But the desert is not only the place where men can experience the physical test of hunger, thirst, and total destitution. It is also the land of temptation, where Satan's

power is manifested. The devil often leads us there to hold out to us the prospect of all the world's splendors and to persuade us that we would be wrong to give them up. By going into the desert, Jesus exposed himself to Satan's seductive power and firmly opposed it, thus prolonging the event of his baptism and his Incarnation. He is not content to descend into the deep waters of the Jordan. Christ descends also to the very depths of human misery, to the regions of broken hearts and ruined relationships, to the most depraved carnal dictatorships and the desolate places of a world marred by sin. The desert teaches us to fight against evil and all our evil inclinations so as to regain our dignity as children of God. It is impossible to enter into the mystery of God without entering into the solitude and silence of our interior desert.

105. All the prophets went off to the desert to meet God. The experience of God is inseparable from the experience of the desert.

106. Saint John the Baptist himself spent thirty years in the desert: "And the child grew and became strong in spirit, and he was in the wilderness till the day of his manifestation to Israel" (Lk 1:80). John the Baptist built his relationship with God in the place of the greatest silence. The desert leads to silence, and silence draws a person into the most profound intimacy of God.

It is inevitable that the contemplative who has perceived God in this tranquil night of the interior and exterior desert should aspire not only to the most recollected cloisters but to remote, austere hermitages. These are forceful truths that are based on experiences of undeniable validity. But does one absolutely have to live in the desert or in a monastery in order to become a contemplative?

107. God opens up for everyone, right in the middle of the world and in ordinary life, paths toward a more radical life of contemplation and sanctity. As Father Marie-Eugène wrote in *I Want to See God*:

> Very numerous are the spiritual persons for whom life in solitude can be only an unrealizable dream. This one is married, has charge of a family; consequently his duties impose on him an absorbing daily task in the midst of the tumult of the world. Another has a vocation to the

exterior apostolate and is engaged in the multiplicity of good works that his zeal has created, or at least must carry on. There was a time when they might have hesitated between the solitary life and that which is now theirs. But the time is no longer. Moreover, they made their choice, acting in obedience to the light of their vocation. They are taken up with obligations from which they cannot withdraw, and that God requires them to fulfil faithfully.

We must ask, then, if apostolic activity—necessary for the extension of the kingdom of God—and accomplishment of the most sacred duties of family life are incompatible with the demands of contemplation and of a very elevated spiritual life. There are many souls who are thirsty for God and who feel their desires sharpening in the excessive activity to which the most authentic of their duties bind them. Could they be condemned never to arrive at the divine plenitude for which they long, because God has taken them away from the solitude of the desert? We cannot think so; for it is the same Wisdom who imposes on them these external duties and who calls every one to the Source of living water. Divine Wisdom is one and consistent in His calls and requirements. "Spirit of the power of God," strong and sweet, Wisdom makes play of obstacles to pour out graces into holy souls throughout the ages, and make of them friends of God and prophets.

108. If the solitude of the desert were absolutely necessary for the development of contemplation, we would have to conclude that all who cannot go there and those who could not bear it are incapable of attaining sanctity, which would be reserved for rare, privileged souls. The examples of Saint Faustina Kowalska, Saint John Bosco, Saint Josemaría Escrivà de Balaguer, Saint Teresa of Calcutta, and Saint John Paul II show that all are called to contemplation, perfect love, and holiness. It is up to each individual to place himself at the disposal of the silent God who awaits us in the deep desert of our heart by avoiding din and turmoil.

In his *Oeuvres spirituelles* [Spiritual works], Father Jérôme declared: "How beneficial, therefore, are those who, by the weight of their silence, play the role of the dike and the breakwaters and stop all the turmoil that comes from within or without by putting themselves in the way. Thanks to them, the lake always remains calm; the ships do not break their moorings; the hulls do not collide."

109. The choice of silence is therefore a gift for humanity. The men and women who enter into the silence offer themselves as a holocaust for their brethren. The exterior world is like an overflowing river running down a slope and threatening to smash everything in its path. In order to control this force, it is necessary to build dikes. And silence is this powerful dike that controls the tumultuous waters of the world and protects from noises and distractions of all sorts. Silence is a dam that restores a kind of dignity to mankind. The monasteries and the spiritual masters are dikes that protect humanity from the threats that weigh upon it. How necessary it is for people to imitate them so as to make silence an effective dam!

110. Persons who live in noise are like dust swept along by the wind. They are slaves of a turmoil that destroys their relationships with God. On the other hand, those who love silence and solitude walk step by step toward God; they know how to break the vicious circles of noise, like animal tamers who manage to calm roaring lions.

111. Saint Cyprian of Carthage writes in his *Epistle to Donatus*:

> While I was still lying in darkness and gloomy night, wavering hither and thither, tossed about on the foam of this boastful age, and uncertain of my wandering steps, knowing nothing of my real life, and remote from truth and light, I used to regard it as a difficult matter, and especially as difficult in respect of my character at that time, that a man should be capable of being born again—a truth which the divine mercy had announced for my salvation—and that a man quickened to a new life in the laver of saving water should be able to put off what he had previously been; and, although retaining all his bodily structure, should be himself changed in heart and soul. "How," said I, "is such a conversion possible...?"...
>
> These were my frequent thoughts. For as I myself was held in bonds by the innumerable errors of my previous life, from which I did not believe that I could possibly be delivered, so I was disposed to acquiesce in my clinging vices; and because I despaired of better things, I used to indulge my sins as if they were actually parts of me, and indigenous to me." (*Ad Donatum*, 3–4)

Man must make a choice: God or nothing, silence or noise.

112. Without the moorings of silence, life is depressing movement, a puny little boat ceaselessly tossed by the violence of the waves. Silence is the outer wall that we must build in order to protect an interior edifice.

113. Indeed, God himself is the one who builds the dike that protects us from the turmoil, from external attacks, and from the storms of this world. This is the assurance that the prophet Isaiah gives us: "In that day this song will be sung in the land of Judah: 'We have a strong city; he sets up salvation as walls and bulwarks'" (Is 26:1). Sheltered by this wall, we live in silence and the heart of God, and our attention is constantly directed toward him, because we want to see God.

Why talk about "walls and bulwarks"? Because originally man was destined to live with God. But by giving in to sin, he was not only driven out of paradise but also out of himself and was abandoned in exteriority and darkness. Through the Incarnation, God came to abolish the consequences of original sin and to restore man's original destiny and vocation. By becoming incarnate and taking on our human condition, Jesus enabled mankind to set out again on the path of interiority. So it is that Saint Gregory the Great applies to the Incarnation and redemption the notions of interiority and exteriority. Christ is the one who, by coming down to earth, wins back for fallen man the joys of contemplation, of the *lux interna* [internal light]. Christ is in a way the wall that protects the spiritual edifice that is the Church. But he is also the outer wall that protects our interior edifice. Saint Gregory says:

> It must be noted that this wall of the spiritual edifice is called exterior. Indeed, the wall built to protect an edifice is ordinarily placed not inside but outside. Why therefore was it necessary to say that it is exterior, since ordinarily this wall is never placed in the interior? Because it is indispensable if we want the wall placed outside to defend what is inside. But what else does he designate by this term but the very Incarnation of the Lord? For if God is an interior wall for us, the God-made-man is an exterior wall. This is why a prophet says to him: "You went forth for the salvation of your people, for the salvation of your anointed" (Hab 3:13). And indeed, this wall, namely, the Incarnate Lord, would not be a wall for us unless he were outside, for he would not protect us inside if he did not appear outside.

114. Similarly, in his book *Silence cartusien*, Dom Augustin Guiller-and writes these magnificent lines: "For us Carthusians, the words that we do not say become prayers. That is our strength, and we can do some good only by this great method of silence. We speak to God about those to whom we do not speak." He continues: "It is necessary for us to have no more fear of ourselves or of others. It is necessary to look real life in the face. This profound, prolonged look is what God will give us, for God is at the basis of everything. This desire (or this love) is what we seek. This is where God calls us. One arrives at this point only after a long journey that separates us from creatures and from ourselves.... The great science and the great light here below is silent love." And he concludes: "In silence, sadness is looking at oneself; joy is looking at God. This is why we have silence: it is necessary to get out of oneself, to think of God instead of thinking about self."

115. Infallibly, silence leads to God, provided man stops looking at himself. For even in the experience of silence, there is a snare: narcissism and egotism.

116. Contemplative silence is a silence of adoration and listening by a person who stands in the presence of God. To stand silently in God's presence is to pray. Prayer demands that we successfully keep quiet so as to hear and listen to God.

Silence requires absolutely availability with respect to God's will. Man must be completely turned toward God and toward his brethren. Silence is a quest and a form of charity, in which God's eyes become our eyes and God's heart is grafted onto our heart. We cannot stay in the presence of the fire of divine silence without being burned.

The friends and the lovers of God are irradiated by him. The more they remain in silence, the more they love God. The more empty of self they are, the more full of God they are. The more they converse with God, face to face, the more their faces beam with the light and splendor of God, like Moses coming out of the meeting tent (Ex 34:29–35).

117. There are souls who claim solitude so as to find themselves, and others who seek it in order to give themselves to God and to others.

118. In silence, God's joy becomes our joy. Being silent in the presence of God is almost being like God.

119. Dom Guillerand put it neatly: "Life is a few minutes spent together while waiting for the definitive great reunion in the fatherland where there is only one minute ... but an eternal minute. And by practicing a little, we will be able to begin living that minute here below through silence and solitude."

Silence and solitude are a small anticipation of eternity, when we will be in God's presence permanently, irradiated by him, the great Silent One, because he is the great lover.

120. Silence and solitude are very simple things, just as God himself is infinitely simple. In *The Prayer of Love and Silence*, Dom Jean-Baptiste Porion wrote:

> It is Our Lord himself who gives us the invitation: *Be ye simple as doves* [Mt 10:16]. Man is a complex being, but it would be a pity if he introduced his complications into his relations with God. God, on the contrary, is simplicity itself. The more complicated we are, therefore, the farther we stray from him; the simpler we are, on the other hand, the closer we come to him.

Silence is a paradise, but man does not see this right away. He is full of contradictions. We ought to be like children in God's presence. But we try in so many ways to make our relationship to God difficult and obscure or even nonexistent. Man has lost the simplicity of childhood. That is why silence is so difficult for him. And man rejects silence even more because he wants to become God himself.

In silence he cannot be a false god but can merely stand in a luminous face-to-face encounter with God.

In The Confessions, *Saint Augustine confides his own experience through these magnificent lines: "Late have I loved Thee, O Beauty so ancient and so new; late have I loved Thee! For behold Thou wert within me, and I outside; and I sought Thee outside and in my unloveliness fell upon those lovely things that Thou hast made. Thou wert with me and I was not with Thee. I was kept from Thee by those things, yet had they not been in Thee, they would not have been at all. Thou didst call and cry to me and break open*

*my deafness: and Thou didst send forth Thy beams and shine upon me and
chase away my blindness: Thou didst breathe fragrance upon me, and I drew
in my breath and do now pant for Thee: I tasted Thee, and now hunger and
thirst for Thee: Thou didst touch me, and I have burned for Thy peace."
Ultimately, where are the dwelling places of solitude and silence?*

121. Jesus himself points out to men the beautiful dwelling places of
solitude and silence. First of all, there is the privacy of our room when
we have closed the doors to be alone, in the secrecy of an intimate
conversation with God. There is also the chiaroscuro of a chapel, a
place of solitude, silence, and intimacy, where the Presence of all
presences awaits us, Jesus in the Eucharist. There are also shrines,
holy places, and monasteries that have been established to enable
us to devote a few days to the Lord. Finally, there are the houses of
God that are our churches, if the priests and the faithful take care to
respect their sacred character, so that they do not become museums,
theaters, or concert halls, but remain places reserved for prayer and
God alone.

122. Let us not hesitate to give pride of place to silent daily prayer
in the solitude of our room. In a perfect symbiosis with the cloisters of monasteries, it is necessary to experience an intimate relationship with God in the sanctuary of our room and to fight the
good fight of faith through prayer and silence. Today, in this pagan
world besotted with idols that boasts of the most abominable sins,
God himself demands through the mouth of the prophet Isaiah that
we go into our rooms to keep ourselves safe from all contamination
and all slavery of sin, but especially to pray intensely with a view
to our conversion: "Come, my people, enter your chambers, and
shut your doors behind you; hide yourselves for a little while....
For behold, the LORD is coming forth out of his place to punish the
inhabitants of the earth.... Or let them lay hold of my protection,
let them make peace with me, let them make peace with me" (Is
26:20–21; 27:5). We can become true contemplatives by living in
peace with God if our houses become temples of God.

123. The distance that must be traveled in order to go to the farthest
limits of our interior territory is so vast and so arduous that it needs
stopping places that consist of houses where silence and solitude are

inviolable pillars. The sacred intimacy of a chapel, a room, or the cloister of a monastery symbolizes the purity of paradise. In that blessed place, solitude and silence attain a form of aesthetic and spiritual perfection.

124. If we walk toward God, there comes a moment when speech is useless and uninteresting because contemplation alone has any importance. And so, more than any other reality, monastic life enables souls to contemplate God. The silence of the monasteries provides the best earthly setting for the person who wants to ascend toward the One who awaits him.

Dom Jean-Baptiste Porion very rightly reflected in *The Prayer of Love and Silence*:

> All life is mysterious in its principle and its operation. Contemplative life is the most profound life of all, and the truest. This is why it is also the most secret as well as the most inexplicable. Too simple and too spiritual for human words to be able to express it completely.... To enter the cloister is to convert, in other words, to turn away from the world and toward God. This is the beginning of Carthusian life and of all religious life as well. Those whom a divine calling leads into solitude have heard the Gospel verse: *"Poenitentiam agite. Vade, vende quod habes."* (Repent. Go, sell what you possess.) Therefore, above all, they have made an effort to be detached from creatures, to break the chains of our servitude. These acts of renunciation and submission will never cease to be necessary. We will always have to struggle against our fallen nature. *"Militia est vita hominis super terram."* (Man's life on earth is a combat.)

125. The cloister makes the *fuga mundi* a reality: the flight from the world to find solitude and silence. It means an end of the turmoil, the artificial lights, the sad drugs of noise and the hankering to possess more and more goods, so as to look to heaven. A man who enters the monastery seeks silence in order to find God. He wants to love God above all else, as his sole good and his only wealth. In his *Homily for the Christmas Novena*, Saint Alphonsus Liguori said:

> In order to be able to love God much in Heaven, it is necessary first to love him much on earth. The degree of our love for God at the end of

our life will be the measure of our love for God during eternity. Do we want to gain certitude that we will no longer be separated from this Supreme Good in the present life? Let us embrace him more and more by the bonds of our love, while saying to him with the Bride in Song of Songs: "I found him whom my soul loves: I held him, and would not let him go." How did the sacred Bride hold her Beloved? "One holds God with the arms of charity", Saint Ambrose replies. Happy, then, the one who can exclaim with Saint Paulinus: "Let the rich own their riches, let Kings possess their kingdoms: as for us, our glory, our wealth, and our kingdom is Christ!" And with Saint Ignatius [of Loyola]: "Only give me your love and your grace, and I am rich enough." Make me love you, and may I be loved by you; I do not desire and do not have to desire anything else.

Benedict XVI expressed better than any other pope this beautiful mystery of contemplative life in his speech at the Collège des Bernardins in Paris on September 12, 2008: "We set out from the premise that the basic attitude of monks in the face of the collapse of the old order and its certainties was *quaerere Deum*—setting out in search of God. We could describe this as the truly philosophical attitude: looking beyond the penultimate, and setting out in search of the ultimate and the true."

126. A monk commits himself to a journey that is noble and long; nevertheless, he already has guidance: the word of the Bible in which he hears God. Hence he must strive to understand him in order to be able to go to him. Thus the progress of monks, while remaining impossible to measure as it advances, is realized at the heart of the Word that is received and meditated on through the liturgy. In this search for God, the monk is intensely gripped by the silence of Christ during his Passion, and he is the one who attracts him.

Renunciation really does play a role, but it is a form of being stripped naked in God, a predisposition to silent listening and adoration. It is a long march toward God in light of the Word of the Bible. Silence is always the enemy of futile prospects, small talk, and affectations.

127. The world can pursue man anywhere he may go to hide, even in the solitude and silence of a cloister. Pride, the passions, and hypocrisy

seek to reassert their worst rights over the soul. When that happens, nestling in silence against the heart of God, with the open Bible over our head like the wings of the Holy Spirit, is still the best antidote, the one thing necessary to chase away from our interior territory all that is useless, superfluous, worldly, and even our own self.

128. The monastic tradition calls "Great Silence" the nocturnal atmosphere of peace that is supposed to reign in the communal areas, as well as in each cell, generally from Compline until Prime, so that each one can be alone with God. But each person ought to create and build for himself an interior cloister, "a wall and a bulwark", a private desert, so as to meet God there in solitude and silence.

129. For Father Jérôme, in his *Écrits monastiques*, it is rather obvious: "What a privilege it is to have this right—an acknowledged right, because it is a religious right—to take refuge in silence! Moreover, it is a privilege only if one has the courage to make use of it." Silence is the privilege of courageous persons. They may fall and lose hope; silence will unceasingly be able to lift them up again because it bears within it a divine presence and a divine origin. Silence is a conversion that is never accomplished easily.

130. In his book *Silence cartusien*, Dom Guillerand also wrote: "I want to become accustomed to looking in the darkness where the light filters through in order to arrive without injuring myself, to listen to this silence in which a voice speaks that says everything without words, to love this love that gives itself by enlightening me and speaking to me in this form that is higher than myself and closer to the light and the truth."

131. Physically, the faces of men of silence are different from those that are disfigured by the noises and pleasures and stratagems of a godless world. Their features, their gazes, and their smiles are lined by the power of silence. Great monks are accustomed to looking in the dark and can ceaselessly find the light that is God. For God is hidden, *Deus absconditus*, wrapped in a veil that silence alone can open partway. The shadow of silence allows a man to fix his attention on God. Silence is mystery; and the greatest mystery, God,

remains silent. I love to recall this remark by the poet Patrice de la Tour du Pin: "In every life, silence says God. Everything that exists thrills to belong to him! Be the voice of silence at work. Cherish life; for it praises God."

132. Monastic life, the life of men of solitude and silence, is an ascent toward the heights, not a rest on the heights. Monks climb higher every day because God is ceaselessly greater. On this earth, we will never be able to reach God. But nothing can accompany our earthly journey toward God better than solitude and silence.

133. Cloisters are not the only places where we can seek God.... Saint Augustine was abruptly snatched from his monastery to be consecrated the Bishop of Hippo. Overwhelmed by an exhausting episcopal office, crushed by the multiplicity of his pastoral duties, Saint Augustine often considered his episcopal activity to be a *sarcina episcopalis*. This popular term from military language refers to the soldier's baggage, his *barda*. The Bishop of Hippo had to load a particularly heavy *barda* on his shoulders every day. Despite his demanding ministry, and although he often had to deal with secular matters, Augustine found the time for silence and solitude in order to read, study, meditate on Sacred Scripture, pray for long hours, compose his dogmatic works, provide catechesis and teaching. Augustine's example is situated in the Church, not an abstract, ideal Church, but in the community in Hippo, whose care-lined faces, miseries, and heartbreaks were well known to him. With that community he prayed, fasted, suffered, and journeyed toward the daily conversion that is indispensable in order to live abundantly through God, with God, and in God. He expresses the experience of this community while commenting on the psalms, in which he finds himself again in his entirety: "From the time that the body of Christ groans being in afflictions, until the end of the world, when afflictions pass away, that man groaneth and calleth upon God: and each one of us after his measure hath his part in that cry in the whole body."

This God who desires him, this God who is present to his brethren, this God present in the innermost depth of his soul, is also the God whom he aspires to embrace, above and beyond all theological research, in silent prayer. Toward him he stretches out his whole being, which is now aflame with love. How many times did he scan the horizon to see whether he was coming so that he could rest in him and rejoice in his Presence! Augustine described himself as a man under God's tent, "delighted by the interior music, drawn by his sweetness", his divine notes that silence the noises of flesh and blood and the slow advance toward the House of God. But he knows that ecstasy lasts but a moment. He falls back into everyday human miseries. He groans in his fragile flesh. He is now borne up by an attempt that is the very reason for his journey. "Sing and keep on walking", he repeats. God is at the end of the road; already he feels the press of his hand . . .

Is silence the exile of speech? At times in your life have you thought that words were becoming too cumbersome, too heavy, too noisy?

134. We need to cultivate silence and to surround it with an interior dike.

In my prayer and in my interior life, I have always felt the need for a deeper, more complete silence. I am talking about a kind of discretion that amounts to not even thinking about myself but, rather, turning my attention, my being, and my soul toward God. The days of solitude, silence, and absolute fasting have been a great support. They have been an unprecedented grace, a slow purification, and a personal encounter with a God who wanted to draw me gradually toward a more substantial interior life so as to maintain an intimate relationship with him. Days of solitude, silence, and fasting, nourished by the Word of God alone, allow man to base his life on what is essential.

Thus I knew that I could acquire a spiritual vigor and freshness like those of a tree planted beside running waters, which stretches out its roots toward the stream. This tree fears nothing when hot weather arrives; its foliage stays green; during years of drought, it is carefree and does not cease to bear fruit (Jer 17:7–8). Silence and the development of my interior life are absolutely necessary; consecrated souls and priests must never forget it.

135. In *The Way of the Heart*, Henri Nouwen bitterly rebukes priests when he writes:

Silence guards the inner heat of religious emotions. This inner heat is the life of the Holy Spirit within us. Thus, silence is the discipline by which the inner fire of God is tended and kept alive.... What needs to be guarded is the life of the Spirit within us. Especially we who want to witness to the presence of God's Spirit in the world need to tend the fire within with utmost care. It is not so strange that many ministers have become burnt-out cases, people say many words and share many experiences, but in whom the fire of God's Spirit has died and from whom not much more comes forth than their own boring, petty ideas and feelings. Sometimes it seems that our many words are more an expression of our doubt than of our faith. It is as if we are not sure that God's Spirit can touch the hearts of people: we have to help him out and, with many words, convince others of his power. But it is precisely this wordy unbelief that quenches the fire....

As ministers our greatest temptation is toward too many words. They weaken our faith and make us lukewarm. Silence is a sacred discipline, a guard of the Holy Spirit.

St. John is particularly clear on this subject: "If you love me, you will keep my commandments. And I will ask the Father, and he will give you another Counselor, to be with you for ever, even the Spirit of truth, whom the world cannot receive, because it neither sees him nor knows him; you know him, for he dwells with you, and will be in you. I will not leave you desolate; I will come to you" (Jn 14:15–18).

After the Ascension, Christ did not leave mankind orphaned. As at the beginning of creation, like a gentle breeze, "the Spirit of God was moving over the face of the waters"; so the Son of God entrusted humanity into the hands of the Holy Spirit, who spreads the love of the Father and silently distributes his light and wisdom. This is why it is scarcely possible to let oneself be guided by the Holy Spirit in the noise and agitation of the world.

Christ is certainly distressed to see and to hear priests and bishops, who ought to be protecting the integrity of the teaching of the Gospel and of doctrine, multiply words and writings that weaken the rigor of the Gospel by their deliberately ambiguous, confused statements. It is not inopportune to remind these priests and prelates, who give the impression of saying the opposite of the Church's traditional teaching in matters of doctrine and morality, of Christ's severe words: "Therefore I tell you, every sin and blasphemy will be forgiven men, but the blasphemy against the Spirit will not be forgiven. And whoever says a word against the Son of man will be forgiven; but whoever speaks against the Holy Spirit will not be forgiven, either in this age or in the age to come." "[He] is guilty of an eternal sin", Mark adds (Mt 12:31–32; Lk 12:10; Mk 3:29).

Of course we have the duty to seek new pastoral approaches. But in his *Commentary on the Gospel of John*, Saint Thomas Aquinas warns us:

> If then, you ask which way to go, accept Christ, for he is the way: "This is the way, walk in it" (Is 30:21). And Augustine says: "Walk like this human being and you will come to God. It is better to limp along on the way than to walk briskly off the way." For one who limps on the way, even though he makes just a little progress, is approaching his destination; but if one walks off the way, the faster he goes the further he gets from his destination. If you ask where to go, cling to Christ, for he is the truth which we desire to reach.

Nouwen's remarks about priests who have misappropriated the Word of God, the sacraments, and the liturgy clearly demonstrate that there is a very close connection between silence and fidelity to the Holy Spirit. Without the asceticism of silence, pastors become rather uninteresting men, prisoners of their boring, pathetic torrents of words. Without the life of the Holy Spirit and without silence, a priest's teaching is nothing but confused chatter devoid of substance. A priest's speech must be an expression [*une forme*] of his soul and the sign of the divine Presence.

Nouwen's reflection is valid for everyone. The closer we are to the Holy Spirit, the more silent we are; and the farther we are from the Spirit, the more garrulous we are.

Every priest and every bishop ought to be able to say, like Saint Augustine: "*Voce Ecclesiae loquor* (I speak with the voice of the Church)" (Serm. 129, 4) and, therefore, with the voice of Jesus Christ; thus, with subtlety and efficacy, he should take upon himself the full responsibility of pastor and guide. Every priest, every bishop will keep in mind that on the terrible Day of Judgment he himself will have to answer before God for the sins of those whom he was unable to reform because of his own negligence.

In a letter, Saint Augustine writes seriously: "The glory of this age passes; on Judgment Day all these honors will be good for nothing. It is not my intention to waste my life on the vanity of ecclesiastical honors. I think of the day when I will have to render an accounting for the flock that has been entrusted to me by the Prince of pastors. Understand my fears, because my fears are great."

136. Lack of respect for silence is a form of blasphemy against the Holy Spirit. If he returns to a discipline of silence, a priest can subject himself to the Holy Spirit. If God's spokesmen do not let the Holy Spirit speak in them, they unfailingly change divine grace into mere, despicable human cleverness.

137. The priest is a man of silence. He must always be listening for God. True pastoral and missionary depth can come only from silent prayer. Without silence, the priesthood is ruined. A priest must be in the hands of the Holy Spirit. If he strays from the Spirit, he will be doomed to carry out a merely human work.

138. It is true that the Holy Spirit is still the "unknown God", according to the title of a little book by Father Victor Dillard, a Jesuit priest who died in Dachau on January 12, 1945. In *Au Dieu inconnu*, he introduced his reflection with this magnificent prayer, which is a supplication and a cry to the Holy Spirit, asking him to let himself be known, understood, touched, and even to reveal his face. For our desire to see him is intense:

> Lord, make me see.... I do not even know how to call on you, what to say: Holy Spirit, O Holy Ghost.... I try to understand you, to isolate you in the divine sea into which I plunge. But my outstretched hand brings me nothing, and imperceptibly I drift away and kneel before the Father or lean over my more familiar interior Christ. My body stops. The senses want their ration of images so as to enable the soul to fly toward you. And you give them only strange material foods: a dove, tongues of fire, breath. Nothing that allows the warm intimacy of a familial human prayer for two. The trouble is that you are too close to me. I would need a bit of distance in order to look at you, to demarcate you, and to demarcate me, too, with respect to you, to satisfy my need for precise contours in order to understand our union.

Father Victor Dillard's prayer expresses the believer's difficulty in picturing the uniqueness of the Divine Person named the Holy Spirit. Nevertheless, he is invoked extensively at the heart of the Eucharistic celebration in prayers that he might sanctify the people of God and all things and come to accomplish the transubstantiation, in other words, the transformation of the substance of the bread and wine into that of the Body and Blood of Jesus Christ in the Eucharist.

139. Christ gave us the great silence of the Holy Spirit. How can we forget him? If people wander away from the devouring fire of the Spirit's silence, they always end up adoring idols. It is necessary to tend the silent fire of Pentecost. Without the Spirit's silence, men are empty husks.

140. Silence is not the exile of speech. It is the love of the one Word. Conversely, the abundance of words is the symptom of doubt. Incredulity is always talkative.

141. We often forget that Christ loved to be silent. He set out for the desert, not to go into exile, but to encounter God. And at the most crucial moment in his life, when there was screaming on all sides, covering him with all sorts of lies and calumnies, when the high priest asked him: "Have you no answer to make?" Jesus preferred silence.

It is a case of true amnesia: Catholics no longer know that silence is sacred because it is God's dwelling place. How can we rediscover the sense of silence as the manifestation of God? This is the tragedy of the modern world: man separates himself from God because he no longer believes in the value of silence.

142. Without silence, God disappears in the noise. And this noise becomes all the more obsessive because God is absent. Unless the world rediscovers silence, it is lost. The earth then rushes into nothingness.

Does the silence of listening exist? Might there be a paradox in trying to understand the other by remaining silent?

143. In order to listen, it is necessary to keep quiet. I do not mean merely a sort of constraint to be physically silent and not to interrupt what someone else is saying, but rather an interior silence, in other words, a silence that not only is directed toward receiving the other person's words but also reflects a heart overflowing with a humble love, capable of full attention, friendly welcome and voluntary self-denial, and strong with the awareness of our poverty.

The silence of listening is a form of attention, a gift of self to the other, and a mark of moral generosity. It should manifest an awareness of our humility so as to agree to receive from another person a gift that God is giving us. For the other person is always a treasure and a precious gift that God offers to help us grow in humility, humanity, and nobility.

I think that the most defective human relationship is precisely one in which the silence of attention is absent.

144. It is necessary to impose silence on the labor of thought, calm the agitation of the heart, the turmoil of cares and worries, and eliminate all artificial distraction. Nothing makes us understand listening better than the correlation between silence and listening, attention and the gift. Thus, Saint John writes in the Prologue to his Gospel: "The light shines in the darkness, and the darkness has not overcome it" (Jn 1:5). The silence of listening is a silent heart-to-heart conversation.

How else can a heart fully receive the other person but in silence? The latter can be explained, not by the intellect, but by the soul.

145. By analogy, music is fully listened to when everything falls silent around us and within us, in the most perfect way, with our eyes closed. The best way I can express this silence of listening is by evoking the magic of the organ when it fills the church with its song. One hears it then, without seeing anything of what is going on high up in the choir loft where it is situated; a sound emerges from a maternal darkness and, beneath the motionless, shadowy vaulted ceiling, envelops us like a winding sheet.

The summit of the silence of listening is surely reached when even the word is presented in silence, without losing any of its vitality, in reading, which is an encounter between a word deprived of sound and an addressee who is totally turned toward his own interior in a perfect solitude of welcome.

What can be said about the silence of memory? We are not speaking here about the silence of sickness, when a person loses his memories and points of reference.

146. Memory is a word made fruitful by the Holy Spirit. It is a tomb, a tilled soil in which man deposits the seed of the word, and the latter takes root and springs up silently, developing a new, more abundant life that bears hope within it.

Having died in the silence of listening, the word flourishes again under the sun of the Spirit that reawakens it to life. Assimilated and made fruitful through meditation, it appears as a new being laden with many fruits: if the grain of wheat does not die, it bears no fruit. The death of the seed is the life of the plant. And the plant, the only being in all nature that is simultaneously silent and animated, is offered to us precisely as the most perfect image of what occurs during the moments that follow silent listening.

Thus the speculative tradition of *lectio divina*, which has run through Christianity from Origen to our day, says that *meditatio* follows *lectio* [reading], and *oratio* [prayer] follows *meditatio*. The reading of the *lectio divina* is by its nature reserved for a situation in which one addresses God, and thus it reflects perfectly the riches of silence.

147. The silence of memory is peace of soul and heart. The silence of memory is a free, upright man.

In his Diary of a Country Priest, *Georges Bernanos writes: "Keeping silent—what a strange expression! Silence keeps us." How are we to understand this sort of human irrationality with respect to silence?*

148. Father Jérôme, a Trappist monk, tried to answer this question. In his *Écrits monastiques*, he wrote:

> Silence is a mystery; or, more exactly, people's attitude toward silence poses a quasi-mysterious problem. All sensible people admire silence; they are all persuaded of its usefulness; but they are almost never

willing to make progress in it.... In order to practice charity: we should take upon ourselves the sorts of "noises" that trouble minds, stop them right there and not let them run along to others. And we should do so simply, because trouble turns people away from God.

Noise surrounds us and assaults us. The noise of our ceaselessly active cities, the noise of automobiles, airplanes, machines outside and inside our houses. Besides this noise that is imposed on us, there are the noises that we ourselves produce or choose. Such is the soundtrack of our everyday routine. This noise, unconsciously, often has a function that we do not dare admit: it masks and stifles another sound, the one that occupies and invades our interior life. How can we not be astonished by the efforts that we constantly make to stifle God's silences?

149. Noise is a desecration of the soul, noise is the "silent" ruin of the interior life. Man always has the tendency to remain outside himself. But we must ceaselessly come back to the interior castle.

150. We discover this noise painfully when we decide to stop what we are doing to enter into prayer. Often the great din colonizes our interior temple. The modern world has multiplied the most toxic noises, which are so many malignant enemies of peace of heart. In a secularized, materialistic, and hedonistic world, in which wars, bombs, and submachine gunfire, acts of violence and barbarism are the common currency, where assaults on the dignity of the human person, the family, and life affect people at their very core, respect for silence has become the least of humanity's worries. And yet God hides himself in silence.

151. Carmelite Brother Philippe de Jésus-Marie writes quite accurately, in a conference on interior silence:

We sense that our soul, originally, is a space of silence, a virgin place, a sanctuary where God wants to dwell in peace with us. But when we appear on the threshold of this interior temple by making a movement of recollection, we discover odd cacophonies that turn this time of prayer into a resonating chamber where all the aspects of our lives come to echo, where all our fears and worries, our desires and our most varied emotions are manifested. The fundamental question, then, is no longer primarily the one about external noise but, rather, the one about the silence of our thoughts.

Alas, the experience described by Brother Philippe de Jésus-Marie is widespread nowadays, particularly in the Western world, and even beyond it.

One day, beyond the invasive noise that is perversely interwoven in so many lives, it will be important to listen once again to the "still small voice", the voice of God, which will say to us again: "What are you doing here, Elijah?" (1 Kings 19:12–13).

152. In *The Interior Castle*, Teresa of Avila describes with particular precision this universal experience: "It seems as if there are in my head many rushing rivers and that these waters are hurtling downward, and many little birds and whistling sounds, not in the ears but in the upper part of the head where, they say, the higher part of the soul is."

153. Carmelite Brother Philippe de Jésus-Marie also writes:

> Therefore during prayer time it is absolutely necessary to resist the urge to board those trains or boats that go by. In order to do that, it is of capital importance not to identify with these thoughts but, on the contrary, to realize that they come to us, that they are not of us, that they are displayed on the backdrop of our interior silence. That is where we will encounter God.... All that he asks of us in his presence is to remain in this silence, which is the most beautiful of all praises that we could offer him.

All of us are in "those trains or boats that go by". Often we enter chapels and churches with the trains and boats. It can even happen that we are not very aware of the noise that we drag behind us into the house of God.

154. I know that it is very difficult to get rid of the manifold problems that can assail us and trouble our silence. How can we ask a mother whose child is seriously ill to hold at bay all the painful thoughts that

constantly assail her? How can we ask a man who has just lost his wife, carried off by a long illness, to set aside the veil of sadness that is breaking his heart so as to rediscover a certain quality of silence?

Yet even if daily life is as difficult as it can be, God nevertheless remains present in each one of us. He is a patient, faithful, and merciful God, who waits untiringly. The most difficult thing is probably to come to our senses, to be quiet, to turn toward the Father, to repent and say: "'How many of my father's hired servants have bread enough and to spare, but I perish here with hunger! I will arise and go to my father, and I will say to him, "Father, I have sinned against heaven and before you; I am no longer worthy to be called your son; treat me as one of your hired servants."' And he arose and came to his father" (Lk 15:17–20). The journey toward heaven consists of rediscovering our silent interior life in which God dwells and waits for us, watching the horizon.

155. In a conference dealing with "The Sound of Silence in the Holy Desert", Carmelite Brother Jean-Gabriel de l'Enfant-Jésus rightly commented:

> Reading the Desert Fathers in this way, you would be tempted to believe that life in the Desert is full of sweet conversations with God, with no other care but this "holy laziness" whose loving contemplation John of the Cross describes in his *Spiritual Canticle*.... Most often, however, the hermit is confronted with the darkness of his sinful soul. Silence and solitude are the place of a spiritual battle against his three enemies: the world, the devil, and the old man (or "the flesh", in the Pauline sense), which is the most stubborn of the three, if we are to believe John of the Cross.

It is necessary to protect precious silence from all parasitical noise. The noise of our "ego", which never stops claiming its rights, plunging us into an excessive preoccupation with ourselves. The noise of our memory, which draws us toward the past, that of our recollections or of our sins. The noise of temptations or of acedia, the spirit of gluttony, lust, avarice, anger, sadness, vanity, pride—in short: everything that makes up the spiritual combat that man must wage every day. In order to silence these parasitical noises, in order

to consume everything in the sweet flame of the Holy Spirit, silence
is the supreme antidote.

156. There is a sort of glory of silence. Saint Ignatius of Loyola did
not hesitate to write in his *Spiritual Exercises*: "The more the soul is in
solitude and seclusion, the more fit it renders itself to approach and
be united with its Creator and Lord."

157. Silence never makes a display of splendor or grandeur. Silence is
simply in the image of God. Silence never blinds us like flashy, gaudy
noises, because it is the simple reflection of divine love.

158. In his book *For Self-Examination*, the philosopher Søren Kierkegaard summed up the problem explicitly and brilliantly:

> If, in observing the present state of the world and life in general, from
> a Christian point of view one had to say ...: It is a disease. And if I
> were a physician and someone asked me "What do you think should
> be done?" I would answer, "... The very first thing that must be
> done is: create silence, bring about silence; God's Word cannot
> be heard, and if in order to be heard in the hullabaloo it must be
> shouted deafeningly with noisy instruments, then it is not God's Word;
> create silence! Ah, everything is noisy; and just as a strong drink is said
> to stir the blood, so everything in our day, even the most insignificant
> project, even the most empty communication, is designed merely to
> jolt the senses or to stir up the masses, the crowd, the public, noise!
> And man, this clever fellow, seems to have become sleepless in order
> to invent ever new instruments to increase noise, to spread noise and
> insignificance with the greatest possible haste and on the greatest possi-
> ble scale. Yes, everything is soon turned upside down: communication
> is indeed soon brought to its lowest point with regard to meaning, and
> simultaneously the means of communication are indeed brought to
> their highest with regard to speedy and overall circulation; for what is
> publicized with such hot haste and, on the other hand, what has greater
> circulation than—rubbish! O, create silence!"

159. The most difficult thing for man is to seek God in silence. This
silent light is not a human word but a humble and poor light.

II

GOD DOES NOT SPEAK,
BUT HIS VOICE IS QUITE CLEAR

Oh, happy and most happy is the soul that merits to be drawn to God and by God, so that, through the unity of the Spirit in God, it loves God alone and not some personal good, and loves itself only in God.... "That they may be one, even as we are one" (John 17:11)! This is the goal, this is the consummation, the perfection: peace, the joy of the Lord, joy in the Holy Spirit, this is the Silence in Heaven (cf. Rev 8:1).

—William of Saint Thierry
Letter to the Brethren of Mont-Dieu

NICOLAS DIAT: *Thomas Merton rightly considers in* The Sign of Jonas *that "the problem of language is the problem of sin. The problem of silence is also a problem of love. How can a man really know whether to write or not, whether to speak or not, whether his words and his silence are for good or for evil, for life or for death, unless he understands the two divisions of tongues— the division of Babel, where men were scattered in their speech because of pride, and the division of Pentecost when the Holy Ghost sent out men of one dialect to speak all the languages of the earth and bring all men to unity: 'that they may be one, Father, Thou in Me and I in Thee that they may be one in us!' (cf. Jn 17:21–22). The apostles and disciples come downstairs and tumble into the street like an avalanche, talking in every language.... [God] manifested Himself through them. That is the only possible reason for speaking—but it justifies speaking without end, as long as the speech grows up from silence and brings your soul to silence once again."*

How then can we understand the mystery of God's silence, which so many men through the ages have found so difficult to accept?

87

ROBERT CARDINAL SARAH:

160. Many of our contemporaries cannot accept God's silence. They do not admit that it is possible to enter into communication other than by words, gestures, or concrete, visible actions. Yet God speaks through his silence. The silence of God is a form of speech. His Word is solitude.

The solitude of God is not an absence, it is his very being, his silent transcendence.

161. Thomas Merton thinks that "The silence of God should teach us when to speak and when not to speak. But we cannot bear the thought of that silence, lest it cost us the trust and respect of men."

We are anxious to respond to so many difficulties, sufferings, and disasters that afflict mankind. We forget that the source of our troubles comes from the illusion that we are something other than mere dust. The man who makes himself God no longer wants to know that he is mortal. Psalm 103 says that God himself "knows our frame; he remembers that we are dust. As for man, his days are like grass; he flourishes like a flower of the field; for the wind passes over it, and it is gone, and its place knows it no more" (Ps 103:14–16).

We should recognize that God is our joy, and in him our dust can become splendor. The love of Christ changes the immense sorrow of mankind into joy; the secret of happiness is to see all our sufferings in the light of Christ's victory over death. All suffering contributes in one way or another to our happiness.

162. Creation itself is a silent word of God. The wordless beauty of nature displays before our eyes the manifold riches of a Father who is ceaselessly present among men. This divine speech is not audible to ears that are too human; nevertheless, it is the most profound speech of all. The sun, the moon, and the stars are absolutely silent to our ears, but they are a word and a message essential to our earthly existence. There is a language of the stars that we can neither know nor comprehend but that God understands perfectly.

The *Canticle of the Three Young Men*, the *Hymn of the Universe*, that we sing every Sunday at Morning Prayer, taken from the Book of Daniel, attests that the sun and the moon, nights and days, the stars, the mountains and the hills, the springs and the fountains, the oceans and the rivers, the beasts of the sea and the birds of the air bless the Lord and sing his praise: "He who is of God hears the words of God" (Jn 8:47).

Why can men not hear the voice of God when he speaks through creation? Indeed, we think that we are the only ones capable of speaking to him and hearing him! In *To Leave Before Dawn / The Green Paradise*, Julien Green writes:

> God speaks to children with extreme gentleness, and what He has to say to them He often says without words. Creation provides Him with the vocabulary He needs, leaves, clouds, running water, a patch of light. It is the secret language that books cannot teach you and which children know very well.... Children can be compared to a vast multitude who have received an uncommunicable secret and who gradually forget the secret, the multitude's fate being taken in hand by so-called civilized nations.... As for me, I have known what children know, and all the reasoning in the world has not been able to tear away from me that unutterable something. Words cannot describe it. It stands on the threshold of speech and, on this earth, remains mute.

163. I am certain that God gives to each believer a heart capable of hearing the language of creation. According to the expression of Ben Sirach the Sage, the Father has "set His eye on [men's] hearts" (Sir 17:8, Douay-Rheims), so that the believer may look at God, his neighbor, and the whole of creation with God's eyes. God has sealed my heart in his heart. God dwells in my heart. From now on, man and God are in league, because they have the same heart and the same eyes: what God sees and hears, the believer can also see and hear. I dare to say that such a love exists.

164. Christ approached from his descent from the Mount of Olives when, joyfully, the whole multitude of his disciples began to praise God in a loud voice for the miracles that they had seen. They said: "Blessed is the King who comes in the name of the Lord! Peace in heaven and glory in the highest!" Some Pharisees in the crowd said to him: "Teacher, rebuke your disciples." Christ's response to the Pharisees is particularly eloquent, because it confirms that creation is also capable of singing the praise of God. He said: "I tell you, if

these were silent, the very stones would cry out" (Lk 19:38–40). As we have heard, the Bible exhorts creation to praise God. The rivers, the birds, the reptiles, the sun, and the moon praise the Lord. The language of God, like that of nature, is not immediately perceptible to our intellect; nevertheless, it still has a great power that wishes to communicate itself to men. By language I mean all merely human expressions that bind men to each other. But I do not renounce entirely the mute language of beauty, of the mountain, of the sea, of the stone, of thunder, of fire, and of all creatures that show forth God and sing his praises.

165. The silence of God is understood by faith, in meditation on the communion that can exist between him and men.

The divine silence is a mysterious revelation. God is not insensitive to evil. At first, we may think that God allows evil to destroy men. But if God remains silent, he nonetheless suffers with us from the evil that tears apart and disfigures the earth. If we seek to be with God in silence, we will understand his presence and his love.

166. God's silence can also be a reproach. We often pretend not to want to listen to this language. Conversely, if there is an earthquake or a major natural disaster, associated with immeasurable human tragedies, we accuse God of not speaking. God's silence questions mankind on its ability to enter into the mystery of life and hope at the very heart of suffering and hardships. The more we refuse to understand this silence, the more we move away from him. I am convinced that the problem of contemporary atheism lies first of all in a wrong interpretation of God's silence about catastrophes and human sufferings. If man sees in the divine silence only a form of God's abandonment, indifference, or powerlessness, it will be difficult to enter into his ineffable and inaccessible mystery. The more man rejects the silence of God, the more he will rebel against him.

167. The silence of God is elusive and inaccessible. But the person who prays knows that God hears him in the same way that he understood the last words of Christ on the Cross. Mankind speaks, and God responds by his silence.

168. How can we understand these long years of the Shoah [Holocaust] and the abominable procession of extermination camps, like the one in Auschwitz-Birkenau, where so many innocent Jews perished? How can we understand God's silence? Why did God choose not to intervene when his people were being massacred? Hans Jonas, the German Jewish philosopher, has attempted to respond to such a painful question in his book *The Concept of God after Auschwitz*: "What did Auschwitz add to that which one could always have known about the extent of the terrible and horrendous things that humans can do to humans and from times immemorial have done?" Hans Jonas naturally calls God into question: "God let it happen. What God could let it happen?" The Almighty God did not intervene to prevent the barbaric massacre of his people. And why did he allow it? Hans Jonas responds: "In order that the world might be, and be for itself, God renounced His being." What does that mean? "To make room for the world, the *En-Sof* (Infinite; literally, No-End) of the beginning had to contract Himself so that, vacated by Him, empty space could expand outside of Him: the 'Nothing' in which and from which God could then create the world. Without this retreat into Himself, there could be no 'other' outside God." We can guess his conclusion: In deciding on this withdrawal into himself so that man can exist, God becomes by that very fact a suffering God, because he will have to suffer because of man and be disappointed in him. God will also be a concerned God, because he will entrust the world to agents other than himself, to free agents. In short, this is a God at risk, a God who incurs a proper risk. But then, that God is not an almighty God. In order for the goodness of God to be compatible with the existence of evil, he must not be almighty. More exactly, it is necessary for this God to have renounced power. In the simple fact of allowing human freedom lies a renunciation of power.

169. But if God is not powerful, then he is not God. He is the Almighty, but, at the same time, he wants to permit man to be truly free. Because the omnipotence of God is the omnipotence of love; and the omnipotence of love is death. The infinity of God is not an infinity in space, a bottomless, shoreless ocean; it is a love that has no limits. Creation is an act of infinite love. For Hans Jonas, the act of creation is a kind of divine "self-restraint". By dint of this, God's

silence and his allowing things to happen can receive an initial explanation. Human suffering mysteriously becomes suffering for God.
In the divine nature, suffering is not synonymous with imperfec-
tion. This problem reminds me of a letter from a mother of a family
touched by the idea of vulnerability in God:

> When my children were little and I thought for them and made deci-
> sions for them, everything was easy: my freedom alone was in ques-
> tion. But the time came when I realized that my role was gradually to
> get them used to making choices, and as soon as I agreed to do that,
> I felt worried. While allowing my children to make decisions, and
> therefore to take risks, I at the same time took the risk of seeing
> freedoms other than mine arise. If, too often, I continued to make
> choices in place of my children, it was, I must admit, to spare them
> from suffering the consequences of a choice that they might have to
> regret. Yet there was another reason at least as important, if not more
> so: in order not to risk a disagreement between their choice and the
> one I would have liked to see them make. It was a lack of love on
> my part, therefore, since by acting that way I essentially tried to shield
> myself from possible suffering, the pain I felt each time my children
> committed themselves to a way different from the one that to me
> seemed best for them. This way I manage to glimpse the fact that God
> the "Father" can suffer. We are his children. He wants us to be free to
> build our own lives, and the infinity of his love makes any constraint
> on his part impossible. Perfect love, without a trace of self-interest but
> that implies the acceptance from the outset of some suffering inherent
> in this total freedom that he wants for us.

To believe in a silent God who "suffers" is to make the mystery of
God's silence more mysterious and more luminous, too; it is to dispel
a false clarity so as to replace it with a "shining darkness". Because I
do not forget the words of the Psalm: " 'Let only darkness cover me,
and the light about me be night,' even the darkness is not dark to
you, the night is bright as the day" (Ps 139:11–12). This psalm could
strengthen man when his darkest demons besiege him and when he
is tempted to revolt against God.

The silence of God is an invitation to maintain silence ourselves
in order to examine thoroughly the great mystery of man in his joys,
pains, suffering, and death.

How can we respond to people who tell themselves more or less vaguely: "God is not interested in me. He is always silent!"?

170. It is not easy to find adequate language to speak respectfully and fruitfully to those who feel abandoned by God. It is necessary to be armed with fraternal compassion and a prudent pedagogy and to allow oneself to be supported by prayer, the work of the Spirit who opens the heart to the Word of God. With friendship and tact, the important thing is to ask these people to accept the mystery of the divine silence by making an act of surrender and of faith in the salvific dimension of suffering. If man remains fixed on materialistic and rationalist certainties, he always bets on this hypothetical abandonment of God. Love, by its essence, implies a leap into the unknown. Modernity likes to see in the silence of God an easy proof of his non-existence: if evil and suffering exist, there can be no God.

171. I still hear the sobbing voice of a seven-year-old Muslim child who, with tears in his eyes, was lamenting: "Does Allah exist? Why did he let my dad be killed? Why did he not do something to prevent this crime?" In his mysterious silence, God manifests himself in the tear shed by the child who suffers, and not in the order of the world that would justify this tear. God has his mysterious way of being close to us in our trials.

172. External manifestations are not always the best evidence of closeness. Our closest friends are sometimes far from us, which does not prevent them from loving us dearly. A father is not necessarily close to his children throughout their lives, but he remains no less concerned about them.

173. God is a Father who may seem distant. But this Father is as interested in us as if he were as close as possible to our heart. Sometimes, God lifts us to the top of the Cross, letting us grow tall in the trial in order to test our growth and our intimacy with him. It is necessary to undergo suffering as a part of our humanity. Contemplation of the Cross helps us. Teilhard de Chardin wrote in a letter: "If we fully understand the meaning of the Cross, we will no longer run the risk of finding life sad and ugly. We will only become more

attentive to its incomprehensible seriousness." And, prefacing the book that records the notes of his sister, who was an invalid throughout her life, he wrote: "O Marguerite, my sister, while I, given body and soul to the positive forces of the universe, was wandering over continents and oceans, my whole being passionately taken up in watching the rise and fall of all the earth's tints and shades, you lay motionless, stretched out on your bed of sickness; silently, deep within yourself, you were transforming into light the world's most grievous shadows. In the eyes of the Creator, which of us, tell me, which of us will have had the better part?"

This look from the Cross gives rise in us to a prayer similar to that of Jesus: "Father, into your hands I commit my spirit!" (Lk 23:46).

174. I can imagine that a person who never prays is incapable of understanding God's silent speech. Nevertheless, when we are lovers, we always notice the slightest gesture of the one whom we love. It is the same with prayer. If we are accustomed to praying often, we can grasp the meaning of God's silence. There are signs that only two fiancés can understand. The person of prayer is also the only one to grasp the silent signs of affection that God sends him.

175. God is a discreet friend who comes to share joys, pains, and tears without expecting anything in return. We must believe in this friendship.

The Book of Revelation by Saint John speaks in a particularly poetic manner of the "silence in heaven". What is the meaning of these lines that have given rise to so many interpretations?

176. In heaven, speech does not exist. There on high, the blessed communicate with each other without any words. There is a great silence of contemplation, communion, and love.

177. In the divine homeland, souls are completely united to God. They are nourished by the vision of him. Souls are completely taken by their love for God in absolute delight. There is a great silence because souls have no need for words in order to be united to God. Anguish, passions, fears, sorrows, jealousies, hatreds, and impulses

disappear. Nothing exists except the unique heart-to-heart with God. The embrace of souls and God is eternal. Heaven is the heart of God. And this heart is silent forever. God is perfect tenderness that has no need of any speech in order to be diffused. Paradise is like a huge burning bush that is never consumed, however forcefully the love that burns there spreads. There above, love burns with an innocent flame, with a pure desire to love infinitely and to plunge into the intimate depth of the Trinity.

178. Benedict XVI expresses with striking clarity the importance of the love of God. In the very first lines of his encyclical *Deus caritas est*, he wrote:

> We have come to believe in God's love: in these words the Christian can express the fundamental decision of his life. Being Christian is not the result of an ethical choice or a lofty idea, but the encounter with an event, a person, which gives life a new horizon and a decisive direction. Saint John's Gospel describes that event in these words: "God so loved the world that he gave his only Son, that whoever believes in him should ... have eternal life" (Jn 3:16). In acknowledging the centrality of love, Christian faith has retained the core of Israel's faith, while at the same time giving it new depth and breadth. The pious Jew prayed daily the words of the Book of Deuteronomy which expressed the heart of his existence: "Hear, O Israel: the Lord our God is one Lord, and you shall love the Lord your God with all your heart, and with all your soul and with all your might" (6:4-5). Jesus united into a single precept this commandment of love for God and the commandment of love for neighbor found in the Book of Leviticus: "You shall love your neighbor as yourself" (19:18; cf. Mk 12:29-31). Since God has first loved us (cf. 1 Jn 4:10), love is now no longer a mere "command"; it is the response to the gift of love with which God draws near to us.

179. In the Book of Revelation by Saint John, there are some mysterious descriptions. The silence of heaven is a silence of love, prayer, offering, and adoration. Thus, "when the Lamb opened the seventh seal, there was silence in heaven for about half an hour.... And another angel came and stood at the altar with a golden censer; and he was given much incense to mingle with the prayers of all the saints ...; and the smoke of the incense rose with the prayers of the saints from the hand of the angel before God" (Rev 8:1, 3-4).

180. Saint Augustine's prayer for the dead is particularly beautiful:

> If you knew the gift of God and what heaven is. If you could hear the
> song of the angels from here and see me in the midst of them. If you
> could see unfolding before your eyes the horizons and eternal fields,
> the new paths where I walk! If, for a moment, you could contemplate
> as I do the beauty before which all beauties pale. What? You saw
> me, you loved me in the country of shadows, and you could not
> see me or love me in the country of immutable realities! Believe me,
> when death comes to break your bonds as it broke those that chained
> me and when, on a day that God knows and that he has determined,
> your soul comes into this heaven where mine has preceded, on that
> day you will see me again, you will find my affection purified. God
> forbid that upon entering a happier life, unfaithful to the memories
> and the true joys of my other life, I became less loving. You will
> see me again, then, transfigured into ecstasy and happiness, no longer
> awaiting death, but advancing moment to moment with you into new
> paths of Light and Life. Wipe away your tears, and weep no more if
> you love me.

181. To speak about a "silence in heaven" is a truly daring adventure.
In certain journeys, it is wise and prudent to let oneself be guided by
the experience of those who know the conditions and the geographical setting. What an extraordinary adventure to try to reflect on the
silence of heaven! To set out on the route of this mystery, it is necessary to be roped to others. Alone we can only stammer ...

182. The Fathers of the Church often reflected on these questions.
They knew that silence is the supreme freedom of man with God.
Saint Gregory the Great has some words of rare profundity on silence.
In the *Pastoral Rule*, he wrote: "For the human mind, after the manner of water, when closed in, is collected unto higher levels, in that it
seeks again the height from which it descended; and, when let loose,
it falls away in that it disperses itself unprofitably through the lowest
places.... For, because it has not the wall of silence, the city of the
mind lies open to the darts of the foe" (III, 14).

183. I often think of my predecessor in the See of Conakry, Archbishop Raymond-Marie Tchidimbo. He remained for almost nine

years in a sordid prison. It was forbidden for him to talk to anyone. In this silence, so terrible in appearance, like an icy and black insult, he had to turn to God in order to survive. The silence imposed by his jailers became his sole expression of love, his only offering to God, his only ladder to rise to heaven and converse with God, face to face, as a man speaks with his friend. Mysteriously, his dungeon allowed him to understand a little the great silence of heaven. During the long months, he expected to be savagely murdered, to be electrocuted or beaten. He could understand that the mystery of evil, the mystery of suffering, and the mystery of silence are intimately connected. Thanks to an intimate encounter with God in the silence, he faced the daily trials with serenity. He knew that his life would not end in a miserable jail. He knew that his prison was like a plowed field; every day he sowed his life there as a seed is sown, fully aware that those who sow in tears will sing when they reap. He knew that he was at the door of the true life. Beyond the distress, beyond so many physical and moral humiliations, silence gave him strength, courage, humility, and selflessness.

184. Paradoxically, the silence of someone sentenced to death carries in it all sorts of hope. The condemned already sees on this earth the great silence of heaven. The silence of the abominations leads like a tunnel toward the hope of silence in God. Because, for the worst criminals, the only necessity is to push on the door of true silence and to put their hands into the silent hands of God: "This is the end, this is the consummation, the perfection, the peace, the joy of the Lord, the joy in the Holy Spirit, this is the silence in heaven." The silence of prayer is like a Eucharistic silence, a silence of adoration, a silence in God.

185. Benedict XVI, in his homily during the Mass on the Feast of *Corpus Christi*, June 7, 2012, stated:

To be all together in prolonged silence before the Lord present in his Sacrament is one of the most genuine experiences of our being Church, which is accompanied complementarily by the celebration of the Eucharist, by listening to the word of God, by singing and by approaching the table of the Bread of Life together. Communion and contemplation cannot be separated, they go hand in hand. If I am truly to communicate with another person I must know him, I must be able to be in silence close to him, to listen to him and look at him lovingly. True love and true friendship are always nourished by the reciprocity of looks, of intense, eloquent silences full of respect and veneration, so that the encounter may be lived profoundly and personally rather than superficially.

This is the real anticipation of the silence of God that we are all called to know.

186. It may be enough to look with simplicity and admiration at the faces of the old monks, lined and burned by God's silence, in order to approach such a beautiful mystery. The monks are humanly damaged, banished by the children of the world, and yet spiritually irradiated, marked by the beauty of Christ.

187. Mother Teresa had a face charred by God's silences, but she bore within her and breathed love. By dint of remaining long hours before the burning flame of the Blessed Sacrament, her face was tanned, transformed by a daily face-to-face encounter with the Lord.

188. The aestheticism of silence does not depend on human factors; it is divine. The silence of God is an illumination, simple and sublime, little and grandiose.

Seen from this earth, eternity can seem long and silent . . .

189. The silence of eternity is the consequence of God's infinite love. In heaven, we will be with Jesus, totally possessed by God and under the influence of the Holy Spirit. Man will no longer be capable of saying a single word. Prayer itself will have become impossible. It will become contemplation, a look of love and adoration. The Holy Spirit will inflame the souls who go to heaven. They will be completely given over to the Spirit.

190. On this earth, it is important to listen for the silences of the Holy Spirit. Saint Paul writes with assurance: "Likewise the Spirit helps us

in our weakness; for we do not know how to pray as we ought, but the Spirit himself intercedes for us with sighs too deep for words" (Rom 8:26).

191. In heaven, souls are united to the angels and saints through the Spirit. Then, there is no more speech. It is an endless silence, nestled in God's love. The liturgy of eternity is silent; souls have nothing else to do but to join the choir of angels. They are exclusively in contemplation. Here below, to contemplate is already to be in silence. In heaven, this silence becomes a silence of fullness, in the vision of God. The silence of eternity is a silence of wonder and admiration. "And after my skin has been thus destroyed, then from my flesh I shall see God, whom I shall see on my side, and my eyes shall behold, and not another" (Job 19:26–27). Indeed, the silence of eternity is connected to the fullness of God; it is a Trinitarian silence.

192. The Church knows how difficult it is for man to understand the silence of eternity. Here on earth, there are few things that can make us grasp the immensity of divine love. During the Mass and the Eucharist, the consecration and the elevation are a small anticipation of the eternal silence. If this silence is authentic, we can glimpse the silence of heaven.

Adoration of the Blessed Sacrament is a time when the quality of interior silence can allow us to enter a little into God's silence. Adoration is a little drop of eternity.

The silence of eternity is a silence of love.

A prayer of Kierkegaard attempts to penetrate the understanding of God's silence: "Never let us forget that You speak also when You are quiet; give us confidence, too, when we are awaiting Your coming, that You are quiet out of love just as You speak out of love. Thus, whether You are quiet or speak, You are always the same Father, the same paternal heart, whether You guide us by Your voice or raise us by Your silence." Likewise, the silences of Christ can be difficult to understand . . . .

193. Jesus comes to this earth during a peaceful and silent night, while mankind is sleeping. Only the shepherds remain awake (Lk 2:8). His birth is surrounded by solitude and silence. For thirty years, no one

hears him. Christ lives in Nazareth in great simplicity, buried in the silence and the humble workshop of Joseph the carpenter (Mt 13:55). It is certain that he already lives in prayer, penance, and interior recollection. This hidden life of Jesus is in the silent shadow of God. The Son of Mary lives constantly in the Beatific Vision, in profound communion, inseparably united to the Father.

194. The silence of Jesus is the very silence of God the Father. Did Jesus not say to Philip: "He who has seen me has seen the Father; how can you say, 'Show us the Father'? Do you not believe that I am in the Father and the Father is in me?" (Jn 14:9–10). We must never grow weary of repeating this sentence by Saint John. It means that the unity of God and man in Jesus manifests in time the eternal unity of the Father and the Son in the Holy Spirit. The silence of the Father is the silence of the Son; the voice of the Son is the voice of the Father. To hear Jesus is to hear the Father.

195. In Nazareth, God was constantly and silently with God. God spoke to God in silence. In examining this silence, men reenter the unfathomable, silent mystery of the Trinity.

196. Christ's public life is rooted in and supported by the silent prayer of his hidden life. The silence of Christ, God present in a human body, is hidden in the silence of God. His earthly speech is inhabited by the silent speech of God.

The whole life of Jesus is wrapped in silence and mystery. If man wants to imitate Christ, it is enough for him to observe his silences.

The silence of the crib, the silence of Nazareth, the silence of the Cross, and the silence of the sealed tomb are one. The silences of Jesus are silences of poverty, humility, self-sacrifice, and abasement; it is the bottomless abyss of his kenosis, his self-emptying (Phil 2:7).

197. At the moment of his supreme sacrifice, the silence of Jesus is extremely poignant. He speaks only once to respond to Pilate, who says to him: "Are you the King of the Jews? What have you done?" Jesus answers: "My kingship is not of this world" (Jn 18:36). He includes in his kingdom Abraham, Isaac, Jacob, John the Baptist, all the saints in heaven, but also the community of his disciples who

make up the Church. Although the latter are in the world, they are not of the world. Jesus tells Pilate three times that his kingdom is not of this world (Jn 18:36), because he notices that the latter desires to know the truth and to defend it. Pilate is convinced of the innocence of Jesus, but he is assaulted by the howls of hatred and the accusations that are pouring in. On learning that Jesus is a Galilean, he decides to entrust him to Herod Antipas, tetrarch of the province of Galilee. The chief priests and the scribes are present, and they raise the stakes to elicit a sentence from Herod. Jesus is baselessly accused of all sorts of crimes. Among the grievances, there is the sacrilegious assertion that Jesus claims to destroy the Temple and to be the Son of God. In order to incite Herod against Jesus, they also protest loudly, claiming that Christ and John the Baptist have agreed to slander him because of his adulterous relationship with Herodias, the wife of his brother Philip.

In fact, Herod has taken Philip's wife as his bride. In order to make the situation worse, they recall that Jesus has praised John the Baptist, defending him in a public speech (Mt 11:9–11). Moreover, Jesus has no respect for the tetrarch and has even insulted him, calling him a "fox" (Lk 13:32). The chief priests and the scribes are there; they accuse Jesus spitefully and relentlessly (Lk 23:10). Herod and his courtiers treat him with contempt and mock him (Lk 23:11). "But he made no answer" (Lk 23:9). Jesus is unwilling to respond to Herod because he sees him as a vicious, dissolute, cruel man who hates the truth, to the point of beheading John the Baptist, who was the voice of Jesus Christ, because he made the truth known to him. How then would the Lord not have kept silence before the one who has taken the life of his voice?

Herod sends Jesus back to Pilate; the latter again summons the high priests, the rulers, and the people (Lk 23:13), and says to them: "You brought me this man as one who was perverting the people; and after examining him before you, behold, I did not find this man guilty of any of your charges against him; neither did Herod, for he sent him back to us. Behold, nothing deserving death has been done by him; I will therefore chastise him and release him" (Lk 23:14–16). In the face of all the false accusations of the chief priests and the elders, Jesus makes no answer, because they are nothing but clamor, confusion, jealousy, and uncontrolled hatred (Mt 27:14). Jesus, in being silent, intends to show his contempt for the lies, for he is the truth, the light, and the only way that leads to Life. His cause does not need to be defended. We do not defend the truth and the light: their splendor is their own defense. This prompted Saint Ambrose (in his *Commentary on the Gospel of Luke* 10, 97) to say: "The Lord is accused and keeps silent. And it is with good reason that he keeps silent; it is because he has no need of defense. Those who try to defend themselves are those who fear being defeated. His silence meant not, as the saying goes, that he was giving consent, but rather that he thought too little of those accusations to dignify them with a response."

Pilate, surprised at the silence and serenity of Jesus, says to him: "Do you not hear how many things they testify against you?" (Mt 27:13). Jesus is so imperturbable, so calm, and so peaceful that one might think he does not hear the howling of the crowd, which is drunk with hatred. But recall that it is written: "Yes, I am like a man who does not hear, and in whose mouth are no rebukes. But for you, O LORD, do I wait; it is you, O LORD my God, who will answer. For I pray, 'Only let them not rejoice over me, who boast against me when my foot slips!' For I am ready to fall, and my pain is ever with me" (Ps 38:14–17).

And so Pilate adds: "Have you no answer to make? See how many charges they bring against you" (Mk 15:4). And the Lord answers nothing, so that the governor is even more surprised (Mt 27:14). He does not understand the cause of such an extraordinary silence. He is confronted with God's silence, in the midst of the howling of men who are drunk with irrational hatred! The priests, at least, ought to have remembered what was written by the prophet Isaiah:

> He was oppressed, and he was afflicted,
> yet he opened not his mouth;
> like a lamb that is led to the slaughter,
> and like a sheep that before its shearers is silent,
> so he opened not his mouth.
> By oppression and judgment he was taken away;
> and as for his generation, who considered
> that he was cut off out of the land of the living,
> stricken for the transgression of my people?
> And they made his grave with the wicked

and with a rich man in his death,
although he had done no violence,
and there was no deceit in his mouth. (Is 53:7–9)

We have just experienced with Jesus before Pilate and Herod the excitement of the high priests, the elders, and the crowd. This event may seem to us surprising and scandalous, but it contains for us a doctrine and a teaching: in the school of Jesus, with our heart, understanding, and will wide open, let us allow God to introduce us into his silence and diligently learn to love and to live in this same silence.

198. Today, the silences of Christian martyrs who will be massacred by the enemies of Christ imitate and prolong those of the Son of God. The martyrs of the first centuries, like those of our sad time, all show the same silent dignity. Silence then becomes their only speech, their only testimony, their last testament. The blood of martyrs is a seed, a cry, and a silent prayer that rises up to God.

Christ started his public ministry by withdrawing into the desert for forty days . . .

199. I have already mentioned Jesus' withdrawal into a spiritual and mystical desert, that of the first thirty years of his life in Nazareth.

It is important to stop for a moment at his stay in the desert of Judea, for forty days and forty nights, before his public life, as though to store up reserves of silence with a view to this immense mission that will lead him so far as to give his life. The Gospels explain how Jesus went frequently into the deserts, seeking solitude, calm, and nocturnal silence. In these moments, he felt the finger of God that drew him into these regions where he lived, allowed himself to be seen, and conversed with man, as a friend speaks to his friend. The man who possesses God in his heart and in his body is eager for silence. We must uproot ourselves from the world, from the crowd, and from all activity, even charitable works, in order to remain for long moments in the intimacy of God.

200. Christ knows that God is never in the tormented noise of the world. He is not unaware of the terrible difficulties that will not fail

to trouble his itinerary. In order to face the Cross, which is still far off, silence and solitude are a necessity. In Gethsemane, when the end is near and the Apostles are sleeping, incapable of understanding in depth the drama that is playing out, he remains one last night in silence, in prayer. In his final moments, nocturnal silence is Christ's companion. The faithful must get used to praying at night, like Jesus. God carries out his works in the night. In the night, all movement is transformed and grows by God's strength.

201. For mankind, Christ's silent recollection is a great lesson. From the crib to the Cross, silence is constantly present, because the problem of silence is a problem of love. Love is not expressed in words. It takes on flesh and becomes one and the same being with the one who loves in truth. Its strength is such that it leads us to give ourselves even unto death, unto the humble, silent, and pure gift of our life.

If we want to prolong Christ's work on this earth, it is necessary to love silence, solitude, and prayer.

Is the death of Jesus therefore a great silence?

202. For three days, the victory of darkness over light plunged the earth into a thick silence and a terrible anguish. The Messiah had died, and the silence of his death seemed to have had the last word. God himself seemed silent. His Son felt alone, abandoned to the torments of the Cross. This was the most terrible moment of his earthly life. He was on the verge of death. Jesus had lost his strength and his blood. When he was nothing more than an exhausted, dying man, he uttered a great cry.

He was leaving this world, and his Father had not shown the slightest word of comfort. Certainly the Virgin Mary, his mother, and Saint John were at the foot of the Cross. But this sweet presence did not prevent him from shouting with all the strength that he had left: "My God, my God, why have you forsaken me?" (Mt 27:46). Jesus suffered from the apparent absence of God, but the confidence that he had always had in his Father did not fade. A few split seconds after this cry of pain, he prayed one last time to the Almighty for his executioners: "Father, forgive them; for they know not what they do." And he expired, saying: "Father, into your hands I commit my spirit!" (Lk 23:34, 46).

203. On this earth, the only silence that must be sought is the one that belongs to God. Because the silence of God alone is victorious. The heavy silence of Christ's death was of short duration, and it gave rise to life.

204. The silence of Jesus' death transforms, purifies, and appeases man. It causes him to be in communion with the sufferings and death of Christ, to come back fully into the divine life. This is the great silence of the Transfiguration because, "unless a grain of wheat falls into the earth and dies, it remains alone; but if it dies, it bears much fruit. He who loves his life loses it, and he who hates his life in this world will keep it for eternal life. If any one serves me, he must follow me" (Jn 12:24–26).

205. Saint John insists on the moral solitude and isolation of Christ before his Passion. He is alone from the beginning because he is God. He is alone because nobody can understand him. Saint John says that a large number of disciples abandoned him because his teaching about the Eucharist and the demands of the Gospel was beyond them.

Today, some priests treat the Eucharist with the utmost contempt. They see the Mass as a talkative banquet where Christians faithful to the teaching of Jesus, divorced-and-remarried persons, men and women in an adulterous situation, unbaptized tourists who participate in the Eucharistic celebrations of the large anonymous crowds can indiscriminately have access to the Body and Blood of Christ. The Church must examine with urgency the ecclesial and pastoral appropriateness of these immense Eucharistic celebrations made up of thousands and thousands of participants. There is a great danger of transforming the Eucharist, "the great mystery of faith", into a vulgar county fair and of desecrating the Body and Precious Blood of Christ. The priests who distribute the sacred species while not knowing anyone and give the Body of Jesus to all, without distinguishing between Christians and non-Christians, participate in the desecration of the Holy Eucharistic Sacrifice. Those who exercise authority in the Church become culpable, by a form of voluntary complicity, in allowing the sacrilege and desecration of the Body of Christ to take place in these gigantic and ridiculous self-celebrations, where so few perceive that "you proclaim the Lord's death until he comes" (1 Cor 11:26).

Some priests unfaithful to the "memory" of Jesus insist more on the festive aspect and the fraternal dimension of the Mass than on the bloody sacrifice of Christ on the Cross. The importance of interior dispositions and the necessity of reconciling ourselves with God by agreeing to let ourselves be purified by the sacrament of confession are no longer in fashion today. More and more, we conceal the warning of Saint Paul to the Corinthians: "For as often as you eat this bread and drink the chalice, you proclaim the Lord's death until he comes. Whoever, therefore, eats the bread or drinks the cup of the Lord in an unworthy manner will be guilty of profaning the body and blood of the Lord. Let a man examine himself, and so eat of the bread and drink of the cup. For any one who eats and drinks without discerning the body eats and drinks judgment upon himself. That is why many of you are weak and ill" (1 Cor 11:26–30).

How can we be recollected in silence and adoration, like Mary at the foot of the Cross, before the God who dies for our sins in the course of each of our Eucharists? How can we be silent and give thanks in the presence of Almighty God who suffers the Passion because of our rebellion, apathy, and infidelities?

We live at the surface of ourselves too often to understand what we are celebrating. The lack of faith in the Eucharist, the Real Presence of Christ, can lead to sacrilege. Jesus is isolated by the growing hatred of the Pharisees, who form against him an increasingly stronger coalition, forcing his listeners to separate themselves from him. Some Christians are forming a coalition to separate Jesus and his doctrine from those who honestly seek the truth. He is more and more alone among men who hate him or do not know how to love him because they are incapable of knowing him as he is. But there will always be a little flock who will want to know him and love him.

It is imperative for men to rediscover the Easter we celebrate in each of our Eucharists. The grace of Easter is a profound silence, an immense peace, and a pure taste in the soul. It is the taste of heaven, away from all disordered excitement. The Paschal vision does not consist in a rapture of the spirit; it is the silent discovery of God. If only the Mass could be, each morning, what it was on Golgotha and on Easter morning! If only the prayers could be as lucid, if the risen Christ could always shine in me in his Paschal simplicity ...

Easter marks the triumph of life over death, the victory of Christ's silence over the great roar of hatred and falsehood. Christ enters into eternal silence. The Church must now continue the mission of Jesus through the daily suffering and death experienced in silence, prayer, supplication, and great fidelity.

206. In a world where shouting and excitement of every kind unceasingly expand their empires, we will need more and more to contemplate and to learn to enter into Christ's silence.

The rejection of silence is a rejection of the love and life that come to us from Jesus.

207. On May 2, 2010, on the occasion of the exposition of the Holy Shroud, Pope Benedict XVI went to the cathedral of Turin to venerate the relic there. He delivered an extraordinary meditation entitled "The Mystery of Holy Saturday", in which he associated the mystery of Holy Saturday and the mystery of silence:

> One could say that the Shroud is the Icon of this mystery, the Icon of Holy Saturday. Indeed it is a winding-sheet that was wrapped round the body of a man who was crucified, corresponding in every way to what the Gospels tell us of Jesus who, crucified at about noon, died at about three o'clock in the afternoon. At nightfall, since it was *Parasceve*, that is, the eve of Holy Saturday, Joseph of Arimathea, a rich and authoritative member of the Sanhedrin, courageously asked Pontius Pilate for permission to bury Jesus in his new tomb which he had had hewn out in the rock not far from Golgotha. Having obtained permission, he bought a linen cloth, and after Jesus was taken down from the Cross, wrapped him in that shroud and buried him in that tomb (cf. Mk 15:42–46). This is what the Gospel of Saint Mark says, and the other Evangelists are in agreement with him. From that moment, Jesus remained in the tomb until dawn of the day after the Sabbath, and the Turin Shroud presents to us an image of how his body lay in the tomb during that period which was chronologically brief (about a day and a half), but immense, infinite in its value and in its significance.
>
> Holy Saturday is the day when God remains hidden, we read in an ancient Homily: "What has happened? Today the earth is shrouded in deep silence, deep silence and stillness, profound silence because

the King sleeps.... God has died in the flesh, and has gone down to rouse the realm of the dead" (*Homily on Holy Saturday*, PG 43, 439). In the *Creed*, we profess that Jesus Christ was "crucified under Pontius Pilate, died and was buried. He descended to the dead. On the third day, he rose again."

Dear brothers and sisters, in our time, especially after having lived through the past century, humanity has become particularly sensitive to the mystery of Holy Saturday. The concealment of God is part of contemporary man's spirituality, in an existential almost subconscious manner, like a void in the heart that has continued to grow larger and larger. Towards the end of the nineteenth century, Nietzsche wrote: "God is dead! And we killed him!" This famous saying is clearly taken almost literally from the Christian tradition. We often repeat it in the *Way of the Cross*, perhaps without being fully aware of what we are saying. After the two World Wars, the *lagers* and the *gulags*, Hiroshima and Nagasaki, our epoch has become increasingly a Holy Saturday: this day's darkness challenges all who are wondering about life, and it challenges us believers in particular. We too have something to do with this darkness.

Yet the death of the Son of God, Jesus of Nazareth, has an opposite aspect, totally positive, a source of comfort and hope. And this reminds me of the fact that the Holy Shroud acts as a "photographic" document, with both a "positive" and a "negative". And, in fact, this is really how it is: the darkest mystery of faith is at the same time the most luminous sign of a never-ending hope. Holy Saturday is a "no man's land" between the death and the Resurrection, but this "no man's land" was entered by One, the Only One, who passed through it with the signs of his Passion for man's sake: *Passio Christi. Passio hominis.* And the Shroud speaks to us precisely about this moment, testifying exactly to that unique and unrepeatable interval in the history of humanity and the universe in which God, in Jesus Christ, not only shared our dying but also our remaining in death: the most radical solidarity.

In this "time-beyond-time", Jesus Christ "descended to the dead". What do these words mean? They mean that God, having made himself man, reached the point of entering man's most extreme and absolute solitude, where not a ray of love enters, where total abandonment reigns without any word of comfort: "hell". Jesus Christ, by remaining in death, passed beyond the door of this ultimate solitude to lead us too to cross it with him. We have all, at some point, felt the frightening sensation of abandonment, and that is what we fear most about death, just as when we were children we were afraid to be alone in the dark and could only be reassured by the presence of a person who loved us. Well, this is exactly what happened on Holy Saturday: the voice of God resounded in the realm of death. The unimaginable occurred: namely, Love penetrated "hell". Even in the extreme darkness of the most absolute human loneliness we may hear a voice that calls us and find a hand that takes ours and leads us out. Human beings live because they are loved and can love; and if love even penetrated the realm of death, then life also even reached there. In the hour of supreme solitude we shall never be alone: *Passio Christi. Passio hominis.*

This is the mystery of Holy Saturday! Truly from there, from the darkness of the death of the Son of God, the light of a new hope gleamed: the light of the Resurrection. And it seems to me that, looking at this sacred Cloth through the eyes of faith, one may perceive something of this light. Effectively, the Shroud was immersed in that profound darkness that was at the same time luminous; and I think that if thousands and thousands of people come to venerate it—without counting those who contemplate it through images—it is because they see in it not only darkness but also the light; not so much the defeat of life and of love, but rather victory, the victory of life over death, of love over hatred. They indeed see the death of Jesus, but they also see his Resurrection; in the bosom of death, life is now vibrant, since love dwells within it. This is the power of the Shroud: from the face of this "Man of sorrows", who carries with him the passion of man of every time and every place, our passions too, our sufferings, our difficulties and our sins—*Passio Christi. Passio hominis*—from this face a solemn majesty shines, a paradoxical lordship. This face, these hands and these feet, this side, this whole body speaks. It is itself a word we can hear in the silence. How does the Shroud speak? It speaks with blood, and blood is life! The Shroud is an Icon written in blood; the blood of a man who was scourged, crowned with thorns, crucified and whose right side was pierced. The Image impressed upon the Shroud is that of a dead man, but the blood speaks of his life. Every trace of blood speaks of love and of life. Especially that huge stain near his rib, made by the blood and water that flowed copiously from a great wound inflicted by the tip of a Roman spear. That blood and that water speak of life. It is like a spring that murmurs in the silence, and we can hear it, we can listen to it in the silence of Holy Saturday.

208. Paradoxically, in the Gospels, Christ rarely asked his disciples to keep silent, except after Peter's profession of faith (Mt 16:20)

and at the time of the Transfiguration (Mt 17:1–13). He leads them instead to the desert to introduce them to silence and conversation with God. But he orders the storms, the winds, and the devils to be silent. Jesus imposes silence on everything that brings evil, vice, and death.

209. In a homily given in Nazareth on January 5, 1964, Paul VI said:

> Nazareth is a kind of school where we may begin to discover what Christ's life was like and even to understand his Gospel.... First, we learn from its silence: If only we could once again appreciate its great value. We need this wonderful state of mind, beset as we are by the cacophony of strident protests and conflicting claims so characteristic of these turbulent times. The silence of Nazareth should teach us how to meditate in peace and quiet, to reflect on the deeply spiritual, and to be open to the voice of God's inner wisdom and the counsel of true teachers. Nazareth can teach us the value of study and preparation, of meditation, of a well-ordered personal spiritual life, and of silent prayer that is known only to God.

210. Why are men so noisy during the liturgies while Christ's prayer was silent? The words of the Son of God come from the heart, and the heart is silent. Why do we not know how to speak with a silent heart? The heart of Jesus does not speak. It radiates with love because its language comes from the divine depths.

Can we talk about the silences of the Holy Spirit? In God or Nothing, *you explain that the Spirit is often the great misunderstood one.*

211. The Holy Spirit has no face and no speech. He is silent by his divine nature. The Spirit acts in silence from all eternity. God speaks, Christ speaks, but the Holy Spirit is always expressed through the prophets, saints, and men of God.

The Holy Spirit never makes noise. He leads to the truth by remaining the great intermediary. In silence, he leads mankind toward Christ by repeating his teaching. The only time where the Holy Spirit came with noise was at Pentecost, in order to reawaken sleeping mankind and to draw it from its torpor and sin:

When the day of Pentecost had come, they were all together in one place. And suddenly a sound came from heaven like the rush of a mighty wind, and it filled all the house where they were sitting. And there appeared to them tongues as of fire, distributed and resting on each one of them. And they were all filled with the Holy Spirit and began to speak in other tongues, as the Spirit gave them utterance.

Now there were dwelling in Jerusalem Jews, devout men from every nation under heaven. And at this sound the multitude came together, and they were bewildered, because each one heard them speaking in his own language. (Acts 2:1–6)

212. The Spirit dwells in the interior of man by regenerating him without manifest noise. The Spirit is a silent force. Free as the wind, the Spirit blows unpredictably. If we do not drive away his fire, he sets the world ablaze.

213. In *Against Heresies*, Saint Irenaeus wrote: "[The Holy Spirit] has been entrusted to the Church, ... that all members receiving it may be vivified; and the [means of] communion with Christ has been distributed throughout it, that is, the Holy Spirit." The Spirit is communion.

Today, the world is not sufficiently attentive to the Holy Spirit. Without attention to the Spirit, men are divided; they scatter, hate one another, and are divided as at Babel. Then wars are started, and sects abound. Without the Spirit, unbelief advances; with the Spirit, God comes close.

I am sad to see how much we abuse the Holy Spirit. In their imagination and in disregard of the will that intends that we be one, some men, on their own initiative, create their own churches, their own theologies, and their own beliefs, which in fact are only petty subjective opinions. The Holy Spirit has no opinions. He only repeats what Christ taught us in order to lead to the whole truth.

I say this in all seriousness: The absence of the Holy Spirit in the Church creates all the divisions. Where the Church is, there is the Spirit of God. Where the Spirit is, there is the Church.

The Holy Spirit is a bond of communion between the Father and the Son. He is the breath of life that we cannot grasp. He is invisible, but fully present.

214. When we are docile to the Holy Spirit, we are sure to be walking toward the truth because we are entirely subject to his inspirations. At the first Council of Jerusalem, thanks to the great silence of the Spirit, prayer, and fasting, the Apostles had the audacity to affirm the truth of God and not that of men (Acts 15). All the councils are placed under the protection of the Spirit. During conclaves, the Spirit points out God's choice to the cardinals; the latter must submit to his will and not to human political strategies. If we thwart the Holy Spirit by miserable, petty human calculations, secret meetings, and media consultations, we run headlong into tragedy and we are gravediggers of the divine nature of the Church.

215. The rejection of the Spirit is a blasphemy and a mortal sin because it is a matter of rejecting the truth. Without the Spirit, the Church is in danger of becoming a new tower of Babel. The different and deviant languages drown out the testament of the Son of God. Some pretentious, cynical ideologues threaten the truth of Jesus. Confusion, relativism, and chaos point toward a fatal prospect.

In the Gospels, why is Mary so silent?

216. The entire life of the Mother of Jesus is bathed in silence. Among the evangelists, only Luke and John have the Blessed Virgin actually speak.

Saint Luke records the words of Mary in the account of the Annunciation:

> The angel Gabriel was sent from God to a city of Galilee named Nazareth, to a virgin betrothed to a man whose name was Joseph, of the house of David; and the virgin's name was Mary. And he came to her and said, "Hail, full of grace, the Lord is with you!" But she was greatly troubled at the saying, and considered in her mind what sort of greeting this might be. And the angel said to her, "Do not be afraid, Mary, for you have found favor with God. And behold, you will conceive in your womb and bear a son, and you shall call his name Jesus.
>
> > He will be great, and will be called the Son of the Most High;
> > and the Lord God will give to him the throne of his father
> > David,

and he will reign over the house of Jacob for ever;
and of his kingdom there will be no end."

And Mary said to the angel, "How shall this be, since I have no husband?" And the angel said to her,

"The Holy Spirit will come upon you,
and the power of the Most High will overshadow you;
therefore the child to be born will be called holy,
the Son of God.

And behold, your kinswoman Elizabeth in her old age has also conceived a son; and this is the sixth month with her who was called barren. For with God nothing will be impossible." And Mary said, "Behold, I am the handmaid of the Lord; let it be to me according to your word." And the angel departed from her. (Lk 1:26–38)

In *L'Humble Présence*, Maurice Zundel said that "silence is the only thing that reveals the depths of life." The great works of God are the fruit of silence. God alone is witness of them and, along with him, those who see from within, who keep silence and live in the presence of the silent Word, like the Virgin Mary. For Zundel, Mary became a disciple of the Word:

She listens, she consents, she gives herself, she loses herself in its depths. Every fiber of her being resounds with this appeal: "Let me hear your voice" (Song 2:14). Mary grants a hearing to the silent Word. Her flesh then can become the cradle of the Eternal Word.... In her, each man sees himself called to the same destiny: he becomes a dwelling of God, of the silent Word. Because if it is true that God created human nature for no other reason than to receive from it the Mother that he needed to be born, then every man is called, through the silent reception of the Word, to become the Temple of the Word, the "Basilica of silence".

217. In fact, Mary is so silent that the evangelists say little about the Mother of God. She is entirely absorbed by contemplation, adoration, and prayer. She hides herself in her Son; she exists only for her Son. She disappears in her Son.

218. Saint Luke mentions Mary's words a second time when she loses the Child Jesus, then finds him again in the Temple among the doctors of the law:

Now his parents went to Jerusalem every year at the feast of the Passover. And when he was twelve years old, they went up according to custom; and when the feast was ended, as they were returning, the boy Jesus stayed behind in Jerusalem. His parents did not know it, but supposing him to be in the company they went a day's journey, and they sought him among their kinsfolk and acquaintances; and when they did not find him, they returned to Jerusalem, seeking him. After three days they found him in the temple, sitting among the teachers, listening to them and asking them questions; and all who heard him were amazed at his understanding and his answers. And when they saw him they were astonished; and his mother said to him, "Son, why have you treated us so? Behold, your father and I have been looking for you anxiously." And he said to them, "How is it that you sought me? Did you not know that I must be in my Father's house?" And they did not understand the saying which he spoke to them. And he went down with them and came to Nazareth, and was obedient to them; and his mother kept all these things in her heart.

And Jesus increased in wisdom and in stature, and in favor with God and man. (Lk 2:41–52)

Saint John relates a single conversation of Mary in the episode of the wedding feast at Cana:

There was a marriage at Cana in Galilee, and the mother of Jesus was there; Jesus also was invited to the marriage, with his disciples. When the wine failed, the mother of Jesus said to him, "They have no wine." And Jesus said to her, "O woman, what have you to do with me? My hour has not yet come." His mother said to the servants, "Do whatever he tells you." Now six stone jars were standing there, for the Jewish rites of purification, each holding twenty or thirty gallons. Jesus said to them, "Fill the jars with water." And they filled them up to the brim. He said to them, "Now draw some out, and take it to the steward of the feast." So they took it. When the steward of the feast tasted the water now become wine, and did not know where it came from (though the servants who had drawn the water knew), the steward of the feast called the bridegroom and said to him, "Every man serves the good wine first; and when men have drunk freely, then the poor wine; but you have kept the good wine until now." This, the first of his signs, Jesus did at Cana in Galilee, and manifested his glory; and his disciples believed in him.

After this he went down to Capernaum, with his mother and his brethren and his disciples; and there they stayed for a few days. (Jn 2:1–12)

In the Gospels of Mark and Matthew, there is no mention of Mary's words.

In God's plan, the Virgin is inseparably bound up with the Word. The Word is God, and the Word is silent. She is completely under the influence of the Holy Spirit, who does not speak. The attitude of Mary is that of listening. She is completely turned to the word of the Son. She is consent, she is obedience.

Mary does not speak. She simply wants to submit to God like a trusting child. Her *fiat* is total and joyful. She intends to receive God's will through Jesus.

The Mother of Jesus is lost in wonder and the silence of joy at the feet of the Child on Christmas; she suffers and is in anguish when Herod threatens the Infant God, at the foot of the Cross. She remains in the silence of consent, the kind that is summed up in this remarkable sentence: "I am the handmaid of the Lord; let it be to me according to your word" (Lk 1:38).

219. From the Gospels, we do not know how Mary's sorrow was manifested at the foot of the Cross. Art has depicted the Mother of God in the *Stabat Mater Dolorosa*, but the evangelists remain silent about her state of soul. Nevertheless, Mary is associated interiorly and totally in the mystery of redemption by the Cross.

Mary's *fiat* is a silence to which the Mother of Christ will remain faithful for eternity. Noiselessly, Mary offers her life and that of her Son to the Eternal Father. Noiselessly, she says *fiat* in advance to the death of Jesus. As a mother, she sees the terrible agony of Jesus, whose body is covered with wounds and bruises. She stands, clinging to the Cross, and the blood of her Son flows down on her face and arms. Imitating Jesus, Mary can say: "No one takes it from me, but

I lay it down of my own accord" (Jn 10:18). The Virgin is crucified and dies mystically with her Son.

After the death of Christ, Mary supports the Apostles with her prayer; she asks that they may receive the strength and light of the Spirit. By her physical, prayerful, discreet presence, she engenders the Church and encourages her Son's companions. When the Apostles are dispersed, she reconstitutes the community of disciples and builds up the Church in silence and prayer. Ever since the Upper Room, the Church has drawn her missionary breath in prayer and the acceptance of the Spirit.

In the light of Pentecost, Mary is the first to understand the mystery of the Church. As Christ was born in poverty, in the silence of the night, and by the power of the Spirit, so too the Church could not come into existence in the midst of glories and worldly noise. The Spouse of Christ proceeds from the Holy Spirit, who bursts into the Upper Room where the community is in prayer with Mary.

Mary's *fiat* finds its completion in the emergence of the first Church through the power of the Spirit.

220. During his general audience on November 22, 1995, John Paul II declared:

> Mary's example enables the Church better to appreciate the value of silence. Mary's silence is not only moderation in speech, but it is especially a wise capacity for remembering and embracing in a single gaze of faith the mystery of the Word made man and the events of his earthly life.
>
> It is this silence as acceptance of the Word, this ability to meditate on the mystery of Christ, that Mary passes on to believers. In a noisy world filled with messages of all kinds, her witness enables us to appreciate a spiritually rich silence and fosters a contemplative spirit.

221. "Hear this faint, continuous noise that is silence. Listen to what we hear when nothing makes itself heard", wrote Paul Valéry in *Tel quel*. This is the motto of the Virgin Mary. This is the motto of a strong woman. This is the motto of a silent woman.

222. Pierre de Bérulle rightly wrote in his *Oeuvres de piété*: "This silence of the Virgin is not a silence of stammering and powerlessness.

It is a silence of light and delight; it is a silence more eloquent in the praises of God than eloquence itself. It is a powerful and divine challenge in the order of grace."

In my country, at the end of the daily rosary, we often sing this hymn to Mary: "May your sweet presence enlighten us forever, O Virgin of silence. Give us your great peace." From now on, Mary lives in the home of Saint John, as Jesus had wished on the Cross. We can imagine that she lived in silence and in a profound peace. She meditated often on the Passion of Jesus, the wonderful summit of their common missions. The more time passed, the more silent, recollected, and contemplative she became. She prayed and fasted. She joyfully accepted so many sacrifices in order to extend the Passion of her Son for the salvation of the world. Her prayer was a perpetual silence in God.

III

SILENCE, THE MYSTERY, AND THE SACRED

We should learn not to give any name to God, lest we imagine that in so doing we have praised and exalted him as we should, for God is "above names" and ineffable.

— Meister Eckhart, *Sermons*

NICOLAS DIAT: What relation do you find between silence and the sacred?

ROBERT CARDINAL SARAH:
223. The notion of sacredness is abused, particularly in the West. In the countries that claim to be secular, emancipated from religion and from God, there is no longer any connection with the sacred. A certain secularized mentality attempts to be liberated from it. Some theologians assert that Christ, by his Incarnation, put an end to the distinction between sacred and profane. For others, God becomes so close to us that the category of the sacred is consequently outmoded. Thus, some in the Church still have not managed to detach themselves from an entirely horizontal pastoral approach centered on social work and politics. In these assertions or these behaviors, there is a lot of naïveté and perhaps genuine pride.

224. In June 2012, in his homily for the Feast of Corpus Christi, Benedict XVI solemnly declared: "[Christ] did not abolish the sacred but brought it to fulfillment, inaugurating a new form of worship, which is indeed fully spiritual but which, however, as long as we are journeying in time, still makes use of signs and rites. . . . Thanks to Christ, the sacred is truer, more intense and . . . also more demanding!"

This is a serious question because what is at stake is our relation to God. Confronted with his grandeur, majesty, and beauty, how can we not be overcome with a joyous, holy fear? If we do not tremble before the divine transcendence, it is because we are damaged, all the way down to our human nature. I am astounded by the frivolousness, weakness, and vanity of so many discussions that claim to empty the sacred of all meaning. So-called enlightened theologians ought to enroll in the school of the people of God. The simplest faithful know that the sacred realities are one of their most precious treasures. Spontaneously they intuit that one can enter into communion with God only through an interior and exterior attitude marked by the sacred. The people are right; it would be arrogant to claim to have access to God without getting rid of a profane attitude and a non-religious, hedonistic paganism.

225. In Africa, the sacred is something quite obvious for the Christian people, but also for believers of all religions. Many Westerners look down on the sacred as something infantile and superstitious, but this disdain results from the self-importance of spoiled children. I do not hesitate to say that the men of the Church who want to distance themselves from the sacred harm humanity by depriving it of loving communion with God.

God desires to communicate to us his friendship and intimacy, but he can do so only if we are open to him in a fair, true attitude. Before the Entirely Other, man must acknowledge his littleness, misery, and nothingness. Remember what Jesus said to Saint Catherine of Siena: "I am the one who is; you are the one who is not."

226. Without radical humility that is expressed in gestures of adoration and in sacred rituals, no friendship with God is possible.

Silence manifests this connection in an obvious way. True Christian silence makes itself sacred silence first so as to become silence of communion.

227. Before the divine majesty, we are at a loss for words. Who would dare speak up in the presence of the Almighty? When God reveals his glory to Isaiah, the prophet cries out: "Holy, holy, holy!" He uses the Hebrew word *kadosh*, which means holy and sacred at the same time. Then he exclaims: "I am lost!" We could just as well translate it: "I am reduced to silence!" (Is 6:5).

228. People of all cultures and of all religions know: before God, we are lost, and in the presence of his grandeur, our words no longer have meaning. They are not up to the Infinite. In Africa, after the songs and the dances, a sacrifice to the deity is surrounded by an impressive sacred silence.

Of course, the sacred silence of Christians goes farther. It is not about a taboo that God inflicts on mankind so as to preserve his power jealously. On the contrary, the true God prescribes the sacred silence of adoration so as to communicate himself to us better. But Isaiah explains: "Listen to me in silence!" (Is 41:1).

229. In 1995, in his Apostolic Letter *Orientale Lumen*, Saint John Paul II recalled:

> All, believers and non-believers alike, need to learn a silence that allows the Other to speak when and how he wishes.... In the humble acceptance of the creature's limits before the infinite transcendence of a God who never ceases to reveal himself as God-Love ..., I see expressed the attitude of prayer.... We must confess that we all have need of this silence, filled with the presence of him who is adored.

230. To refuse silence filled with confident fear and adoration is to refuse God the freedom to take hold of us by his love and presence. Sacred silence allows man to place himself joyfully at God's disposal. It enables him to overcome the arrogant attitude that would claim that God is at the disposal of all the whims of his children. What creature can boast of possessing the Creator in this way? On the contrary, sacred silence offers us a way of leaving the profane world and the incessant turmoil of our immense metropolitan cities so as to allow God to take hold of us. Sacred silence is truly the place where we can encounter God, because we come to him with the proper attitude of a man who trembles and stands at a distance while hoping confidently.

231. Sacred silence is therefore the only truly human and Christian reaction to God when he breaks into our lives. It seems that God himself teaches us that he expects from us this worship of silent, sacred adoration. "When you praise the Lord, exalt him as much

as you can; for he will surpass even that. When you exalt him, put forth all your strength, and do not grow weary, for you cannot praise him enough. Who has seen him and can describe him? Or who can extol him as he is?" Ben Sirach the Sage asks (Sir 43:30–31). When God appears, praise alone should flow from our heart. Conversely, every form of display that gives the impression of a spectacle must disappear. Why show the vanity of a profane action or of a worldly word in the presence of his infinite grandeur? "The LORD is in his holy temple; let all the earth keep silence before him" (Hab 2:20). Only at that moment can he take the initiative to meet us. For God always loves first. Our sacred silence becomes a silence of joy, of intimacy, and of communion: "The words of the wise [are] heard in quiet" (Eccles 9:17).

232. Silence teaches us a great rule of the spiritual life: familiarity does not promote intimacy; on the contrary, a proper distance is a condition for communion. Humanity advances toward love through adoration. Sacred silence, laden with the adored presence, opens the way to mystical silence, full of loving intimacy. Under the yoke of secular reason, which only makes us feel guilty, we have forgotten that worship and the sacred are the only entrances to the spiritual life.

233. Sacred silence is a cardinal law of all liturgical celebrations. In 1978, in an article in *Communio*, the theologian Hans Urs von Balthasar wrote:

> No liturgy designed by men could be "worthy" of the subject of their homage, of God at whose throne the heavenly choirs prostrate themselves with covered faces, having cast off their crowns and ornaments before offering adoration. The attempt to return to him who "created all according to his will" the honour that all creatures received must *a priori* compel to its knees an earthly community of sinners. *Domine non sum dignus!* [Lord, I am not worthy!] If this community, meeting for praise and worship, should have anything else in mind than adoration and self-oblation—for example, self-development or any other project in which they place themselves thematically in context next to the Lord who is to be worshipped, then they naively deceive themselves. This topic can be touched only with fear and trembling.

234. How can we fail to mention here the liturgy of Good Friday, when the celebrant comes into the sanctuary? He prostrates himself, stretching out on the floor in front of the altar, and remains in that position for a long interval in great silence. This silent gesture is eloquent. Man acknowledges his nothingness, and he literally has nothing to say in view of the sacred mystery of the Cross. Humbly, he can only prostrate himself and adore. But this adoration is not crushing; on the contrary, it opens us up to an attitude of abandonment and trust.

235. Since the reform of Paul VI, and despite the intention of that great pope, sometimes in the liturgy there is an air of misplaced, noisy familiarity. Under the pretext of seeking to make access to God easy and approachable, some have wanted everything in the liturgy to be immediately intelligible. This egalitarian intention may seem commendable. But in thus reducing the sacred mystery to good ideas, we prevent the faithful from approaching the true God. Under the pretext of pedagogy, some priests indulge in endless flat, horizontal commentaries. These pastors are afraid that silence in the presence of the Most High might disconcert the faithful. In *Orientale Lumen*, however, Saint John Paul II cautions us:

> On the contrary, the Christians of the East turn to God as Father, Son and Holy Spirit, living persons tenderly present, to whom they utter a solemn and humble, majestic and simple liturgical doxology. But they perceive that one draws close to this presence above all by letting oneself be taught an adoring silence, for at the culmination of the knowledge and experience of God is his absolute transcendence.

236. How can we claim to approach "Him who is beyond all things" by adopting a negligent, careless attitude? In a very beautiful homily entitled "On the Grave and the Cross", Saint John Chrysostom already exhorted his faithful to take care during the procession at communion. He asked them to approach only if they were full of "fear, veneration, and reverence", and he expressed his astonishment: "The angels who guarded Jesus' tomb did so with fear and recollection, while you—who are going, not to an empty tomb, but to the table where the living Lamb offers himself—approach in a disorderly

fashion, noisily, each one joking with his neighbor?" What would he say today about our processions? How many priests walk toward the altar of sacrifice while chattering, discussing, or greeting the people who are present instead of losing themselves in a sacred silence full of reverence . . .

237. At the beginning of our Eucharistic celebrations, how is it possible to eliminate Christ carrying his Cross and walking painfully under the weight of our sins toward the place of sacrifice? There are so many priests who enter triumphantly and walk up toward the altar, greeting people left and right, so as to appear sympathetic. Just look at the sad spectacle of some Eucharistic celebrations. . . . Why so much frivolousness and worldliness at the moment of the Holy Sacrifice? Why so much profanation and superficiality, given the extraordinary priestly grace that renders us able to make the Body and Blood of Christ substantially present by the invocation of the Spirit? Why do some think that they are obliged to improvise or invent Eucharistic Prayers that conceal the sacred prayers in a wash of petty, human fervor? Are Christ's words insufficient, making it necessary to multiply merely human words? In such a unique and essential sacrifice, is there any need for such a display of imagination and subjective creativity? "In praying do not heap up empty phrases as the Gentiles do; for they think that they will be heard for their many words", Jesus warns us (Mt 6:7). Many fervent Christians who are moved by the Passion and death of Christ on the Cross no longer have the strength to weep or to utter a cry of pain to the priests and bishops who make their appearance as entertainers and set themselves up as the main protagonists of the Eucharist. These believers tell us nevertheless: "We do not want to gather with men around a man! We want to see Jesus! Show him to us in the silence and humility of your prayer!"

Sacred silence is a good belonging to the faithful, and clerics must not deprive them of it.

238. In 2011, during the World Youth Day in Madrid, Pope Benedict XVI was supposed to address the young people from all over the world during the great vigil. As he was about to speak, a storm arose, and there was a cloudburst. The pope waited with the young people for the storm to calm down. Finally, when the weather

became more clement, a master of ceremonies brought the Holy
Father the speech that he had prepared. But the pope preferred to
use the remaining time for the essential thing. Instead of speaking, he
invited the young people to enter with him into the silence of adoration. Kneeling before the Blessed Sacrament, Benedict XVI preached
by his silence. There were more than a million young people behind
him, drenched to the skin, standing in the mud; nevertheless, over
that immense crowd reigned an impressive sacred silence that was literally "filled with the adored presence". It is an unforgettable memory, an image of the Church united in great silence around her Lord.

From another angle, what is the connection between silence and mystery?

239. Words often bring with them the illusion of transparency, as
though they allowed us to understand everything, control everything, put everything in order. Modernity is talkative because it is
proud, unless the converse is true. Is our incessant talking perhaps
what makes us proud?

Never before has the world spoken so much about God, about
theology, about prayer, and even about mysticism. But our human
language lowers to a paltry level everything that it tries to say about
God. Words spoil anything that surpasses them. Now, mystery is by
definition that which is above our human reason. In his *Mystical Theology*, pseudo-Dionysius the Areopagite wrote that, confronted with
this reality that is beyond everything, confronted with the mystery,
we are led to the "dazzling obscurity of the secret Silence ... sur-
charging our blinded intellects with the ... invisible fairness of glories
which exceed all beauty."

240. There is a real warning that our civilization needs to hear. If our
intellects can no longer close their eyes, if we no longer know how
to be quiet, then we will be deprived of mystery, of its light, which is
beyond darkness, of its beauty, which is beyond all beauty. Without
mystery, we are reduced to the banality of earthly things.

241. Often I wonder whether the sadness of Western urban societies,
filled with so much depression and moral distress, so many suicides,
does not come from the loss of the sense of mystery. In losing the

capacity for silence in the presence of the mystery, people cut themselves off from the sources of joy. Indeed, they find themselves alone in the world, without anything that surpasses and supports them. I know of nothing more frightening than that! How else can we understand the reflection of Blaise Pascal in his *Pensées*:

> When I see the blindness and the wretchedness of man, when I regard the whole silent universe, and man without light, left to himself, and, as it were, lost in this corner of the universe, without knowing who has put him there, what he has come to do, what will become of him at death, and incapable of all knowledge, I become terrified, like a man who should be carried in his sleep to a dreadful desert island, and should awake without knowing where he is, and without means of escape.

Without silence, we are deprived of mystery, reduced to fear, sadness, and solitude. It is time to rediscover silence! The mystery of God, his incomprehensibility, is the source of joy for every Christian. Every day we rejoice to contemplate an unfathomable God, whose mystery will never be exhausted. The eternity of heaven itself will be the joy, ever new, of entering more profoundly into the divine mystery without ever exhausting it. Only silence can express this joy: "We are silent because the words by which our souls would fain live cannot be expressed in earthly language", said the Carthusian Augustin Guillerand, in the anthology *They Speak by Silences*.

242. In order to preserve the mystery, it is necessary to protect it from profane banality. Silence performs this role admirably. A treasure must be placed out of reach; what is precious always remains veiled. Even our body is covered with clothing, not because it would be shameful or impure, but because it is sacred and mysterious. In the liturgy, the chalice is veiled; the ciborium and the tabernacle are covered with a veil when they contain the Real Presence. Silence is an acoustic veil that protects the mystery. Do we not automatically lower our voice to say the most important things, words of love? In the past, in the Latin liturgy, the very mysterious words of the Canon and of the consecration, pronounced *submissa voce* [in a low voice], were draped in a veil of silence.

243. In his Apostolic Letter *Orientale Lumen*, Saint John Paul II writes this magnificent line: "This mystery is continuously veiled, enveloped in silence, lest an idol be created in place of God."

There is a great risk that Christians may become idolaters if they lose the meaning of silence. Our words inebriate us; they confine us to what is created. Bewitched and imprisoned by the noise of human speech, we run the risk of designing worship to our specifications, a god in our own image. Words bring with them the temptation of the golden calf! Only silence leads man beyond words, to the mystery, to worship in spirit and in truth. Silence is a form of mystagogy; it brings us into the mystery without spoiling it. I understand why Thérèse of Lisieux wrote in her letter to Céline, dated October 14, 1890: "Virginity is a profound silence." We must rediscover that reserve, that modesty, that virginal sense, that silent delicacy in order to approach the holy mysteries of the liturgy, the great mysteries of theology.

Let us learn to keep silence even in the midst of suffering. Today there are many who howl with the wolves to defend a view of the liturgy, of which they want to be the sole custodians; these ideologues noisily immolate on the altar of their idols those whom they consider reactionary. God willing, may their idols breathe in the sweet-smelling aroma of their sacrifice ...

It seems to me that silence veils the mysteries, not to hide them, but to reveal them. The mysteries can be uttered only in silence. Thus, in the liturgy, the language of the mysteries is silent.

Nevertheless God speaks, but his speech, too, is a mystery ...

244. In his beautiful book *A New Song for the Lord*, Joseph Cardinal Ratzinger recalled: "Wherever God's word is translated into human words there remains a surplus of the unspoken and unspeakable which calls us to silence." God reveals himself, but our human words fail to express his immensity, depth, and mystery. He forever remains beyond our words. And how small God would be if we understood him!

I realize that theologians study this mystery and translate into human words the results of their research. But these words will be tolerable only if the study of them is rooted in silence and leads to silence. Otherwise, they will become vain chattering. Theology must rediscover a contemplative language. By adopting the ways of the secular sciences, exegetes and theologians run the risk of straying far from the mystery of God's Word. "Though we speak much we cannot reach the end, and the sum of our words is: 'He is the all' ", Scripture says (Sir 43:27).

245. In order to speak about God, it is necessary to begin by keeping quiet. I am thinking here about preachers, too. A homily is not a summary of theological knowledge or of exegetical interpretations. Priests, who are marked with the priestly character, are thereby in a way the mysterious instruments of the Word of God. The homily is therefore strictly reserved to men who have been invested with the sacred order of priests and deacons; it cannot be delegated to laypersons, not even to the most competent. Essentially this is not about any academic competence or a profession: "For the lips of a priest should guard knowledge, and men should seek instruction from his mouth" (Mal 2:7; Titus 1:7–9; 1 Tim 3:13), Scripture says. The words in a homily are not a lesson; they are the echo of the words of the Master as he taught on the roads of Galilee. And so priests must prepare their homilies in the silence of prayer and contemplation.

246. In a discussion of the liturgy, Cardinal Ratzinger was not afraid to assert:

> If we do not understand the place of silence, we run the risk of by-passing the Word of God, also. Therefore we must enter into this depth of silence in which the mystery greater than all human words is communicated. This step is essential.... God is above all the great silence. It is necessary to escape the multiplication of words in order to rediscover the Word. If there is no silence by which to enter into their depth, the words themselves become incomprehensible. And the liturgy, the presence of the great mystery of God, must therefore be also the place where we have the opportunity to enter into the depths of our souls.

Before the depth of the mystery of God, Saint Augustine writes in his *Expositions on the Psalms*, we experience the limitations of words. And so we rejoice wordlessly. We cannot name the ineffable God: "If you cannot tell him forth in speech, yet ought not to remain silent, what else can you do but jubilate? In this way the heart rejoices without words and the boundless expanse of rapture is not circumscribed by syllables", the Holy Doctor says.

247. From this joyous experience of mystery is born sacred song. The chant of the Christian liturgies ought to distance itself from certain verbose hymns so as to rediscover the contemplative grandeur of the chant of the monks of the East and the West.

Gregorian chant is not contrary to silence. It has issued from it and leads to it. I would even say that it is as though woven of silence. At the Grande Chartreuse, what a moving experience it is to chant with the monks, in the half-light of the evening, the great *Salve Regina* at Vespers! The last notes die out one by one in a filial silence, enveloping our trust in the Virgin Mary. This experience is essential for understanding Joseph Ratzinger's reflection in his book, *A New Song for the Lord*: "Silence ... lets the unspeakable become song and also calls on the voices of the cosmos for help so that the unspoken may become audible. This means that church music, coming from the Word and the silence perceived in it, always presupposes a new listening to the whole richness of the Logos."

During the reign of Paul VI, in 1969, did the liturgical reform cause a loss of silence in the liturgy?

248. As Cardinal Godfried Danneels remarked in a conference with a provocative title, "An Attitude of Service, not of Manipulation", "the main fault of the Western liturgy, as it is celebrated, is that it is too wordy." I think that it is necessary to pose the question at the root of the matter. It is not just about artificially adding a little more silence in the Church's liturgies.

Of course, the liturgy provides for times of silence that must be respected, before each prayer, before the *Confiteor*, after the reading of the Word of God, and after Communion. These times allow the soul to breathe. The offertory, too, can be a silent moment.

249. I am familiar with the regrets expressed by many young priests who would like the Canon of the Mass to be recited in complete silence. The unity of the whole assembly, communing with the

words pronounced in a sacred murmur, was a splendid sign of a contemplative Church gathered around the sacrifice of her Savior. In *The Spirit of the Liturgy*, Cardinal Ratzinger wrote:

> Anyone who has experienced a church united in the silent praying of the Canon will know what a really *filled* silence is. It is at once a loud and penetrating cry to God and a Spirit-filled act of prayer. Here everyone does pray the Canon together, albeit in a bond with the special task of the priestly ministry. Here everyone is united, laid hold of by Christ, and led by the Holy Spirit into that common prayer to the Father which is the true sacrifice—the love that reconciles and unites God and the world.

Nevertheless, the intention of the liturgical reform was commendable: the Council Fathers wanted to rediscover the original function of the Eucharistic Prayer as a great public prayer in the presence of God. But we notice also a strong temptation to look for variety by introducing improvisations into the Canon. The liturgy now runs the risk of trivializing the words of the Eucharistic Prayer. And so I think that Cardinal Ratzinger was correct when he wrote in his "The Regensburg Tradition and the Reform of the Liturgy", with reference to the Canon, "Must we not relearn this silent, inner co-praying with each other and with the angels and saints ... and with Christ himself", so that we do not lose "the real inner event of the liturgy, the departure from human speech into being touched by the eternal"? In his day he had proposed practical solutions and forcefully declared that the audible recitation of the Eucharistic Prayer in its entirety was not the only means of getting everyone to participate in this act. We must work for a more balanced solution and offer the possibility of intervals of silence in this area.

250. Silence is an attitude of the soul. It cannot be decreed without appearing overrated, empty, and artificial. In the Church's liturgies, silence cannot be a pause between two rituals; silence itself is fully a ritual, it envelops everything. Silence is the fabric from which all our liturgies must be cut. Nothing in them should interrupt the silent atmosphere that is its natural setting.

Now, celebrations become tiring because they unfold in noisy chattering. The liturgy is sick. The most striking symptom of this sickness is perhaps the omnipresence of the microphone. It has become so indispensable that one wonders how priests were able to celebrate before it was invented.... I sometimes have the impression that celebrants fear the free, personal interior prayer of the faithful so much that they talk from one end of the ceremony to the other so as not to lose control of them. I think that such attitudes betray a profound lack of understanding of the insights of Vatican Council II. More than ever, the council's teaching on the liturgy contained in *Sacrosanctum Concilium* must guide us. Fifty years after its promulgation, we are not yet done exploring its depth. It is high time to let the council teach us rather than to utilize it to justify our concerns about creativity.

251. The goal of *Sacrosanctum Concilium* was the participation of everyone in the mystery that is made present in the sacred liturgy. In order to understand this intention, it is absolutely necessary to remember that one of the means proposed by the council for implementing it is sacred silence. Truly, it is about becoming participants in a sacred mystery that infinitely surpasses us: the mystery of the death of Jesus out of love for the Father and for us. Christians have the ardent obligation to be open to an act that is so mysterious that they will never be able to perform it by themselves: the sacrifice of Christ. In the thought of the Council Fathers, the liturgy is a divine action, an *actio Christi*. In the presence of it, we are overcome with a silence of admiration and reverence. The quality of our silence is the measure of the quality of our active participation.

252. In 1985, in his famous book-length interview with Vittorio Messori, Cardinal Ratzinger stressed: "[Some have lost] sight of what is *distinctive* to the liturgy, which does not come from what *we do* but from the fact that something is *taking place* here that all of us together cannot 'make'."

253. Silence poses the problem of the essence of the liturgy. Now the latter is mystical. Eastern Christians rightly speak about the "Divine Liturgy" and the "holy mysteries". As long as we approach the liturgy with a noisy heart, it will have a superficial, human appearance. Liturgical silence is a radical and essential disposition; it is a conversion of the heart. Now, to convert, etymologically, is to turn around,

to turn toward God. There is no real silence in liturgy unless we are turned toward the Lord in our heart. But true silence is the silence of our passions, the heart purified of carnal impulses, washed of all our hatreds and resentments, oriented toward the holiness of God. The more resplendent the priest's chastity, the more he becomes, through his union with Christ, "a pure Victim, a holy Victim, a spotless Victim" and draws the whole people of God to "put on the new man, created after the likeness of God" (Eph 4:24).

254. It is not enough simply to prescribe more silence. In order for everyone to understand that the liturgy turns us interiorly toward the Lord, it would be helpful if during the celebrations all of us together, priests and the faithful, turned bodily toward the east, symbolized by the apse. This way of doing things is still absolutely legitimate. It is in keeping with the letter and the spirit of the council. There is no lack of testimonies from the early centuries of the Church. As Xavier Accart judiciously notes in his marvelous book, *Comprendre et vivre la liturgie* [Understanding and Living the Liturgy].

> "When we stand to pray, we turn toward the east", Saint Augustine explains, echoing a tradition that goes back, according to Saint Basil, to the Apostles themselves. Since the Churches were designed for the prayer of the first Christian communities, the *Apostolic Constitutions* recommended in the fourth century that they be "oriented". And when the altar is in the west, as in Saint Peter's Basilica in Rome, the celebrant must turn toward the rising of the sun and thus be facing the people. The concern of the Church Fathers, therefore, was not so much to celebrate with one's back or face to the people ... but rather to face east.

Then he adds:

> This bodily orientation of prayer, however, is only the sign of an interior "orientation". Origen emphasizes—does he not?—that such a choice "symbolizes the soul that looks toward the rising of the true light" when he writes in the *Gospel Parables*: "From the east the favor granted by God comes to you; for from there is the man, 'the Orient is his name' (Zacharias 6:12, Douay-Rheims), who has been established 'mediator between God and man' (1 Tim 2:5). This is for you

therefore an invitation to 'look toward the east' (Bar 4:36) always, whence rises for you the 'Sun of righteousness' (Mal 4:2), whence the light is born for you; so that you might never 'walk in the darkness' and 'the last day' may not overtake you in darkness (cf. Jn 12:35, 48)."

Does the priest not invite the people of God to follow him at the beginning of the great Eucharistic Prayer by saying: "Lift up your hearts", to which the people respond, "We lift them up to the Lord"?

As Prefect of the Congregation for Divine Worship and the Discipline of the Sacraments, I am anxious once again to recall that celebration *versus orientem* is authorized by the rubrics of the *Missal* because it is part of apostolic tradition. There is no need for particular authorization to celebrate in this way, with the people and the priest turned toward the Lord. If physically it is not possible to celebrate *ad orientem*, it is necessary to place a cross on the altar, in plain sight, as a reference point for all. Christ on the Cross is the Christian Orient.

255. Celebration toward the east fosters silence. Indeed, there is less temptation for the celebrant to monopolize the conversation. Facing the Lord, he is less tempted to become a professor giving a lesson throughout the Mass, reducing the altar to a podium centered on the microphone instead of the Cross. On the contrary, turned toward the east and the Cross, the celebrant becomes aware that he is, as Pope Francis often recalls, a shepherd who walks in front of the sheep. The priest remembers that he is an instrument in the hands of Christ the priest, that he must keep quiet so as to let the Word break through, that his human words are ridiculous compared to the one Eternal Word. I am convinced that we priests do not use the same tone of voice when we celebrate facing east. We are much less tempted to make a spectacle of ourselves, to mistake ourselves for actors, as Pope Francis says!

Thus the whole assembly is as though drawn in after the priest by the silent mystery of the Cross. It ought to be possible in the parishes to implement regularly this way of celebrating Mass.

This renewed entrance into the mystery would allow everyone to experience a silent, contemplative approach to doctrine and theology. These disciplines are the result, not of a laborious effort by a self-enclosed community, but, rather, of receptiveness in silence to the Word of God that precedes us and surprises us. The pope recalled in the Bull of Indiction of the Jubilee Year of Mercy that we must rediscover "the value of silence in order to meditate on the Word that comes to us".

256. Celebrating Mass facing east, by breaking up the face-to-face, private get-together, helps to prevent turning the liturgy into the community's celebration of itself. On the contrary, when we turn toward the Lord, the liturgy allows us to return to the world with a new impetus and a truly missionary strength, so as to bring to it, not our poor, hollow, noisy experience, but the one Word, heard in silence.

257. I refuse to waste our time pitting one liturgy against another or the rite of Saint Pius V against that of Blessed Paul VI. Rather, it is about entering into the great silence of the liturgy; it is necessary to know how to be enriched by all the Latin or Eastern liturgical forms that give a privileged place to silence. Without this contemplative spirit, the liturgy will remain an occasion for hateful divisions and ideological confrontations instead of being the place of our unity and of our communion in the Lord. It is high time to enter into this liturgical silence, turned toward the Lord, which the council intended to restore. What I am about to say now does not contradict my submission and obedience to the supreme authority of the Church. I deeply and humbly desire to serve God, the Church, and the Holy Father with devotion, sincerity, and a filial attachment. But here is my hope: God willing, when he wills and as he wills, the reform of the reform will take place in the liturgy. Despite the gnashing of teeth, it will happen, for the future of the Church is at stake. To ruin the liturgy is to ruin our relationship to God and the concrete expression of our Christian faith. The Word of God and the doctrinal teaching of the Church are still heard, but souls that desire to turn toward God and to offer him the true sacrifice of praise and adoration are no longer impressed by liturgies that are too horizontal, anthropocentric, and festive, often resembling noisy, popular cultural events. The media have totally invaded the Mass and transformed it into a spectacle, when actually it is the Holy Sacrifice, the memorial of the death of Jesus on the Cross for

the salvation of our souls. The sense of mystery disappears through changes, permanent adaptations that are decided on autonomously and individually so as to seduce our modern, profane mentalities that are marked by sin, secularism, relativism, and the rejection of God. In many Western countries, we see the poor leaving the Catholic Church because she has been taken by storm by ill-intentioned persons who make themselves out to be intellectuals and despise the little ones and the poor. This is what the Holy Father should denounce loudly and clearly. For a Church without the poor is no longer the Church but a mere "club". Today, in the West, how many empty, closed church buildings are destroyed or redesigned for profane use, regardless of their sacral character and original purpose. Nevertheless, I know that many priests and faithful Catholics live out their faith with extraordinary zeal and fight every day to preserve and enrich the houses of God.

We must urgently rediscover the beauty, sacred character, and divine origin of the liturgy by remaining staunchly faithful to the teaching of the *Catechism of the Catholic Church*. In a conversation with Father Emonet, Charles Cardinal Journet tragically declared: "Liturgy and catechesis are the two jaws of the pincers with which the devil wants to steal the faith away from the Christian people and seize the Church so as to crush, annihilate, and destroy her definitively. Even today the great dragon is keeping watch on the woman, the Church, ready to devour her child." Yes, the devil wants us to be opposed to each other at the very heart of the sacrament of unity and fraternal communion. Satan lashes out with his tail, trying to ravage the whole earth. But Jesus reassures us by saying to Peter: "Simon, behold, Satan demanded to have you, that he might sift you like wheat, but I have prayed for you that your faith may not fail; and when you have turned again, strengthen your brethren" (Lk 22:31–32).

Silence is also mentioned frequently in the liturgical norms issued by many popes.

258. Prayer is a conversation, a dialogue with the Triune God: although at some moments we address God, at others we keep silence so as to listen to him.

259. Of course, the Eastern rites do not foresee times of silence during the Divine Liturgy. In fact, when the priest himself is not chanting—that is, when he prays silently, particularly during the anaphora, the Eucharistic Prayer, except for the words of the consecration, which are chanted aloud—you notice that the deacon, the choirs, or else the faithful sing uninterruptedly. Nevertheless, they are intensely aware of the apophatic dimension of their prayer, which is expressed by all sorts of adjectives and adverbs describing the Supreme Master of the Universe and Savior of our souls. For example, the "preface" of the Byzantine Rite says: "You are God—ineffable, inconceivable, invisible, incomprehensible." Essentially, the Divine Liturgy is something of a plunge into the Mystery; it is celebrated behind the iconostasis, and the priest, who stands at the altar of sacrifice, often prays in silence. For Eastern Christians the iconostasis is the veil that protects the mystery. Among the Latins, silence is a sort of sonic iconostasis.

260. In the West, in all its rites—Roman, Roman-Lyonnais, Carthusian, Dominican, Ambrosian—the priest's silent prayer is not accompanied uninterruptedly by the singing of the choir or of the faithful. The Latin Mass has always included times of complete silence. Until the reform by Blessed Paul VI, this was the case especially during the Canon, which was recited by the celebrant silently, *in secreto*, except in the rare instances of sacramental concelebration. It is true that in some places there was an attempt to fill up the void of this silence of several minutes—which in reality was only apparent—with the sound of the organ or by polyphonic singing, but this practice was not in keeping with the spirit of the rites.

261. Vatican Council II prescribed that a time of silence should be maintained during the Eucharistic Sacrifice. Thus, the Constitution *Sacrosanctum Concilium* decreed that "to promote active participation, the people should be encouraged to take part by means of acclamations, responses, psalmody, antiphons, and songs, as well as by actions, gestures, and bodily attitudes. And at the proper times all should observe a reverent silence." The *General Instruction of the Roman Missal* of Blessed Paul VI, revised in the year 2002 by Saint John Paul II, specified many places in the Mass where such a silence must be observed.

We find first this general reminder:

> Sacred silence also, as part of the celebration, is to be observed at the designated times. Its nature, however, depends on the moment when it occurs in the different parts of the celebration. For in the Penitential Act and again after the invitation to pray, individuals recollect themselves; whereas after a reading or after the Homily, all meditate briefly on what they have heard; then after Communion, they praise God in their hearts and pray to him.
>
> Even before the celebration itself, it is a praiseworthy practice for silence to be observed in the church, in the sacristy, in the vesting room, and in adjacent areas, so that all may dispose themselves to carry out the sacred action in a devout and fitting manner.

It is sad, and almost a sacrilege, to hear occasionally priests and bishops chattering incessantly in the sacristy, and even during the entrance procession, instead of recollecting themselves and contemplating in silence the mystery of the death of Christ on the Cross, which they are preparing to celebrate and which ought to inspire in them nothing but fear and trembling.

262. In the 1969 *Missal*, silence is first prescribed during the penitential preparation: "The Priest calls upon the whole community to take part in the Penitential Act, which, after a brief pause for silence, it does by means of a formula of general confession." Then, for the collect: "... the priest calls upon the people to pray and everybody, together with the priest, observes a brief silence so that they may become aware of being in God's presence and may call to mind their intentions." Similarly,

> The Liturgy of the Word is to be celebrated in such a way as to favor meditation, and so any kind of haste such as hinders recollection is clearly to be avoided. In the course of it, brief periods of silence are also appropriate, accommodated to the assembled congregation; by means of these, under the action of the Holy Spirit, the Word of God may be grasped by the heart and a response through prayer may be prepared. It may be appropriate to observe such periods of silence, for example, before the Liturgy of the Word itself begins, after the First and Second Reading, and lastly at the conclusion of the Homily.

This advice applies also to the homily, which must be received and assimilated in an atmosphere of prayer. Finally it becomes a genuine prescription addressed to the faithful for the Eucharistic Prayer, when "the people, for their part, should associate themselves with the priest in faith and in silence."

We find again the option of remaining silent after Holy Communion or to prepare to listen to the "Post-Communion" prayer. At a Mass celebrated without the people, a moment of silence is recommended to the celebrant: "After the purification of the chalice, the priest should observe a brief pause for silence."

263. Silence is therefore by no means absent from the Ordinary Form of the Roman Rite, at least if priests follow its guidelines and celebrate in the spirit of its recommendations. Unfortunately, too often we have forgotten that the council includes silence as part of *actuosa participatio* also, which promotes truly deep, personal participation, allowing us to hear interiorly the Word of the Lord. Now in some liturgies no trace of this silence is left. Apart from the homily, all other speeches or introductions of persons should be forbidden during the celebration of Holy Mass.

264. Today you often get the impression, as Nicola Bux states in his book on *Benedict XVI's Reform*, that:

> Catholic worship ... has gone from adoration of God to the exhibition of the priest, the ministers, and the faithful. Piety has been abolished as a word and liquidated by liturgists as devotionalism, but they have made the people ... put up with liturgical experiments and rejected spontaneous forms of devotion and piety. They have even succeeded in imposing applause on funerals in place of mourning and weeping. Did Christ not mourn and weep at the death of Lazarus? Ratzinger rightly observes: "Wherever applause breaks out in the liturgy ... it is a sure sign that the essence of the liturgy has totally disappeared."

What would be your fondest wish concerning the place of silence in the liturgy?

265. I call Catholics to genuine conversion! Let us strive with all our heart to become in each of our Eucharistic celebrations "a pure Victim, a holy Victim, a spotless Victim"! Let us not be afraid of liturgical

silence. How I would love it if pastors and the faithful would enter joyfully into this silence that is full of sacred reverence and love for the ineffable God. How I would love it if churches were houses in which the great silence prevails that announces and reveals the adored presence of God. How I would love it if Christians, in the liturgy, could experience the power of silence!

It is necessary to strive to understand the theological reasons for the liturgical discipline with regard to silence. I think that two particularly well-qualified authors can help us in this area and succeed in convincing us that, without silence, an essential and necessary part of the liturgy is lost.

In the first place I want to mention Monsignor Guido Marini, Master of Pontifical Ceremonies. In *La Liturgie: Gloire de Dieu, sanctification de l'homme* [The liturgy: Glory of God, sanctification of man], he speaks about silence in these terms:

> A well-celebrated liturgy, in its various parts, provides for a happy alternation of silence and speech, in which silence animates speech, allows the voice to resonate with an extraordinary depth, and keeps each verbal expression in a proper atmosphere of recollection.... The requisite silence must not ... be considered a pause between one moment in the celebration and the next. Rather, it should be considered a genuine moment of the ritual that complements the words, the vocal prayer, the singing, and the gestures.

Joseph Cardinal Ratzinger had already noted in *The Spirit of the Liturgy*:

> The greater mystery, surpassing all words, summons us to silence. It must, of course, be a silence with content, not just the absence of speech and action. We should expect the liturgy to give us a positive stillness that will restore us. Such stillness will not be just a pause, in which a thousand thoughts and desires assault us, but a time of recollection, giving us an inward peace, allowing us to draw breath and rediscover the one thing necessary.

This is therefore a silence in which we simply look at God and allow him to look at us and to envelop us in the mystery of his majesty and love.

266. We have lost the most profound meaning of the offertory. This, nevertheless, is the moment when, as the name indicates, the whole Christian people offers itself, not alongside of Christ, but in him, through his sacrifice that will be consummated at the consecration. Vatican Council II admirably underscored this aspect by insisting on the baptismal priesthood of the laity, which consists essentially of offering ourselves with Christ in sacrifice to the Father. This teaching of the council was expressed magnificently by the old prayers of the offertory. I have already said that it would be good if we could use them again freely in order to enter silently into Christ's self-offering. As early as the seventh century, Pseudo-Germanus reports that the procession with the offerings began with this warning: "May all observe a spiritual silence while watching at the doors of their souls. By making the sign of the Cross over their faces, may they guard themselves from the tumult of words and vices.... May they guard their lips from all vulgar words so that their hearts may be turned to Christ alone."

If the offertory is seen just as a preparation of the gifts, as a practical, prosaic gesture, then there will be a great temptation to add and invent rituals so as to furnish what is perceived as an empty space. I deplore the long, noisy offertory processions, embellished with endless dances, in some countries in Africa. Some of the faithful bring forward all sorts of produce and objects that have nothing to do with the Eucharistic Sacrifice. These processions give the impression of being folklore displays, which distort the bloody sacrifice of Christ on the Cross and separate us from the Eucharistic mystery; it ought to be celebrated soberly, with recollection, because we too are immersed in his death and offering to the Father. The bishops of my continent should take measures so that the celebration of the Mass does not become a celebration of one's own culture. The death of God for love of us is beyond any culture. It submerges all culture.

Thus it is advisable to insist on the silence of the laity during the Eucharistic Prayer, as Monsignor Guido Marini explains:

> This silence is not synonymous with laziness or a lack of participation. Its purpose is to make all the faithful enter into ... the act of love by which Jesus offers himself to the Father on the Cross for the salvation of the world. This truly sacred silence is the liturgical moment during

which it is necessary to say yes, with all our strength, to Christ's action, so that it might become our action, too, in everyday life.

According to Cardinal Ratzinger, for their part, "the silent prayers of the priest invite him to make his task truly personal, so that he may give his whole self to the Lord." For everyone, the silence "after the reception of Holy Communion ... is the moment for an interior conversation with the Lord who has given himself to us, for that essential 'communicating', that entry into the process of communication, without which the external reception of the Sacrament becomes mere ritual and therefore unfruitful." After the faithful have finished receiving the Body of Christ, the choir should stop singing so as to leave everyone the time for an intimate conversation with the Lord who has just entered the temple of our body.

What a miracle, to receive the Lord of the Universe in the depths of our heart! "Do you not know that you are God's temple and that God's Spirit dwells in you? If any one destroys God's temple, God will destroy him. For God's temple is holy, and that temple you are" (1 Cor 3:16–17). Indeed, God truly expects of people sanctity of life, the virtues of silence, humility, and simplicity.

At this stage of our reflection, can we speak, therefore, about silence as a Christian ascetical value?

267. In the negative sense, silence is the absence of noise. It can be exterior or interior. Exterior silence involves the silence of words and actions, in other words, the absence of noise from doors, vehicles, jackhammers, airplanes, the noisy mechanism of cameras, often accompanied by dazzling flashes, and also that horrible forest of cell phones that are brandished at arm's length during our Eucharistic liturgies.... Virtuous or mystical silence obviously must be distinguished from disapproving silence, from the refusal to speak up, from the silence of omission through cowardice, selfishness, or hardness of heart.

268. Exterior silence is an ascetic exercise of self-mastery in the use of speech. First of all, it may be helpful to recall what asceticism is. This word is not praised to the skies by our consumer society—far from

it!—and, we must admit, it frightens our contemporaries, including very often the Christians who are influenced by the spirit of the world.

Asceticism is a means that helps us to remove from our life anything that weighs it down, in other words, whatever hampers our spiritual life and, therefore, is an obstacle to prayer. Yes, it is indeed in prayer that God communicates his Life to us and manifests his presence in our soul by irrigating it with the streams of his trinitarian love. And prayer is essentially silence. Chattering, the tendency to externalize all the treasures of the soul by expressing them, is supremely harmful to the spiritual life. Carried away toward the exterior by his need to say everything, the chatterer cannot help being far from God, superficial, and incapable of any profound activity.

The wisdom books of the Old Testament are full of exhortations aimed at avoiding sins of the tongue, in particular, slander and calumny (Prov 10:8, 11, 13). The prophetic books, for their part, mention silence as the expression of reverential fear of God; it is then a preparation for the theophany of God, in other words, the revelation of his presence in our world (Lam 3:26; Hab 2:20; Is 41:1; Zech 2:13). The New Testament is not outdone in this respect. Indeed, there is the Letter of James, which clearly remains the classic passage about controlling the tongue. However, we know that Jesus himself warned us against wicked words, which are the expression of a depraved heart (Mt 15:19), and even against idle words, for which an accounting will be demanded of us (Mt 12:36).

In reality, true, good silence always belongs to someone who is willing to let others have his place, and especially the Completely-Other, God. In contrast, external noise characterizes the individual who wants to occupy too important a place, to strut or to show off, or else who wants to fill his interior emptiness, as is the case in many public places where deafening noise and pride prevail.

269. As for interior silence, it can be achieved by the absence of memories, plans, interior speech, worries.... Still more important, thanks to an act of the will, it can result from the absence of disordered affections or excessive desires. The Fathers of the Church assign an eminent place to silence in the ascetical life. Think of Saint Ambrose, Saint Augustine, Saint Gregory the Great, not to mention

the Rule of Saint Benedict of Nursia on "taciturnity", or his words
about grand silence at night, where he adopts the teaching of Cas-
sian. Starting with those spiritual masters, all the medieval founders
of religious orders, followed by the mystics of the Catholic Counter-
Reformation, insisted on the importance of silence, even beyond its
ascetical and mystical dimension.

Is silence, therefore, an essential condition for contemplative prayer?

270. The Gospels say that the Savior himself prayed in silence, particularly at night, or while withdrawing to deserted places. Silence
is typical of the meditation by the Word of God; we find it again
particularly in Mary's attitude toward the mystery of her Son. The
most silent person in the Gospels is of course Saint Joseph; not a single word of his does the New Testament record for us. Saint Basil
considers silence not only as an ascetical necessity of monastic life but
also as a condition for encountering God. Silence precedes and prepares for the privileged moment when we have access to God, who
then can speak to us face to face as we would do with a friend.

271. We arrive at the knowledge of God by way of causality, analogy,
eminence, but also negation: once we affirm the divine attributes,
which are known by natural reason (this is the kataphatic way), we
must deny the mode of limited realization thereof that we know
here below (this is the apophatic way). Silence is an essential part of
the apophatic way of gaining access to God, which was so highly
prized by the Fathers of the Church, especially the Greeks; this
makes them demand silence of arguments when faced with the mystery of God. I am thinking here of Clement of Alexandria, Gregory
Nazianzen, and Gregory of Nyssa.

It is nonetheless true that silence is above all the positive attitude
of someone who prepares to welcome God by listening. Yes, God
acts in the silence. Hence this very important remark by the great
Saint John of the Cross in his *Maxims on Love*: "The Father spoke one
Word, which was His Son, and this Word He always speaks in eternal silence, and in silence must It be heard by the soul." The Book
of Wisdom had already noted in this regard the manner in which
God intervened to deliver the chosen people from captivity in Egypt:

that unforgettable act took place during the night: "For while gentle silence enveloped all things, and night in its swift course was now half gone, your all-powerful word leaped from heaven, from the royal throne" (Wis 18:14). Later, this verse would be understood by Christian liturgical tradition as a prefiguration of the silent Incarnation of the Eternal Word in the crib in Bethlehem.

And so we have to be silent: this is of course an activity and not a form of idleness. If our "interior cell phone" is always busy because we are "having a conversation" with other creatures, how can the Creator reach us, how can he "call us"? We must therefore purify our mind of its curiosities, the will of its plans, in order to be totally open to the graces of light and strength that God wants to give us profusely: "Father, not my will, but yours be done." Ignatian "indifference" is therefore a form of silence, too.

IV

GOD'S SILENCE IN THE FACE
OF EVIL UNLEASHED

For the man of today, compared to those of the time of Luther and to those holding the classical perspective of the Christian faith, things are in a certain sense inverted, or rather, man no longer believes he needs justification before God, but rather he is of the opinion that God is obliged to justify himself because of all the horrible things in the world and in the face of the misery of being human, all of which ultimately depend on Him.

—Benedict XVI, interview with Jacques Servais, S.J.,
October 2015, published in the English edition
of *L'Osservatore Romano* on March 17, 2016

NICOLAS DIAT: What is the relation between silence and evil? Why is God able to remain silent in the face of sorrowful events?

ROBERT CARDINAL SARAH:
272. Evil raises an immense question, an enigma that is impossible to resolve. No one in any era of human history has succeeded in giving a satisfying response to the problem of evil. In his book *Croire: Invitation à la foi catholique pour les femmes et les hommes du XXIe siècle* [Believing: Invitation to the Catholic faith for women and men of the 21st century], the theologian Bernard Sesboüé writes: "When we wonder about evil, we actually do not know what we are asking. For we seek to understand something that is incomprehensible. Evil is the irrational par excellence, something irretrievable, something that reason really cannot make sense of. . . . Our reflection on evil can only be modest, and it always leaves much to be desired." What can we say when faced with the suffering and death of a child who is brutally snatched from the affection of his parents? Why have so many lives

been mutilated in the gulags and extermination camps of totalitarian systems? Why are children born with terrible handicaps? Why are there so many horrible sicknesses and so much unjust suffering? There is no answer to these questions; we will never be able to say that the veil has been lifted, suffering can be explained.

273. Man is incapable of scrutinizing all the immensity of the heavens and the tens of millions of galaxies. Yet he can descend into the most unsuspected depths of suffering.

His intellect is capable of solving extraordinary problems. The technological prowess of our century seems limitless; man thinks that his eyes have seen everything. He has dried up the sources of the rivers and "the thing that is hidden he brings forth to light" (cf. Job 28:11). But we will never go so far as to fathom and understand the mystery of evil. Wisdom belongs to God alone. The only certainty in this world lies in interior silence, in filial piety that trusts and surrenders. We often find ourselves confronted with what could be called "innocent evil", in other words, the reality of evil inscribed in the nature of things, independently of any human responsibility.

274. The earth that shelters and nourishes us is a gigantic force that is constantly in motion. It often proves to be cruel, brutal, and pitiless. I am thinking of the volcanic eruptions that destroyed entire cities. Pompeii was entirely buried under a thick layer of ashes in 79 B.C., during a powerful eruption of Mount Vesuvius. How can we fail to mention earthquakes, the shocks of which are even more deadly and destructive? We remember the earthquakes in Aquila, in the Abruzzi region, on April 6, 2009, in Haiti on January 12, 2010, in Nepal in 2015, some terrible tsunamis in Indonesia and Sri Lanka on December 26, 2004, and in Japan on March 11, 2011, which engulfed buildings and hundreds of thousands of human lives. I will never be able to forget typhoon Hayan or Yolanda that devastated the Philippines in November 2013.

Men are the innocent, powerless victims of blind natural forces. Our revulsion is heightened when these sufferings and human losses cannot be blamed on anyone; according to our human logic, they call God into question directly. Why does he allow such devastation and so much suffering?

275. In unexpected ways, evil and suffering affect us on a daily basis. We also endure the horrors of deliberate, barbaric hatred and violence, planned and executed by human wickedness, at the obvious instigation of Satan. Faced with suffering, given the assaults of evil caused by nature or by man, there is no one but God who can help us to remain standing.

276. Christians know that God does not will evil. And if this evil exists, God is the first victim of it. Evil exists because his love is not accepted; his love is misunderstood, rejected, and resisted. The world, in its harmony and beauty, can be formed only in a dialogue of love in which God exchanges with us, and we with him. If evil affects God himself, it is because there is a divine wound that we must heal, a wound that unceasingly calls for our generosity. Thus, all of Christianity, all of divine revelation from Genesis on, is the cry of God's innocence. The more monstrous the evil, the more evident it is that God, in us, is the first victim.

277. It is difficult for man to understand evil when he does not appreciate its properly divine dimensions. In his book *Un autre regard sur l'homme* [Another look at man], Maurice Zundel writes:

> And this is the meaning of the Cross: evil can have divine dimensions, evil is ultimately God's pain. In evil, God is the one who is pained, and this is why evil is so terrible. But if God is the one who is pained by evil, then at the heart of this evil there is this love that will never cease to accompany us, to protect our lot, and to suffer with us. It is necessary to say much more: God will be struck by evil, by all evil, before us, in us, and for us, as at Golgotha.

Certainly, it is not easy to imagine how God can be touched by our evil. Job himself wondered: "If I sin, what do I do to you, you watcher of men?" (Job 7:20). How can God be struck by evil? Imagine a mother with her sick child. She can suffer for her child through love and identification. A completely healthy mother can experience her child's agony more painfully than the child himself by reason of this very identification of love with the beloved. Her love is capable of this. How can anyone think that God's love is less maternal than a mother's love, when all the love of all mothers, including that of the Most Blessed Virgin Mary herself, is only a drop in this ocean of God's maternal tenderness? This is why no creature is struck without God being struck in it, before it, and for it.

"Can a woman forget her sucking child, that she should have no compassion on the son of her womb? Even these may forget, yet I will not forget you. Behold, I have graven you on the palms of my hands; your walls are continually before me. Your builders outstrip your destroyers, and those who laid you waste go forth from you" (Is 49:15–17).

278. Like the psalmist, the man of faith turns to God to declare to him: "My eyes are toward you, O LORD God; in you I seek refuge; leave me not defenseless! Keep me from the trap which they have laid for me, and from the snares of evildoers" (Ps 141:8–9).

I behave this way because Jesus Christ, the Son of God who "reflects the glory of God and bears the very stamp of his nature, upholding the universe by his word of power" (Heb 1:3), went before me in the most atrocious suffering. Jesus is connected with men because he is one of them, taking on the human condition, its trials and sufferings. He is also connected to God because he is his own Son. Jesus is in a unique situation that makes him the head of the new human family, "the first-born among many brethren" (Rom 8:29). He shares our trials and bears all our sufferings. Since the death of Jesus on the Cross, the man of faith can no longer take any stance toward evil except at Jesus' side, relying firmly on him. He must stand beside Mary, the Virgin standing at the foot of the Cross, so as to complete in his flesh "what is lacking in Christ's afflictions for the sake of his body, that is, the Church" (Col 1:24).

279. The horrors perpetrated by men and the works of the devil are a mystery that mankind will never be able to understand thoroughly. Evil, whether physical or moral, is always unjust and ignoble. It demeans and destroys man. It tarnishes the image of God engraved on man.

280. Faced with evil, the human being rebels. He seeks in every way he can to get rid of it. Confronted with evil, there is only one

possible attitude: combat and resistance. Here is the recommendation of Saint Peter: "Be sober, be watchful. Your adversary the devil prowls around like a roaring lion, seeking some one to devour. Resist him, firm in your faith" (1 Pet 5:8–9).

281. Prayer must be a form of resistance in order to repel difficulties. It allows us to be clad in the armor of God. Man turns to God humbly, asking him to intervene on his behalf.

282. How did Christ confront evil? How did Mary respond to evil? How did the Mother of God react when she saw the disfigured face of her Son on the Cross?

The Virgin has no strength left in the face of such an outburst of hatred and violence. She is exhausted, overwhelmed, broken. Nevertheless, Mary possesses a great interior strength, and she remains standing and silent. She takes refuge in prayer, self-offering, and serene acceptance of God's mysterious will, in communion with her Son. The Mother of God loves a God who makes no noise and burns up human violence in the fire of his merciful love. At that moment she hears her Son beg God: "Father, forgive them; for they know not what they do" (Lk 23:34). The union of her silence with the prayers of heaven enables her to remain standing at the foot of the Cross. Mary does not rebel, she does not shout. She accepts suffering thanks to her prayer. Did not Jesus himself prepare to endure his Passion by a night of prayer in the garden of Gethsemane and by many other nights, alone on the mountain or away in a deserted place?

283. Christ alone can give man the strength to confront evil and come to terms with it. He offers himself as the only power capable of helping mankind to conquer suffering. "Apart from me you can do nothing" (Jn 15:5). By the strength of his Cross, he has the power to save mankind. The most beautiful cry possible is an outburst of love for God. Suffering is often the expression of an immense love. It is redemptive. Suffering and sorrow show that we are alive, guiding the physician more precisely in his diagnosis. It is necessary to accept suffering and to cope with it in silence. There is no injustice in the world that does not find a prayerful response in God.

I know how difficult it is to stand up to suffering and to come to terms with it. I know that it is difficult for us to accept suffering. We turn to God, shouting, "Why this chalice? Why so many horrors and so much barbaric violence?"

284. God does not will evil. God does not want war. God does not will death or suffering. God does not want injustice. Nevertheless, he allows all these earthly evils. Why such a mystery?

The Father intends that we come to terms with our whole life here below. And evil is part of the human condition. He willed that his own Son should experience the most abject evil for the redemption and salvation of the world.

Might there be an alternative: Either rebellion or the silence of prayer?

285. God always watches over us. Man may experience the darkest nights, endure the worst outrages, confront the most tragic situations, yet God is with him. Often man forgets that God is present. If he is an unbeliever, he supposes that God does not exist. If he has a faith that has grown lukewarm because of the secularized atmosphere of the times, he despairs, thinking that God has abandoned him. But the Father stays with him despite all possible denials.

286. Confronted with evil, man gets organized by gathering the means necessary for his defense. His action is just, but sometimes it provokes greater evils. Our true grandeur lies in the humility of faith; the purer our belief, the more profound it is and the closer it brings us to God, who is infinitely great. Someone who is close to God becomes powerful; he can conquer the evil that corrodes the world, and he is capable of integrating it into his prayer of intercession.

287. Silence and prayer are not a form of defection. They are the strongest weapons against evil. Man wants to "do", but above all else he must "be". In silent prayer, man is fully human. He resembles David before Goliath. For prayer is the noblest, most sublime, and most vigorous act, which elevates man to the level of God.

288. Prayer is offering oneself to God like the fragrance of incense that ascends to God's Throne to disappear in him. God also gives

himself to those who give themselves to him. I know that, in the silent depths of my heart, I can come just as intimately close to God, whatever the circumstances may be or whatever sufferings evil may impose on me.

Saint John Vianney, a man of silence, a great shepherd of souls, who was totally dedicated to the proclamation of the Word of God and to the Mystery of Reconciliation, whose face was transfigured by the Eucharist, offers the most sublime definition of prayer:

> See, my children, a Christian's treasure is not on earth, it is in heaven. Well, then! Our thoughts must go where our treasure is. Man has a fine function: to pray and to love. You pray, you love: that is man's happiness on earth!
>
> Prayer is nothing other than a union with God. When your heart is pure and united with God, you feel within yourself a balm, a sweetness that is inebriating, a light that is dazzling. In this intimate union, God and the soul are like two pieces of wax that have melted together: you can no longer separate them. It is a very beautiful thing, this union of God with his little creature. It is an incomprehensible blessing.
>
> We have not deserved to pray, but God, in his goodness, has allowed us to speak to him. Our prayer is like incense that he receives with the utmost pleasure.
>
> My children, you have a little heart, but prayer enlarges it and makes it capable of loving God.... Prayer is a foretaste of heaven, a stream flowing from paradise. It never leaves us without sweetness. It is a kind of honey that sinks into the soul and sweetens everything. Troubles melt away in the presence of prayer that is made well, like snow before the sun.

289. Silence is not a form of passivity. By remaining silent, man can avoid a greater evil. It is not an earthly dereliction of duty to place your trust in heaven.

Certainly, but how does one keep silence in the face of injustice? How can one not cry out in incomprehension and rebellion?

290. In trying to control everything and to place everything under the banner of rebellion, a man runs the risk of leaving nothing up to God. He finds himself alone, faced with his own limits and helplessness. Now man without God is lost. Without faith lived out in confident silence, he turns away from his God and Redeemer.

291. In the absence of God, it is easy to observe the bitter failures of human debates and of political solutions with regard to evil ...

What is God's instruction? In the parable of the good grain and the chaff, Christ invites us to let the wheat and the weeds grow until the hour of the harvest. Then the time will come when evil will be destroyed by good. Persevering patience, supported by Providence, is an ally in all our daily battles. The combat against evil plays out over time, and it is important to persevere and not to lose hope. God is fashioning hearts, and evil never has the last word. In the darkest night, God works in silence. We have to enter into God's time and into this great silence that is a silence of love, trust, and active abandonment. Let us never forget that silent prayer is the strongest and surest act in the struggle against evil.

292. We must involve God in our combat against injustice. I like to keep saying that our true weapons are love and prayer. The silence of prayer is our only equipment for combat. The silence of invocation, the silence of adoration, the silence of waiting: these are the most effective weapons. Love alone is capable of putting out the flames of injustice, because God is love. Loving God is everything. All the rest has not the slightest value to the extent that it is not transformed and elevated by Christ's love. The choice is simple: God or nothing ...

293. Modern man intends to become the master of time, the only one responsible for his own existence, future, and well-being. He wants to program his life and control his destiny. He organizes his efforts as though God did not exist. He does not need him. On the other hand, God invites us to trust, to be patient, and to work slowly toward the elimination of evil, which requires a long, thankless battle. This combat involves four pillars set up on God in faith: silence, prayer, penance, and fasting.

Is rebellion a trap, to which silence must always be preferred? Your experience of a violent, authoritarian Marxist regime in Guinea certainly provides you with food for thought on this subject. Confronted with the dictator Sékou Touré, what path did you choose?

294. A man of God does not seek any political office. He does not aspire to bring about any change in the political system, nor does

he call for the existing government to be overturned. His mission is essentially moral and spiritual, aimed at the interior renewal of man, love of God and neighbor. Nevertheless, when confronted with some ideological orientations, one cannot let the evil advance. In Guinea, I thought it necessary to call by their names the horrors and scandals perpetrated by the dictatorship, but I did not want to incite the people to rebellion. My intention was to denounce the injustices of the bloody regime of Sékou Touré and to point out the sufferings of the people, particularly the economic and social disaster. The country had won its independence, but the population was deprived of freedom, hunted down, and bound by the chains of fear and ignorance. I called for a change for the good of all, those who governed and those who were governed. For my country possesses all the human and natural resources needed to make its children happy and to help them to live with dignity. I knew that my words would be that much stronger because they had as their rock an intense life of penance, prayer, and silence, rooted and lived in God.

Often, dictators are sincerely persuaded that they are doing good. Alexander Solzhenitsyn made it perfectly clear that the Soviet leaders were convinced that they were leading the country toward an earthly paradise. Sékou Touré, because of a faulty formation of his conscience and an erroneous mind-set, thought that he was bringing progress and prosperity to Guinea.

295. Thanks to the aid of silent prayer, man becomes capable of describing realities in all their raw truth. It is necessary to affirm the principles of the Gospel after encountering God in silence. A man of God will legitimately speak in God's name only after encountering him in the silence of the interior desert and conversing with him face to face, "as a man speaks to his friend" (Ex 33:11). When you really have encountered God, it is impossible to compromise the Gospel and the precepts of divine revelation with the political and ideological positions of a world that rebels against the law of God and of nature.

296. Far from noise and easy distractions, in solitude and silence, if we are intent solely on transmitting the divine will, it will be granted to us to see with God's eyes and to call things as he perceives and judges them.

297. There is no genuine action or major decision except in the silence of the prayer that precedes them.

298. Today the danger lies in the unbridled activism of the modern world. We are always called to fight, to comb the countryside, to overthrow our adversaries, and to destroy them. Indeed, man is driven to compound one evil with another, whereas he ought to let the weeds grow with the wheat. Silence will give us the patience to wait for the moment when the useless plants will fall by themselves. Thanks to silence, we will know how to bide our time and to wait for God's hour with perseverance so as to forge an alliance with him and to work under his guidance.

299. For there is a time to fight and a time to make use of silence. If we truly possess the pedagogy of silence that comes from God, we will have a little of heaven's patience.

300. The devil invites mankind to rebellion and disorder. With his litany of subterfuges, he sows discord and incites us to pour out our hatred upon each other. "Old Scratch" always makes noise and a lot of racket so as to prevent us from resting in God. The devil will not be able to reach us in the stronghold of silence. Let us guard against multiplying sins by satisfying our little egotistical or revolutionary passions.

301. Confronted with the injustice of his arrest, Christ remained silent. The Apostles tried to draw their swords to defend the Son of God. But Jesus told Peter: "Put your sword into its sheath; shall I not drink the chalice which the Father has given me?" (Jn 18:11; Mt 26:52).

302. The Church must not think that an effective response to injustice lies in militant, political, and demagogic activity. Human battles lead only to confrontation, destruction, and ruin. They are nothing compared with the infinite silence of the Father.

In order to confront the misfortunes of the world, Pope Francis calls the Church to be a "field hospital". How can this image be interpreted in terms of our present reflection on silence?

303. There is Pope Francis' initial insight, which is generous and essentially pastoral, and then there is the secular, reductionist interpretation by the media. Alas, this contrast is nothing new. In speaking about Vatican II, Benedict XVI had already denounced the conflict between the vision of the Council Fathers and the relativistic, falsely progressive media interpretation. We must acknowledge, however, that this is a *hapax legomenon*, an expression occurring only once in the history of ecclesiology and of images for the Church.

The Church is a faithful, loving mother. She is a mother before she is a hospital facility. She is the Body of Christ, the Bride of Christ. She represents the roof under which God's family gathers. She educates, teaches, and nourishes, concerned about the physical and moral health of the faithful: this, incidentally, is the area covered by the image of the Church as a field hospital. She is the Mystical Body of Christ and the family of God on earth. *Mater et Magistra*: the Church teaches with certainty the divine truths to a world that thirsts for the Son of God, the way, the truth, the life, and the redeemer of our souls. She is an assembly of prayer, praise, and adoration, as in the Upper Room: "All ... with one accord devoted themselves to prayer, together with the women and Mary the mother of Jesus, and with his brethren" (Acts 1:14). Mary is therefore a "pre-eminent and singular member of the Church, ... its type and excellent exemplar in faith and charity" (LG 53). Finally, she is the mother of priests, who must continue Christ's work for the salvation of souls. This work consists essentially in sanctifying themselves and sanctifying the people of God, praying intensely and incessantly to bring people to God so as to live abundantly every day in him in the Eucharist.

Without the Eucharist, we can neither live nor give God the first place in our lives and activities. The priests and the faithful must respond to the silence of indifference with the silence of prayer. The sickness of apathy is treated by the sacraments, the teaching, and the witness of the saints.

304. The social mission is fundamental, but the salvation of souls is more important than any other work. Saving souls entails not only caring for them but above all drawing them to God, converting them, so as to bring the prodigal children back to the house of the Father of mercies. The primary and fundamental role of the Church today remains the salvation of souls.

305. In a secularized, decadent world, if the Church allows herself to be lured by materialistic, media-savvy, and relativistic sirens, she runs the risk of making Christ's death on the Cross for the salvation of souls futile. The Church's mission is not to solve all the social problems of the world; she must repeat tirelessly the first words of Jesus at the beginning of his public ministry in Galilee: "The time is fulfilled, and the kingdom of God is at hand; repent, and believe in the gospel" (Mk 1:15).

306. I do not think that the Church can fail to take an interest in issues that concern the lives and existence of men. Through her schools and universities, her clinics and hospitals, her institutes of professional formation, her manifold works of charity, the Church actively participates in the fight against poverty. She works to avoid the scandal of having "some countries with a majority of citizens who are counted as Christians have an abundance of wealth, whereas others are deprived of the necessities of life and are tormented by hunger, disease, and every kind of misery. The spirit of poverty and charity [is] the glory and witness of the Church of Christ" (GS 88).

307. The absence of God in modern societies has dug a pit of darkness and injustice. All that God expects of us is our consent, our loving response to his redeeming love.

308. Indifference toward God is the root of one form of noisy rebellion. The latter is an illusion that consists of thinking that we can do without God so as to live better here below. Hence, God's silence becomes an almost objective ally, the tangible proof of humanity without a Creator. In postulating that he is autonomous with respect to the divinity, modern man has reached the point where he no longer tolerates even God's silence.

In this rebellion there is no place for silence; I fear that the media interpretation of the vision of the "field hospital" is part of this sort of rebellion.

309. Before accusing others, it is important to look at oneself. We have a limitless capacity for throwing stones at our neighbor's face. We would do better to admit our own faults. In prayer and

silence, our heart gleams much more than in the blind, autistic frenzy of rebellion.

How can one not rebel, given the bloody wars that ravage humanity? Faced with so many crimes, why is God so silent? Why this deafening silence when children are pitilessly massacred in conflicts?

310. War is always an enterprise of unacceptable destruction, elimination, and annihilation. The other is no longer worth anything. He becomes mere matter doomed to death. When a country, a government, or a coalition tries to subject and annihilate men or nations, barbarism is never far off. Hatred, jealous interests, the bulimic compulsion of the rich and powerful nations to seize the natural resources of weak, poor nations by military violence, the will to dominate and avenge are at the origin of so many wars. The other no longer has the right to life. Indeed, war is an enterprise of evil, because the devil, who detests pity, triumphs with delight. How can we not be scandalized and horrified by the action of American and Western governments in Iraq, Libya, Afghanistan, and Syria? Countries and peoples are destroyed, heads of state are assassinated, for the sake of purely economic interests. In the name of the goddess Democracy, or of a will to geopolitical or military hegemony, they do not hesitate to start a war so as to disorganize and create chaos, especially in the weakest regions, thus sending out onto the roads endless troops of refugees who have neither resources nor a future.

How many families are displaced, reduced to inhumane poverty, exile, and cultural uprooting? How many sufferings in these lives of continuous wandering and flight, how many atrocious deaths in the name of Liberty, another Western goddess? How much blood is shed for a hypothetical liberation of peoples from the chains that supposedly keep them in the yoke of oppression? How many families are decimated in order to impose a Western concept of society?

In these antechambers of horror, the Church is not spared. She must disappear or change her doctrine and her teaching so as to allow for the emergence of a religion without borders and a new global ethics that is said to be consensual, cut off from all the foundational references of revealed truth and yet itself ambivalent and devoid of content.

311. Why is God silent about so many sufferings that are intended, planned, and executed by men themselves? In Africa I was able to witness the most indescribable atrocities. In my archdiocese I sheltered missionaries and religious who were fleeing from Sierra Leone and Liberia, countries prey to conflicts of unprecedented violence. They were horrified to have seen hands cut off, bodies torn apart by land mines, faces lacerated by torturers who no longer had any humanity. For several months I hosted in my residence Archbishop Joseph Ganda of Freetown, the Apostolic Nuncio, Archbishop Antonio Lucibello, and his secretary. They had had to flee Freetown, the capital of Sierra Leone, after having abandoned Monrovia. Those are indelible memories. But no one thought even for an instant to attribute those crimes to God by declaring the criminals innocent and accusing God's silence.

312. I think that it is always necessary to cry out to God. It is good to ask for help and aid from heaven, while expressing the confusion, distress, and sadness that fill our hearts. Christians should know that there is no other way of reaching God. When I traveled in countries that were going through violent, profound crises, I observed how much prayer could help those who no longer had anything. Silence was the last trench that no one could enter, the only room in which to remain in peace, the state in which suffering lowered its weapons for a moment. Silence strengthens our weakness. Silence arms us with patience. Silence in God restores our courage.

When we are ruined, humiliated, belittled, slandered, let us keep silence. Let us hide in the holy sepulcher of Our Lord Jesus Christ, far from the world.

Then the power of the torturers no longer matters. The criminals can destroy everything in their fury, but it is impossible to break into the silence, the heart and the conscience of a man. The beating of a silent heart, hope, faith, and trust in God remain unsinkable. Outside, the world becomes a field of ruins, but inside our soul, in the greatest silence, God keeps watch. War, barbarism, and the parades of horrors will never get the better of God, who is present in us.

The poison of war comes to an end in the silence of prayer, in the silence of trust, in the silence of hope. At the heart of all the barbarities, it is necessary to plant the mystery of the Cross.

I am thinking also of the wars waged by gossip and slanders. Speech can assassinate, a word can kill, but God educates us in the school of forgiveness. He teaches us to pray for our enemies. He surrounds our heart with an enclosure of tenderness so that it may not be sullied by rancor. And he constantly murmurs: "The disciples of my beloved Son have no enemies. Your heart must not have enemies, either." I speak from personal experience. I painfully experienced assassination by gossip, slander, and public humiliation, and I learned that when a person has decided to destroy you, he has no lack of words, spite, and hypocrisy; falsehood has an immense capacity for constructing arguments, proofs, and truths out of sand. When this is the behavior of men of the Church, and in particular of ambitious, duplicitous bishops, the pain is still deeper. But men look at outward appearances, and God sees the heart (1 Sam 16:7). Relying on his view alone, we must remain calm and silent, asking for the grace never to give in to rancor, hatred, and feelings of worthlessness. Let us stand firm in our love for God and for his Church, in humility.

The key to a treasure is not the treasure. But if we give away the key, we also hand over the treasure. The Cross is an exceptionally precious key, even when it appears to be folly, the subject of ridicule, and a scandal; it is repugnant to our mentalities and our search for easy solutions. We would like to be happy and live in a peaceful world without paying the price. The Cross is an astonishing mystery. It is the sign of Christ's infinite love for us. In a sermon by Saint Leo the Great on the Passion, we find this extraordinary passage:

Christ being lifted up upon the cross, let the eyes of your mind not dwell only on that sight which those wicked sinners saw, to whom it was said by the mouth of Moses, "And thy life shall be hanging before thine eyes, and thou shalt fear day and night, and shalt not be assured of thy life" [Deut 28:66].... But let our understandings, illumined by the Spirit of Truth, foster with pure and free heart the glory of the cross which irradiates heaven and earth, and see with the inner sight what the LORD meant when He spoke of His coming Passion: "... Now is the world's judgment, now shall the prince of this world be cast out. And I, if I be lifted up from the earth, will draw all things unto Me." O wondrous power of the Cross! O ineffable glory of the Passion!

313. Through the Cross, Jesus reconciled us with God; he destroyed the barrier that separated us from one another, and he overcame the obstacles that closed off the road to eternal happiness. Christ suffered for us; he leaves us an example so that we might follow in his footsteps. By contemplating the Cross and by making this prayer our own, all dialogue, all forgiveness, and all reconciliation will be possible for us.

This conviction is also part of the tradition of mystical Islam. I would like to tell a story taken from the golden legend of the Muslim holy men. One day the good woman Sutura went to find Tierno Bokar, the wise man of Bandiagara—a village in Mali located on the plateau by the same name, bordered by high cliffs, at the foot of which lived the Dogons, a people famous for its austere art, its complex beliefs about the origins of the universe, and its profound sense of transcendence. She told him: "Tierno, I am very quick-tempered. The slightest gesture affects me severely. I would like to receive a blessing from you or a prayer that will make me gentle, affable, and patient." No sooner had she spoken than her son, a three-year-old toddler who was waiting for her in the yard, came in, took up a small board and struck her with it violently between the shoulders. She looked at the toddler, smiled, and drew him against her and said affectionately while patting him, "Oh! What a naughty boy, mistreating his mother!" "Why did you not lose your temper at your son, when you say you are so quick-tempered?" Tierno Bokar asked her. "But Tierno," Sutura replied, "my son is only a child; he does not know what he is doing; one does not get angry with a child of that age." "My good Sutura," Tierno said to her, "go back home. And when someone irritates you, think of this small board and tell yourself: Despite his age, this person is acting like a three-year-old child! Be indulgent; you can do it, because you just were with your son who struck you so hard. Go, and that way you will no longer get angry. You will live happily, cured of your ailment. The blessings that will then descend on you will be far superior to those that you could obtain from me: they will be blessings from God and from the Prophet himself. Someone who endures and forgives an offense", he continued, "is like a large silk-cotton tree that the vultures befoul while resting on its branches. But the disgusting appearance of the tree lasts only part of the year. Every winter, God sends a series of downpours that wash it from top to bottom and clothe it in new foliage. Try to spread to God's creatures the love that you have for your child. For God sees creatures in the way that a father looks at his children. Then you will be set at the topmost rung of the ladder, where, through love and charity, the soul sees and evaluates the offense only so as to forgive it more wholeheartedly." Tierno's words had such a powerful effect on her that, from that day on, Sutura considered everyone who offended her as children and responded to them only with sweetness, love, and smiling, silent patience. She corrected herself so perfectly that, in the last days of her life, they used to say: "Patient as Sutura." Nothing could anger her. When she died, she was not far from being considered a saint.

314. The Cross is a great school of contemplation, prayer, and forgiveness. We have to learn to stand silently at the foot of the Cross while contemplating the Crucified Lord as the Virgin Mary did. The Cross is a mountain to climb; at the top, it is granted to us to look at men and the world with the very eyes of God. Faced with serious trespasses that seem unforgivable, the act of faith urges man to contemplate the mystery of Calvary. Then he can see the event of Jesus' Passion as the greatest possible trespass but also the place of the greatest forgiveness. In the silence of his heart, he hears Jesus' prayer, which is so difficult to reproduce in concrete actions without the help of divine grace: "Father, forgive them; for they know not what they do" (Lk 23:34).

The Bible, particularly the Old Testament, is full of wars and fratricidal episodes. Silence is not compatible with such vengeful preoccupations . . .

315. The Old Testament is the most realistic, truest, and most authentic expression of the truth about the heart of man. When man is still uncouth and not very docile, far from a God of mercy and pity, when he has not yet been transformed, "born anew, not of perishable seed but of imperishable, through the living and abiding word of God" (1 Pet 1:23), he is violent, barbaric, and pitiless toward his enemy.

Even today, who dares to claim to love his adversary and work for his success? We have kept the spirit and behavior of a man of the Old Testament. For there is "nothing new under the sun", says Qoheleth in Ecclesiastes (1:9).

So many Christians and people downtrodden by the barbaric persecution and violence of wicked men go through the experience of
the Lord Jesus "in the days of his flesh". Psalm 22, which we recite
at the Office of Readings on Good Friday, expresses our own experience when faced with death:

> My God, my God, why have you forsaken me?
>   Why are you so far from helping me, from the words
>   of my groaning?
> O my God, I cry by day, but you do not answer;
>   and by night, but find no rest.
>
> Yet you are holy,
> enthroned on the praises of Israel.
> In you our fathers trusted;
> they trusted, and you delivered them.
> To you they cried, and were saved;
> in you they trusted, and were not disappointed.
>
> But I am a worm, and no man;
> scorned by men, and despised by the people.
> All who see me mock at me,
> they make mouths at me, they wag their heads;
> "He committed his cause to the LORD; let him deliver
>   him,
> let him rescue him, for he delights in him!"
>
> Yet you are he who took me from the womb;
> you kept me safe upon my mother's breasts.
> Upon you was I cast from my birth,
> and since my mother bore me you have been my God.
> Be not far from me,
> for trouble is near
> and there is none to help.
>
> Many bulls encompass me,
> strong bulls of Bashan surround me;
> they open wide their mouths at me,
> like a ravening and roaring lion.

I am poured out like water,
and all my bones are out of joint;
my heart is like wax,
it is melted within my breast;
my strength is dried up like a potsherd,
and my tongue cleaves to my jaws;
 you lay me in the dust of death.

Yes, dogs are round about me;
a company of evildoers encircle me;
 they have pierced my hands and feet—
I can count all my bones—
 they stare and gloat over me;
they divide my garments among them,
and for my clothing they cast lots.

But you, O LORD, be not far off!
O my help, hasten to my aid!
Deliver my soul from the sword,
my life from the power of the dog!
Save me from the mouth of the lion,
my afflicted soul from the horns of the wild oxen!

I will tell of your name to my brethren;
in the midst of the congregation I will praise you:
You who fear the LORD, praise him!
All you sons of Jacob, glorify him,
and stand in awe of him, all you sons of Israel! . . .

316. Wars, violence, and barbarity run through all the history of
Israel. In those ancient times, in order to survive, it was necessary to
fight and destroy the enemy. How could violence be attenuated? The
law of retaliation was decreed, not only by Hebrew law, but by many
nations in the Mediterranean basin. Hammurabi, King of Babylon
(1792–1750 B.C.), ordered a code written in the form of a collection
of court decisions, which was then engraved on a basalt stele that was
discovered in Susa.

The Old Testament shows many episodes of violence; it is nevertheless the book that exalts the incomparable power of prayer. After

they left Egypt and crossed the desert, the Hebrews encountered the Amalekites, a powerful tribe of Edomite nomads who occupied a territory corresponding to the south of Judea. According to the Bible, they were always hounding the Hebrews. During the fighting between the two peoples, Moses tried to involve God in the battle. He was his surest ally. Moses went up on the mountain, with Aaron and Hur, to beseech heaven. When he prayed in silence, with the support of his two companions who held up his hands so that they would be raised until sunset, the Hebrews prevailed. In contrast, when Moses lowered his arms, because of fatigue, the Amalekites prevailed (Ex 17:8–16). In the secret of prayer, God made his people victorious. Man's strength brings only ephemeral triumphs. Only the silence of a heart-to-heart conversation with God is a solid rock.

After David and Solomon, a major change took place gradually. David still had his hands covered with blood, but he was a man of silence, prayer, and peace. In him the coming of the Messiah was gradually wrought. His heart, which was full of mercy and respect for human life, was revealed miraculously on three occasions. When circumstances would have allowed him to kill Saul, he spared his life twice (1 Sam 24 and 26). He forgave Abigail's husband, who had mistreated his messengers (1 Sam 25:14–38), and he bitterly wept over the death of Saul and Absalom, his son who had rebelled against him. David had a profound sense of sin and repentance; his heart was sincere and entirely commended to God. Psalm 51 is a marvelous testimony.

Similarly, in the New Testament, the Gospel of Matthew lets us hear the voice of Rachel shortly after the birth of Jesus. It was at the time of the massacre of the infants in Bethlehem. Rachel weeps in silence so as to enter into hope and to hear the consolations that come from God: "A voice was heard in Ramah, wailing and loud lamentation, Rachel weeping for her children; she refused to be consoled, because they were no more" (Mt 2:18). Rachel is unwilling to dry her tears, because she does not accept facile comfort, hackneyed words, and she is determined that death should not become a rhetorical topic or something that a speech would enable a person to cope with. Her tears are the herald of the tears of the women of Jerusalem who accompany the Crucified Lord because they know that by his death on the Cross, "God himself will be with them; he will wipe away every tear from their eyes, and death shall be no more, neither shall there be mourning nor crying nor pain any more, for the former things have passed away" (Rev 21:3–4).

As President of the Pontifical Council Cor unum, in other words, the one in charge of the pope's charitable work, under Benedict XVI and Francis, you faced many humanitarian catastrophes. How can one not cry out in rebellion in view of such tragedies?

317. I always thought that there are two kinds of horrors. There is the deliberate barbarity perpetrated by men, for example in concentration camps, gulags, tortures, decapitations, all the cruelties of which man is sadly capable. If men were aware that a human being is in the image of God, they would not let themselves go to such extremes. How can anyone dare to destroy God's work? Man's hatred for man is a denial of God. To kill a human being or a human embryo, knowingly, voluntarily and deliberately, is an inexcusable crime. For God said: "Thou shalt not kill." And this law is absolute.

And then there are the effects of nature unleashed: typhoons, earthquakes, or tsunamis that put men in situations of extreme destitution. I have met individuals who had lost the fruits of a lifetime of work. But my experience showed me that men are strong enough to rebuild in the face of such catastrophes. They spontaneously turn their hearts to God to ask him to repair the misfortune. When his material life is reduced to nothing, man commends himself into God's hands all the more forcefully. Why shout, weep, or groan? The loudest cry, the tears that are at the deepest part of our suffering, the most plaintive groaning, is the confident silence and the faint sigh that commend everything into God's hands.

In the psalms, the speech of the man who has placed himself in the presence of God is magnificent:

> I am utterly spent and crushed;
> I groan because of the tumult of my heart.
>
> Lord, all my longing is known to you,
> my sighing is not hidden from you....

Those who seek my life lay their snares,
those who seek my hurt speak of ruin,
and meditate treachery all the day long.

But I am like a deaf man, I do not hear,
like a mute man who does not open his mouth.
Yes, I am like a man who does not hear,
and in whose mouth are no rebukes. . . .

Those who are my foes without cause are mighty,
and many are those who hate me wrongfully.
Those who render me evil for good
are my adversaries because I follow after good.

Do not forsake me, O LORD!
O my God, be not far from me!
Make haste to help me,
O Lord, my salvation! (Ps 38:8–9, 12–14, 19–21)

318. When man does violence to man, the rebuilding is always difficult, long, and hazardous. In evil, humanity is capable of unequaled refinement and imagination. And yet, Father Jacques Mourad, a Syro-Catholic priest who was held hostage by ISIS for almost five months, was able to say upon leaving that hell: "God gave me two things, silence and kindness." I am quite impressed by these very sober, just words.

In fact, silence can make it possible to survive in the most precarious situations. Tortures, ill treatment, and torments, however diabolical they may be, will start to be calmed by a silence that is directed toward God. In a mysterious but real way, he supports us by suffering with us. He is inseparably united to man in all his tribulations; it is one thing to rebel against God because he remained silent during our sufferings; it is another thing to entrust our suffering to him in silence, to offer it to him so that he might transform it into an instrument of salvation by associating it with Christ's suffering.

319. In the face of horror, there are no responses more important than prayer. Man silently turns his gaze toward God, who allows himself without fail to be moved by tears. The human struggle is necessary

in order to combat the powers of evil. But silence is the mysteriously effective hidden instrument. How did the gulags of the Soviet Union fall? By the silent prayer of John Paul II and of the entire Church, sustained by Our Lady of Fatima. Sophisticated political strategies did not get the better of Marxist Communism. Prayer had the last word. The silence of the rosary obtained the unthinkable, and the Western bloc was quite surprised ...

320. There is a time for human action, which is often uncertain, and a time for silence in God, which is truly victorious. Far from vengeful, noisy, ideological rebellion, I believe in the fruitfulness of silence. Prayer and silence will save the world.

Is it not so that poverty is the situation in which it is difficult to remain silent?

321. Were not Jesus, Mary, and Joseph poor? Did they shout in protest against their poverty? So many monks and nuns, Mother Teresa of Calcutta and her missionary sisters: Are they not poor, and are they not silent? But it is not just those in consecrated life. In Africa, in Asia, and elsewhere, I have had the opportunity to meet with poor people who have great nobility and an incomparable dignity. Although they live in extreme material poverty, these people firmly believe in God and are radiant with joy, peace, and inner harmony. Man's wealth is God. The most horrible and most inhumane poverty is the lack of God.

322. The absence or the rejection of God is the most extreme human destitution. No one in this world can satisfy man's desire. God alone satisfies and more than satisfies, to an infinite extent. In the *Confessions*, Saint Augustine writes:

O, Lord ... Thou hast made us for Thyself and our hearts are restless till they rest in Thee.... Who shall grant me to rest in Thee? By whose gift shalt Thou enter into my heart and fill it so compellingly that I shall turn no more to my sins but embrace Thee, my only good? What art Thou to me? Have mercy, that I may tell. What rather am I to Thee, that Thou shouldst demand my love and if I do not love Thee be angry and threaten such great woes? Surely not to love Thee is already a great woe. For Thy mercies' sake, O Lord my God, tell me what Thou art to me. *Say unto my soul, I am Thy salvation.* So speak that I may hear, Lord, my heart is listening; open it that it may hear Thee say to my soul *I am Thy salvation.* Hearing that word, let me come in haste to lay hold upon Thee. Hide not Thy face from me. Let me see Thy face even if I die, lest I die with longing to see it.

323. I am surprised by the way in which poverty is understood in the world today, and even by many members of the Catholic Church. In the Bible, poverty is always a state that brings God and man closer together. The poor of Yahweh populate the Bible. Monasticism is an impulse toward God alone: the monk leads his life in poverty, chastity, and absolute obedience, and lives on God's Word in silence. Perversely, the modern world has set for itself as an odd objective the eradication of poverty. Above all, there is a kind of disturbing confusion between misery and poverty. This way of picturing life is not in keeping with the language of revelation. Poverty corresponds to an idea that God has of man. God is poor, and he loves poor people. God is poor, because God is love, and love is poor. Someone who loves can be happy only in a total dependence on the beloved person. God is absolute poverty; in him there is no trace of possessiveness.

324. In Deuteronomy we find these extraordinary words that allow us to understand the divine mind and will:

> You shall remember all the way which the LORD your God has led you these forty years in the wilderness, that he might humble you, testing you to know what was in your heart, whether you would keep his commandments, or not. And he humbled you and let you hunger and fed you with manna, which you did not know, nor did your fathers know; that he might make you know that man does not live by bread alone, but that man lives by everything that proceeds out of the mouth of the LORD. (Deut 8:2–3)

325. Poverty is a test and an austerity that God imposes on those who claim to live in his company. He wants to know the truth of their heart and their fidelity to his commandments. Poverty is a sign of love. It unburdens us of all that is heavy and that weighs down our

progress toward what is essential. It helps us in the great contemporary battle to rediscover the true values of life.

If you are faced with a decisive battle, look at young David when Goliath challenged the army of Israel. Compared with him, the Philistine Goliath was heavily armed. His height was six cubits and a span. On his head he had a bronze helmet. He was clothed in a coat of mail weighing five thousand shekels of bronze. He also wore greaves, and a javelin of bronze across his shoulder. His spearhead weighed six hundred shekels of iron, and a shield-bearer went before him. Saul wanted to clothe David with his armor. So he placed a helmet on his head and clothed him in a coat of mail and belted a sword on him. But David was unable to walk with all that weight. He said, "I cannot go with these." And David put them off (1 Sam 17). If we are loaded down with an excess of wealth and material goods, if we do not strip ourselves of the ambitions and devices of the world, we will never be able to advance toward God, toward what is essential in our lives. Without the virtues of poverty, it is impossible to wage battle against the Prince of this earth.

On the other hand, rebellion is quite a healthy reaction against misery. It is not possible to bear the destitution in which part of mankind is immersed. I want to make a distinction between poverty, a resemblance to God, "glory of the Church", and misery, with its parade of misfortunes, against which rebellion is necessary. In *Gaudium et Spes* this distinction is presented quite clearly:

> Christians should cooperate willingly and wholeheartedly in establishing an international order that includes a genuine respect for all freedoms and amicable brotherhood between all. This is all the more pressing since the greater part of the world is still suffering from so much poverty that it is as if Christ Himself were crying out in these poor to beg the charity of the disciples. Do not let men, then, be scandalized because some countries with a majority of citizens who are counted as Christians have an abundance of wealth, whereas others are deprived of the necessities of life and are tormented with hunger, disease, and every kind of misery. The spirit of poverty and charity are the glory and witness of the Church of Christ. (GS 88.1)

326. Poverty implies detachment and separation from anything superfluous that would be an obstacle to the growth of the interior life.

Monks are poor, and they seek to get rid of worldly trappings. The greatest of the poor is God, who lives only in love.

In poverty, we are absolutely dependent on the other.

327. Unless we seek to suppress all the superficial aspects of our lives, we will never be united to God. By detaching ourselves from everything superfluous, we enter little by little into a form of silence. Throughout her life, Mother Teresa sought to live in great poverty so as to find God better in silence. Seeking God in her heart was the only wealth she had. She could spend hours before the Blessed Sacrament without uttering a single word. The nun drew her poverty from the humility of God. The Father possesses nothing, and Mother Teresa wanted to imitate him. She asked that her sisters be absolutely and sincerely detached from all material goods.

328. The Church, too, must turn away from worldly languages and conventional talk, the better to find God in silence. In Nazareth, Jesus was conceived in the utmost poverty, but he already had the wealth of silence in God.

If the Church talks too much, she falls into a form of ideological logorrhea.

How are we to define what is superfluous, preventing us from encountering God in silence?

329. Men have to try not to bother about goods that are not necessary. Things are superfluous if a person accumulates them unnecessarily, solely out of greed and avarice. A Christian has the obligation to imitate Christ: "though he was rich, yet for your sake he became poor, so that by his poverty you might become rich" (2 Cor 8:9). The vows of poverty taken by priests and religious correspond to this requirement. This has nothing to do with manifesting a sort of Jansenism that leads to self-hatred. "Blessed are the poor in spirit, for theirs is the kingdom of heaven" (Mt 5:3). Jesus does speak about detachment from all superfluous riches. "The poor have the good news preached to them", Christ announces to John the Baptist in the Gospel of Luke (7:22), in order to express the openness of the poor to the Gospel and God's special love for them.

Likewise, in the Book of Revelation, Saint John exclaims: "You say, I am rich, I have prospered, and I need nothing; not knowing that you are wretched, pitiable, poor, blind, and naked" (Rev 3:17). God always resists the powerful, and he gives his grace to the poor.

The heart of the Christian faith lies in the poverty of a God who gives everything through love, going so far as to give his own life.

If we manage to be with God in silence, we possess what is essential. Man does not live by bread alone, but by a word that comes from the mouth of God. The materialistic civilization that now prevails in the West favors nothing but immediate profit, economic success, and pointless leisure activities. In this domain of King Money, who could ever be interested in God's silence? The Church would commit a fatal mistake if she exhausted herself in giving a sort of social face to the modern world that has been unleashed by free-market capitalism. The good of man is not exclusively material.

330. The big difference between God and man hinges on the problem of possession. If a human being does not possess some material goods, he feels that he is nothing, lost, weak. Most of our troubles result from some form of lack of poverty. Man allows himself be caught in the nets of his lowest instincts to possess. He wants to accumulate material goods in order to satisfy himself and enjoy them. But these superfluous goods obstruct the eyes, shut the heart, and sap our spiritual energy. However, there are also many rich people who live an exceptional spiritual life with God and show immense generosity to the poor.

Of course, we must forcefully recall the legitimate right of peoples to have access to the material means of subsistence, the things that they need in order to live. In Africa, I know how often this principle is trampled on by those who govern. This is why there is an urgent need to evangelize the hearts, minds, and behavior of all my African brethren. In the Encyclical Letter *Caritas in Veritate*, Benedict XVI writes:

Paul VI ... taught that life in Christ is the first and principal factor of development and he entrusted us with the task of travelling the path of development with all our heart and all our intelligence, that is to say with the ardor of charity and the wisdom of truth. It is the primordial truth of God's love ... that opens our lives to gift and makes it possible to hope for a "development of the whole man and of all men", to hope for progress "from less human conditions to those which are more human", obtained by overcoming the difficulties that are inevitably encountered along the way. (CiV 8)

Only the Gospel will be able to heal our human relations so as to establish societies characterized by fraternity and solidarity. God is at the heart of every person, at the center of all our activities, and even at the heart of our poverty and misery.

331. But if we want to enter into God, it is necessary to be poor. For the Father has possessed nothing for all eternity. By nature, we are far from the infinite simplicity of God. Human ambition is reluctant to be destitute. Man lacks consistency. He prefers the noise of matter to the silence of love. Let us never forget this beatitude announced by Jesus: "Blessed are you poor, for yours is the kingdom of God" (Lk 6:20).

Faced with injustice, Albert Camus did not call to silence but to rebellion. "I rebel, therefore we exist", he wrote in The Rebel: An Essay on Man in Revolt. *But also: "What is a rebel? A man who says no, but whose refusal does not imply a renunciation." At first sight, it is rather difficult to say that he is wrong. . . . Are rebellion and fighting words more important than silence?*

332. In his book, *Un autre regard sur l'homme*, Maurice Zundel writes:

> Camus did not know that, behind this scandal and this misfortune of man abandoned to a universe capable of crushing him, there was an infinite, eternal love that never ceases to watch over us, await us, and call us! But without us, this love can do nothing because it is only love, and love is essentially freedom, freedom that addresses our freedom and can do nothing without it, without its consent. Camus was unable to resolve the problems of evil on this side of the veil, but he profoundly sensed it and expressed it magnificently.

In the presence of inhumane suffering, certainly there can be sound, just rebellion. But if it is a question of rebellion against God, consciously or unconsciously, the combat is useless, imaginary, and ridiculous. God is not responsible for the misery that men themselves have generated.

333. Rebellion is not necessarily the fairest attitude. I am even certain that it is never a lasting response. In a sense, rebellion is an empty noise because in fact it offers no response and no hope whatsoever.

The Rebel: An Essay on Man in Revolt is the work of an atheist walled up in himself, without any horizon and, therefore, without any exit that could give him access to the Invisible One who directs his life.

334. I often wonder about the peace that may dwell in the heart of a man who rejects God. In the *Confessions*, Saint Augustine writes: "O, Lord ... Thou hast made us for Thyself and our hearts are restless till they rest in Thee." Without God, man is torn, anxious, worried, agitated, and he cannot arrive at interior rest. True life is not in rebellion but in silent adoration. Of course, we have no answer to the problem of evil; yet our task is to make it less intolerable and to offer a remedy without pride, discreetly, insofar as we can, as Mother Teresa of Calcutta and many other saints did.

335. Media society moves from sentimental rebellion to moral rebellion, like a desperate Sisyphus figure ceaselessly climbing the mountain. It demands its rebellion, its hatred of what it idiosyncratically defines as unjust and unfair, proud of its correct opinions, which are, however, the most pretentious ideas we could ever find. Cynical and shameless, it despicably revels in its dislikes.

336. Modern existence is a propped-up life built entirely on noise, artificiality, and the tragic rejection of God. From revolutions to conquests, from ideologies to political battles, from the frantic quest for equality to the obsessive cult of progress, silence is impossible. What is worse: transparent societies are sworn to an implacable hatred of silence, which they regard as a contemptible, backward defeat.

337. A man without silence is a stranger to God, exiled in a distant land that remains at the surface of the mystery of man and the world; but God is at the deepest part of man, in the silent regions of

his being. In his book, *Saint Grégoire le Grand: Culture et expériences chrétiennes* [Saint Gregory the Great: Culture and Christian experiences], Bishop Claude Dagens explains well the anthropology of the author of the *Moralia*. Saint Gregory assigns an important place to the ideas of interiority and exteriority in his depiction of human destiny: "Man", Bishop Dagens writes, "was destined to live within the divine world: this was his place of origin. By giving in to sin, he personally excluded himself from this privileged place. From now on, exteriority, to which he is consigned under the form of sin, blindness, and exile, prevents him from attaining the interiority he still remembers nostalgically, in other words, holiness, light, the joy of being in his true homeland." Having surrendered to sin, he is like the sand of the sea: "The sand of the sea is forced without by the chafing of the waters, in that man too in transgressing, because he bore the billows of temptation unsteadily, was carried out of himself from within" (*Moralia*, 7, 2, 2 – PL 75, 768C).

How can one keep silence in the presence of sickness?

338. In Psalm 39, which is sometimes entitled "The Nothingness of Man before God", I particularly like this brilliant speech:

> I said, "I will guard my ways,
>   that I may not sin with my tongue;
> I will bridle my mouth,
>   so long as the wicked are in my presence."
>
> I was mute and silent,
>   I held my peace to no avail;
> my distress grew worse,
>   my heart became hot within me.
> As I mused, the fire burned;
>   then I spoke with my tongue:
>
> "LORD, let me know my end,
>   and what is the measure of my days;
>   let me know how fleeting my life is!
> Behold, you have made my days a few handbreadths,
>   and my lifetime is as nothing in your sight.

Surely every man stands as a mere breath!
   Surely man goes about as a shadow!
Surely for nought are they in turmoil;
   man heaps up, and knows not who will gather!

And now, Lord, for what do I wait?
   My hope is in you.
Deliver me from all my transgressions.
   Make me not the scorn of the fool!
I am silent, I do not open my mouth;
   for it is you who have done it.
Remove your stroke from me;
   I am spent by the blows of your hand.
When you chasten man
   with rebukes for sin,
you consume like a moth what is dear to him;
   surely every man is a mere breath!

Hear my prayer, O LORD,
   and give ear to my cry;
   hold not your peace at my tears!
For I am your passing guest,
   a sojourner, like all my fathers.
Look away from me, that I may know gladness,
   before I depart and be no more!"

In suffering, exasperation may get the better of us, but it is important to keep silent by remaining in the presence of God. Sickness, physical and psychological decline, human frailty are great mysteries. Bodily trials are an especially good time to look at the mystery of our short life that rolls inexorably onward toward death. It is necessary to be able to place the frailty of our existence before the power of God.

Sickness is an occasion for God to assess the truth of a man. A human being is a puny creature, but his Creator watches over him in his most difficult moments. Physical trials are wrongly considered bad turns of fate. Why do men not manage to understand that God never wills evil?

In sickness, man is naked before God. "More precisely, the spiritual combat is characterized by an astonishing paradox", Bishop Claude Dagens writes in his book on Saint Gregory the Great.

The more man is tested in his flesh, the more his soul is sanctified, as though exterior trials were necessary in order to bring about interior progress. The holy man Job provides a living example—does he not?—of this paradox and this correspondence. Externally prostrated by fleshly wounds, he remains standing interiorly thanks to the rampart of his soul. This is, indeed, God's instruction: in order to incite men to repentance and conversion, the Lord sends them trials.

339. Trials of the flesh are often indispensable in bringing about a spiritual and moral recovery. A man experiencing trials who trusts in the Divine Goodness shows a great faith in God. He exhibits a silent courage and loses himself in fervent prayer while awaiting the answer of the Almighty. I know that the force of prayer is stronger than thunder and gentler than the morning breeze. I know that the lights of prayer are capable of overturning the foundations of the universe, moving mountains, and raising my being and the world toward God so that we can be lost in him.

In the Bible, the noble figure of Job is very evocative. This holy man, who was rich and surrounded by many children, had an abundance of all the goods that a man can desire. But Job's life abruptly upended. Armed bands stole his seven thousand sheep, his five hundred pairs of oxen, and his three thousand camels. A violent wind blew from the desert, and the house where his children were collapsed and killed them all. The Chaldeans divided into three bands, and his servants were put to the sword. Finally, he himself fell ill. Despite this series of misfortunes, Job remained unshakeable in his love for God. He vigorously proclaimed his innocence and professed a faith as solid as a centuries-old rock: "Oh, that my words were written! Oh, that they were inscribed in a book! Oh, that with an iron pen and lead they were graven in the rock for ever! For I know that my Redeemer lives, and at last he will stand upon the earth; and after my skin has been thus destroyed, then from my flesh I shall see God, whom I shall see on my side, and my eyes shall behold, and not another" (Job 19:23–27).

340. Sickness is a terrible, painful reality. It reveals the mystery of man, his frailty, as well as the interior energy that helps him to be ever more fully realized by overcoming the obstacles of life. If we

successfully resist and show generosity and love, sickness can become a path to God, a path of maturity and interior structuring. Then sickness is an occasion to form in ourselves that perfect man, in the strength of maturity, who actualizes the fullness of Christ.

In silence, man can tell how limited earthly time is. In sickness it is possible for us to live almost perfectly attuned to God. The silent examination of conscience, at the heart of the pain, allows man to look at what he has made of his life and what remains for him to accomplish. Sickness is a sublime hope in the great silence of God. If man rebels against sickness, he falls little by little into a sterile despair, a blind alley, an aggressive, anxious refusal. Rebellion is not resistance, which is first and foremost a silent interior step.

341. Great patients are often men who demonstrate an unshakeable peace. They know that the steep decline of their body has brought their mind to an intimate face-to-face encounter with the divine realities. These individuals are often happy about their lot. Whereas average mortals imagine that it is a sad, serious life, these patients are perfectly serene. God already dwells in the silence of the look of a man who is about to pass away.

Yes, sickness is a sublime manifestation of God's mysterious silence, a loving silence that is close to human suffering. Sickness makes man descend the various degrees of being. It reveals to him his own mystery while helping him enter into himself so as to encounter God there, who is found in the innermost depths of his soul.

The Evangelist John writes as follows:

Now a certain man was ill, Lazarus of Bethany, the village of Mary and her sister Martha. It was Mary who anointed the Lord with ointment and wiped his feet with her hair, whose brother Lazarus was ill. So the sisters sent to him, saying, "Lord, he whom you love is ill." But when Jesus heard it he said, "This illness is not unto death; it is for the glory of God, so that the Son of God may be glorified by means of it."

Now Jesus loved Martha and her sister and Lazarus. So when he heard that he was ill, he stayed two days longer in the place where he was. Then after this he said to the disciples, "Let us go to Judea again." The disciples said to him, "Rabbi, the Jews were but now seeking to stone you, and are you going there again?" Jesus answered, "Are there not twelve hours in the day? If any one walks in the day, he does not stumble, because he sees, the light of this world. But if any one walks in the night, he stumbles, because the light is not in him." Thus he spoke, and then he said to them, "Our friend Lazarus has fallen asleep, but I go to awake him out of sleep." The disciples said to him, "Lord, if he has fallen asleep, he will recover." Now Jesus had spoken of his death, but they thought that he meant taking rest in sleep. Then Jesus told them plainly, "Lazarus is dead; and for your sake I am glad that I was not there, so that you may believe. But let us go to him." Thomas, called the Twin, said to his fellow disciples, "Let us also go, that we may die with him."

Now when Jesus came, he found that Lazarus had already been in the tomb four days. Bethany was near Jerusalem, about two miles off, and many of the Jews had come to Martha and Mary to console them concerning their brother. When Martha heard that Jesus was coming, she went and met him, while Mary sat in the house. Martha said to Jesus, "Lord, if you had been here, my brother would not have died. And even now I know that whatever you ask from God, God will give you." Jesus said to her, "You brother will rise again." Martha said to him, "I know that he will rise again in the resurrection at the last day." Jesus said to her, "I am the resurrection and the life; he who believes in me, though he die, yet shall he live, and whoever lives and believes in me shall never die. Do you believe this?" She said to him, "Yes, Lord; I believe that you are the Christ, the Son of God, he who is coming into the world."

When she had said this, she went and called her sister Mary, saying quietly, "The Teacher is here and is calling for you." And when she heard it, she rose quickly and went to him. Now Jesus had not yet come to the village, but was still in the place where Martha had met him. When the Jews who were with her in the house, consoling her, saw Mary rise quickly and go out, they followed her, supposing that she was going to the tomb to weep there. Then Mary, when she came where Jesus was and saw him, fell at his feet, saying to him, "Lord, if you had been here, my brother would not have died." When Jesus saw her weeping, and the Jews who came with her also weeping, he was deeply moved in spirit and troubled; and he said, "Where have you laid him?" They said to him, "Lord, come and see." Jesus wept. So the Jews said, "See how he loved him!" But some of them said, "Could not he who opened the eyes of the blind have kept this man from dying?"

Then Jesus, deeply moved again, came to the tomb; it was a cave, and a stone lay upon it. Jesus said, "Take away the stone." Martha, the

sister of the dead man, said to him, "Lord, by this time there will be
an odor, for he has been dead four days." Jesus said to her, "Did I not
tell you that if you would believe you would see the glory of God?"
So they took away the stone. And Jesus lifted up his eyes and said,
"Father, I thank you that you have heard me. I knew that you always
hear me, but I have said this on account of the people standing by, that
they may believe that you sent me." When he had said this, he cried
with a loud voice, "Lazarus, come out." The dead man came out,
his hands and feet bound with bandages, and his face wrapped with a
cloth. Jesus said to them, "Unbind him, and let him go."

Many of the Jews therefore, who had come with Mary and had
seen what he did, believed in him; but some of them went to the
Pharisees and told them what Jesus had done. So the chief priests and
the Pharisees gathered in council, and said, "What are we to do? For
this man performs many signs. If we let him go on like this, every one
will believe in him, and the Romans will come and destroy both our
holy place and our nation." But one of them, Caiaphas, who was the
high priest that year, said to them, "You know nothing at all; you do
not understand that it is expedient for you that one man should die for
the people, and that the whole nation should not perish." He did not
say this of his own accord, but being high priest that year he prophe-
sied that Jesus should die for the nation, and not for the nation only,
but to gather into one the children of God who are scattered abroad.
So from that day on they took counsel about how to put him to death.

Jesus therefore no longer went about openly among the Jews, but
went from there to the country near the wilderness, to a town called
Ephraim; and there he stayed with the disciples. (Jn 11:1–54)

342. Often God pays more attention to the human body and vener-
ates it more than man himself does. How can anyone live in peace
and joy if his body is continually subjected to pressures of all sorts?

343. Sickness is intrinsically connected with eternity. The real men
of God have no fear of death, because they are waiting for heaven.
The example of Brother Théophane is admirable. A monk from the
Abbey in Sept-Fons, carried off by a brain tumor at the age of twenty-
eight, he wrote this moving message concerning his short life:

What is monastic life? How many have received this calling? How
many, by the end of their life, have become true monks, friends of

God? What graces, fidelity, perseverance, and courage will I need in order to achieve that? And that little additional something that makes a person God's friend? For me, just beginning now, what will be my future? There is my vocation, the faith, the example of the older monks like Father Jérôme, and this insistent hope to attain it one day, like him. To be a monk, a true monk.

The more he suffered, the more he reached spiritual heights. Father Samuel, a Trappist monk from Sept-Fons, wrote an extraordinary book about his short life, his cruel illness, and his death, *Qui cherchait Théophane* [Whom did Théophane seek?], from which I like to quote these sentences:

> Without Christian hope, he most certainly would have despaired or rebelled. And we would have, too. Everyone was tempted by the absurdity of the situation: sickness mowing down such a young life that promised to be so full! We tried to turn our backs on resignation. Brother Théophane learned from the sickness to be able to disregard the appearances of happiness and to acquiesce in apparent failures. If he had been cured, this attitude would have lit up his whole life. In that regard his testimony is invaluable for other sick people who want to be cured and for us, too. We now know that happiness comes at this price. I am talking about a sturdy happiness that a passing incident does not ruin, however serious it may be. Brother Théophane's illness, therefore, made him a sturdier man and cast him, cast us all, upon God's heart. What was Brother Théophane looking for, then? Brother Théophane asked nothing of anyone, not even of God, not even that they love him; he wanted to be happy.

Father Samuel ends his book with this quotation from Genesis: "Judah is a lion's whelp; from the prey, my son, you have gone up. He stooped down, he lurked as a lion, and as a lioness, who dares rouse him up?" (Gen 49:9).

344. I had this wonderful, rich experience with Brother Vincent-Marie of the Resurrection, who belonged to the community of canons regular in Lagrasse. Stricken by multiple sclerosis, he gradually lost his faculties of speech and movement. Despite that painful situation, Brother Vincent remained serene, joyful, and patient. All our

meetings unfolded in silence and prayer. God asked him to be an ongoing holocaust and a silent offering for the world's salvation; next to my friend, I became a pupil, learning the mystery of suffering.

Watching Brother Vincent, confined to his sickbed, silently revealed to me that the most sublime expression of love is suffering. On the eve of his burial, while reading his personal journal, I discovered all the spiritual energy that nourished his interior life. Indeed, in those pages I found a very profound reflection: "I believe that suffering was granted by God to man in a great design of love and mercy. I believe that suffering is for the soul the great worker of redemption and sanctification." Yes, suffering is a state of happiness and sanctification. Listening to the Brother, I thought I was reading Saint Thérèse of the Child Jesus, who wrote: "I found happiness and joy on earth, but solely in suffering, for I've suffered very much here below."

Brother Vincent offers us one final secret for coping with suffering and finding joy in it. I discovered it in his personal journal. He wrote: "Every day I shut myself into a threefold castle: the first is the most pure Heart of Mary ..., against all the attacks of the Evil Spirit; the second is the Heart of Jesus, against all the attacks of the flesh; the third is the holy sepulcher, where I hide myself next to Jesus from the world."

345. The language of suffering and silence contradicts the language of the world. Faced with pain, we see two diametrically opposite routes traced out: the noble way of silence and the stony rut of rebellion, in other words, the path of love of God and the path of love of self.

346. This pathological fear of suffering and silence is particularly acute in the West. On the other hand, African and Asian cultures manifest a remarkable acceptance of pain, sickness, and death, because the prospect of a better life in the next world is profoundly present in them.

What is the appropriate attitude toward a patient who is incurably ill?

347. When the illness becomes incurable, speech no longer matters much. It is necessary to be able to keep silence, to be able to caress the suffering person affectionately so as to convey to him the

closeness, warmth, and compassion of God. It is enough to take his hand and to look at each other without saying anything. The tenderness of a look can bring God's consolation and comfort. In the presence of a suffering sick person, it is not necessary to speak. It is necessary to be compassionate silently, to love, and to pray, with the assurance that the only language that is appropriate for love is prayer and silence.

348. The sick person is initiated into silence by his own state. He finds that he has made more progress than the well person in the mystery of God's silence. A suffering person is in wordless expectation. But his heart throbs with hope and abandonment, which immerse him in God.

349. Sickness is an anticipation of the silence of eternity.

When facing death, what is true silence?

350. When God comes to take a person, two forms of silence set in: the silence of the living, who are petrified by the death, and the silence of the dead person, which causes us to enter into the mystery of Christian hope and true life.

The former are confronted with the mystery of an agitated, sad, painful, disconsolate silence. This silence marks their faces with anxiety, sadness, and the refusal of the death that comes to disturb a tranquil indifference.

351. Nowadays Western societies reject death, traumatized by the pain and grieving that accompany it. Modern man would like to be immortal. This denial of the great passage leads to a culture of death that permeates social relations as a whole. Postmodern civilization denies death, causes it, and paradoxically unceasingly exalts it. The assassination of God allows death to keep prowling all the time, because hope no longer dwells within the horizon of men.

352. When death is sidelined, the result is the detestation of its silence. New funeral customs display a false joy and an adulterated form of bereavement that are unwilling to let silence do the speaking.

Western decadence has reached such an extent that it is no longer uncommon to hear applause and long speeches during funeral services. Mourning is expressed by tears, not by an artificial, uprooted joy. Did Christ not weep for his friend Lazarus when he had died and been buried for four days?

I do not want to fail to recall that death is a difficult time that causes natural confusion among the living. Likewise, tears are the manifestation of an authentic silence. I also know how difficult it is to accept the suddenness of the separation. Sometimes it is a part of our life that passes away. Death carries off segments of the story of the individuals who remain on earth.

353. The great question of death can be truly understood only in silence and prayer. How else can the silence of the departure be comprehended except by the silence of our heart and our lips?

354. Before the silence of death there is often the silence of sickness and suffering. There is only one way to meditate on the meaning of death, and it passes through interior silence.

Indeed, continuity of relations between the dead and the living exists only in silence. The inseparability between the world of life and the world of death is achieved in silence and in a relation that goes beyond bodies. Despite the physical disappearance of the body, our relations with our beloved dead are indestructible, real, and tangible, because their affection is deeply engraved on our hearts.

355. Death is the silence of mystery, the silence of God, and the silence of life.

How can Christians nourish their silence? The definitive answer is given by Christ on the Cross, where they can find a God who suffers and dies. But Christ's victory is the source of hope and silence, so immense is God's gift.

356. Church teaching about death does not seek first to console or to reassure the bereaved with soothing words. Following Christ, she intends to speak about the immortality of the soul and the resurrection of the body. In Preface I for the Dead, we find this statement: "Life is changed not ended, and, when this earthly dwelling turns to

dust, an eternal dwelling is made ready for them in heaven." Faced with such a reality, only silence truly prevails.

357. Why seek to rebel against death? The rejection of death is a dead end. For, above and beyond the departure and the burial, death is a new birth. In confronting death, we are like infants; we do not know how to speak, but life matures and grows invisibly.

358. Death is comprehensible if, in silence, we direct toward Christ a look of faith: from Calvary, where a God with a lacerated, ruined body is brought to earth, to the tomb where death is overtaken after three days, men find the essence and the fragrance of divine silence.

359. Christianity allows mankind to have a simpler, more serene, and more silent view of death, far from the cries and tears of despair.

360. Death is a door, and we must agree to go through it noiselessly, because it opens in order to lead us to life. The Grim Reaper brings men back to their heavenly fatherland. This is the hope that demands all our prayers! We must desire to go through this door with serenity and faith.

For many people, unfortunately, death seems like an endless night with no tomorrow. And yet night brings valuable things that day does not even imagine. A man without faith believes in lights that he thinks are reliable and eternal. But while we are speculating about our future, saying: "I will pull down my barns, and build larger ones; and there I will store all my grain and my goods. And I will say to my soul, Soul, you have ample goods laid up for many years; take your ease, eat, drink, be merry" (Lk 12:18–19), at the very moment when we are posing questions and making decisions, God extinguishes them. The roofs of our houses collapse on us, the lofty towers are undermined by ants, the walls crack and crumble, and the holiest buildings are reduced to ashes while the night watchman constructs a theory about their durability.

I am well aware that such language is absolutely incomprehensible and shocking for those who do not have faith. Materialistic man wants to make out of life one big party, a time to take advantage of all sorts of pleasures, a compulsive enjoyment. Then, as late as possible, death comes to stop this course and leads to the void. There is nothing left. These people move about like animals, without soul or hope. When the fateful day arrives, since the abyss is about to open up beneath their feet, it is just as well to falsify death in one painless moment. For the survivors, a celebration is still possible.... Death is transformed into a noisy, exhibitionistic spectacle, in soulless funeral parlors, in pagan crematoriums and morbid funeral urns. By means of new technologies, they are taking this profanation and disdain for the human body a step farther by liquefying it, as though to deny the divine destiny of man.

361. A man of faith must look to Christ in silence. The martyrs agree to die without making a sound because they know that death is a door. One's demise is the door to life. I am thinking of Father Maximilian Kolbe, who gave his life to save his comrades and accepted death with immense simplicity. On February 17, 1941, he was arrested by the Gestapo and beaten violently because he refused to deny Jesus Christ, then transferred on May 28 to the camp in Auschwitz, with identification number 16670. Even in the darkest years of the invasion of Poland by Hitler, Maximilian Kolbe exhibited all the vigor of his courage and the depth of his faith. Making himself close to everyone, he felt capable of accomplishing anything for love of Jesus, who ceaselessly communicated his strength to him through the intercession of the Blessed Virgin Mary. Maximilian Kolbe was not a man to compromise; he thought that truth could not be disguised "and that all that we can and must do is to seek it, and when we have found it, to serve it to the end. We must serve truth until death." In July 1941, a man escaped from Block 14, where Father Kolbe was. In reprisal, the Nazis selected ten men and sentenced them to die by starvation.

Maximilian Kolbe volunteered to replace one of the ten prisoners, Franciszek Gajowniczek, the father of a family. The ten prisoners were locked up in an underground, dimly lit bunker. Hunger and thirst drove the doomed men insane within a few days, but with the help of prayer Maximilian managed to keep his companions calm so that piety prevailed in the midst of tragedy. After two weeks without food, only Father Kolbe, who had supported his companions and seen them all die, was still alive. He was finally executed on August 14 by an injection of phenol in the arm, and his body was burned in a crematorium furnace on August 15, 1941, the day of the Feast of the Assumption of the Blessed Virgin Mary.

How can one find silence when confronted with the suffering of death? "Is the moment of death not the only moment of true silence in life?" The philosopher Vladimir Jankélévitch answered this question in Penser la mort?: *"Yes, but for someone who looks at the dying person. The one who is about to die is often in such a state that the words silence and solitude no longer have any meaning for him. The one who looks at him can picture this instant as the most extreme moment of silence in contrast to the existence that surrounds him. Although one can be supported, comforted, and helped throughout one's life, the step of death itself, the moment of death, well, that has to be taken all alone."*

362. In order to respond to that statement, I would like to quote once again several lines by Father Samuel in *Qui cherchait Théophane*:

> In his final days, Brother Théophane could hardly talk at all. I decided to recite the Creed, finishing it with several questions: "Do you believe this?" "Yes." "Do you love our Lord?" "Yes." "Do you love the Virgin Mary?" "Yes." Do you want to do God's will?" "Yes!" These energetic yeses were whistled a bit, as in the Auvergnat dialect, because of a pronunciation difficulty that had just appeared. One day I was so touched, and at the same time amused, by these very simple, wholesome, sincere acts that I interrupted the prayer to make a jest, to which he answered in the same tone: "You are a saint!" "Yesss!" It seemed to us, during those final days, that his attention was intermittent. We wondered where to draw the line between free will and automatic responses. Brother Théophane in fact drifted from one to the other. His silence came as much from his recent difficulties in speaking as it did from a mixture of recollection and half-sleep. When I realized this, I always asked him: "Are you tired?" "No." "Do you want to continue?" "Yes." His adherence to God was therefore limited to a frank assent repeated two or three times against a background of well-established habits. Is that not the human dough of all human prayer?

363. Agony and death are always a great, profound sorrow. But an attitude of silence is the best Christian way of welcoming death. The Virgin Mary stood silently at the foot of her Son's Cross.

The moment that opens the door to an encounter that will make us see God, as the testament of Job so vigorously asserted, is the most beautiful silence in earthly life. But it is nothing compared with the silence of heaven.

364. When the soul is detached from the body of the departing person, it rises in an incomparable silence. The great silence of death is the silence of the soul that travels toward another homeland: the land of eternal life.

It is necessary to be in unison with the soul-silence of the deceased. The great works of God always occur in silence. The moment when the body was united to the soul and the moment when that soul came apart from its carnal envelope are moments of silence, eminently divine moments.

365. All that is from God makes no noise. Nothing is sudden, everything is delicate, pure, and silent.

V

LIKE A VOICE CRYING OUT IN THE DESERT: THE MEETING AT THE GRANDE CHARTREUSE

In the withdrawal of monasteries and in the solitude of the cells, patiently and silently, the Carthusians weave the nuptial garment of the Church.

> —Saint John Paul II, *Message to the Prior of the Carthusian Order* for the ninth centenary of Saint Bruno's death

Our principal endeavor and goal is to devote ourselves to the silence and soli-tude of cell. This is holy ground, a place where, as a man with his friend, the Lord and his servant often speak together; there is the faithful soul frequently united with the Word of God; there is the bride made one with her spouse; there is earth joined to heaven, the divine to the human. The journey, how-ever, is long, and the way dry and barren, that must be traveled to attain the fount of water, the land of promise.

Therefore the dweller in cell should be diligently and carefully on his guard against contriving or accepting occasions for going out, other than those nor-mally prescribed; rather, let him consider the cell as as necessary for his salva-tion and life, as water for fish and the sheepfold for sheep. For if he gets into the habit of going out of cell frequently and for trivial reasons it will quickly become hateful to him; as Augustine expressed it, "For lovers of this world, there is no harder work than not working." On the other hand, the longer he lives in cell, the more gladly will he do so, as long as he occupies himself in it usefully and in an orderly manner, reading, writing, reciting psalms, praying, meditating, contemplating and working. Let him make a practice of resorting, from time to time, to a tranquil listening of the heart, that allows God to enter through all its doors and passages. In this way with God's help, he will avoid the dangers that often lie in wait for the solitary; such as following too easy a path in cell and meriting to be numbered among the lukewarm.

The fruit that silence brings is known to him who has experienced it. In the early stages of our Carthusian life we may find silence a burden; however, if we are faithful, there will gradually be born within us of our silence itself something, that will draw us on to still greater silence. To attain this, our rule is not to speak to one another without the President's permission.

Love for our brothers should show itself firstly in respect for their solitude; should we have permission to speak about some matter, let us do so as briefly as possible.

Those who neither are, nor aspire to becoming, members of our Order are not to be allowed to stay in our cells.

Each year for eight days we devote ourselves with greater zeal to the quiet of cell and recollection. Fittingly, our custom is to do this on the anniversary of our Profession.

God has led us into solitude to speak to our heart. Let our heart then be a living altar from which there constantly ascends before God pure prayer, with which all our acts should be imbued.

— *Statutes of the Carthusian Order,* Book I, Chapter 4,
"The Keeping of Cell and Silence"

God has led his servant into solitude to speak to his heart; but he alone who listens in silence hears the whisper of the gentle breeze that reveals the presence of the Lord. In the early stages of our Carthusian life, we may find silence a toilsome burden; however, if we are faithful, there will gradually be born within us of our silence itself something that will draw us on to still greater silence.

On this account, the brothers may not speak indiscriminately of what they wish, or with whom they wish, or for as long as they wish; with few words and with quiet voice, they may speak about matters affecting their work; but apart from this, they may not speak without permission either to monks or to strangers.

Since, therefore, the observance of silence is of vital importance in the life of a brother, this rule must be kept with great care. However, in doubtful cases not foreseen by the law, let each one prudently judge according to conscience and the needs of the moment, whether, and to what extent, it is lawful to speak.

Devotion to the Spirit dwelling within them, and love for their brothers, both require that, when it is lawful to speak they should weigh their words well and be watchful of the extent to which they speak; for a long and uselessly protracted conversation is thought to grieve the Holy Spirit more and cause more dissipation than a few words, that are indeed against the rule, but are quickly cut short. Often a conversation, that was useful in the beginning, soon becomes useless and, finally, worthy of blame.

On Sundays and solemnities, and also on days specially set apart for recollection, they observe silence with special care and remain in cell. Likewise, every day from the evening Angelus to Prime, throughout the monastery should reign perfect silence, which the brothers may not break, unless in a case of true and urgent necessity; for, as appears from the examples of Scripture and the traditions of the monks of old, this time of the night is specially conducive to recollection and meeting with God.

Let the brothers not presume to speak without permission to seculars who approach them, or to chat with them; they may merely return their greeting, as also that of those they happen to meet, and, if questioned, briefly respond and excuse themselves as not having permission for further speech with them.

Observance of silence and interior recollection require special vigilance on the part of the brothers, since many occasions for speaking come their way; in this they cannot attain perfection, unless they diligently strive to live always in the presence of God.

— *Statutes of the Carthusian Order*, Book II,
Chapter 14, "Silence"

NICOLAS DIAT: *Why seek silence? In a letter to his Carthusian brothers, Saint Bruno writes: "Rejoice, therefore, my beloved brothers, over the lot of overflowing happiness that has fallen to you, and for the grace of God that you have received in such abundance. Rejoice that you have succeeded in escaping the countless dangers and shipwrecks of this storm-tossed world, and have reached a quiet corner in the security of a hidden harbour. Many would like to join you, and many there are also those who make a considerable effort to do so, but fail in their attempt. What is more, many are shut out even after having attained it, since it was not in the plan of God to give them this grace." The first Carthusian often exhorted people to "abandon the fleeting shadows of this world", the noises that were already distracting the minds and hearts of the men of the eleventh century. At the start of this extraordinary interview that gathers us at the Grande Chartreuse, can we review the origins of the desire for silence?*

ROBERT CARDINAL SARAH: The authentic search for silence is the quest for a silent God and for the interior life. It is the quest for a God who reveals himself in the depths of our being. Monks are well acquainted with this reality when they decide to leave the world and this "evil and adulterous generation" (Lk 11:29–32; Mt 12:39).

No one advanced our knowledge about man in his most essential reality better than Saint Augustine. He reviewed his past with admirable precision. Augustine wanted to make his readers discover, in the inmost depths of the human being, the absence of God in sin, the need for God in anxiety, the coming of God in salvation, the presence of God in the life of grace. For him, knowledge about man leads to Being, to a God who is closer to us than we are to ourselves.

Throughout his work, the author of the famous expression "*Noverim me, noverim te*" (*Solil.* 2, 1) proclaims that the knowledge of self and the knowledge of God are closely associated. To go in search of God is not to go out of oneself in order to find something in the outside world; on the contrary, it is to turn away from this world and to reflect on oneself. "Instead of going outside, enter into yourself; man's heart is the place where truth dwells" (*De vera religione* 39, 72).

"Here are men", Saint Augustine says in the *Confessions*, "going afar to marvel at the heights of mountains, the mighty waves of the sea, the long courses of great rivers, the vastness of the ocean, and the movements of the stars, yet leaving themselves unnoticed" (*Confessions* X, 8, 15). They do not marvel at themselves.

This is also the spiritual doctrine of Saint Gregory the Great. "Return to yourself, O man, and explore the seclusion of your heart" (*Moralia* 19, 8), he advises. In order to approach God, man must first know himself. In the *Moralia*, he declares that in order to be raised to the vision of God, the soul must first concentrate, recollect itself, and withdraw into itself.

Man cannot hope to know God without having found himself, in other words, without having confessed in the presence of other men his good and evil actions for the praise of God. How can we not admire Augustine when he thunders: "Thou wert there before me, but I had gone away from myself and I could not even find myself, much less Thee" (V, 2).

Silence is an extremely necessary element in the life of every man. It enables the soul to be recollected. It protects the soul against the loss of its identity. It predisposes the soul to resist the temptation to turn away from itself to attend to things outside, far from God.

If man wants to become entrenched in the depths of his heart, in that beautiful interior sanctuary, in order to examine himself and to verify the Presence of God within him, if he wants to know and understand his identity, he needs to be silent and to win his interiority.

How could it be possible to discover oneself in the midst of noise? A person's clear-sightedness and lucidity about himself can mature only in solitude and silence. A silent man is all the more apt to listen and to stand in the presence of God. The silent man finds God within himself. For any prayer and any interior life, we need silence, a hidden, discreet life that prompts us not to think about ourselves. Silence, in important moments of life, becomes a vital necessity. But we do not seek silence for its own sake, as though it were our goal. We seek silence because we seek God. And we will find it if we are silent in the very depths of our heart.

DOM DYSMAS DE LASSUS: Men consider silence to be the mere absence of noise and speech, but the reality is much more complex.

The silence of a couple who are dining alone can express the depth of a communion that no longer needs words; on the other hand, they may no longer be capable of speaking to each other. The first silence is a silence of communion, and the second—a silence of rupture. Each of these two opposite forms conveys a very strong message; the first says: I love you. The second: Our love is over.

How is this message transmitted? By looks, by gestures, and by the heart. The look of love, in the first case, the downcast look in the second, one expressing the desire for a deeper meeting, the other—the failure of the relationship.

In this book, it goes without saying that we wish to speak about the silence of communion and about the riches it brings. Nevertheless, even within this silence, there is a great diversity. A person can keep quiet in order to listen and to receive everything conveyed by the other's silence. He can keep quiet in order to say in some other way what does not belong to the language of words or because he is facing a reality that is too imposing to speak about.

Is there not a silent dialogue between a mother and the child whom she bears? Sometimes she speaks to him, maybe she has already given him a name, but most often she simply feels him. I remember, during one annual visit of my family to the monastery, my sister was pregnant, and suddenly, in the middle of a conversation, she smiled a beautiful smile. Since the context did not explain it, I asked her: "Irene, why are you smiling?" She then answered me: "He is moving." It was not necessary to ask who "he" was.

I like this image of the pregnant woman because it nicely illustrates the question of interiority. There is no need for a lot of words; "he" is there, that is enough. When "he" means God, prayer is near, because adoration and silence are brother and sister.

ROBERT SARAH: I agree completely. Likewise, how can a priest live apart from silence? Because of the great mystery of the Eucharist that he celebrates daily, he must devote a large part of his life to silence, from which the Canon ought to emerge, weighty with power and meaning. Holy Mass is the most sacred, most divine thing that he possesses. It must be surrounded with dignity, silence, and a sacral character. The [Divine] Office prepares us for it. All creatures are mute except the priest, who has the power to speak for all and in the name of all in the presence of the divine Majesty. The priest unites men to God in a few simple phrases that are divine words. He confronts mankind with God by the words of the consecration, in which he utters the very Word of the Father—he brings about the presence of the Word in time, in a special incarnate, sacrificed state.

The priest must know when to be quiet and when to speak. It is important to pray seven times a day, in order to praise God, to profess him at Holy Mass in the presence of men. The priestly dignity requires us to realize the importance of our words. Everything in the priest, body and soul, must proclaim the Glory of God. Speech is then more important than life or death: these words do not necessarily have to be loud on this earth, provided they make themselves heard in heaven. Above all, in order to nourish this speech, it is terribly important to remain silent.

When? Nearly all the rest of the time. The narcissism of excessive speech is a temptation from Satan. It results in a form of detestable exteriorization, in which man wallows on the surface of himself, making noise so as not to hear God. It is essential for priests to learn to keep to themselves words and opinions they have not taken the trouble to meditate on, interiorize, and engrave in the depth of their heart. We must preach the Word of God and certainly not our petty thoughts! "For if I preach the gospel, that gives me no ground for boasting. For necessity is laid upon me. Woe to me if I do not preach the gospel!" (1 Cor 9:16). Now this preaching implies silence.

Otherwise it is a waste of time—petty, sententious chatter. Spiritual exhibitionism, which consists of exteriorizing the treasures of the soul by setting them forth immodestly, is the sign of a tragic human poverty and the manifestation of our superficiality. We often speak because we think that others expect us to do so. We end up no longer knowing how to be quiet because our interior dike is so cracked that it no longer holds back the floods of our words. God's silence, however, should teach us that it is often necessary to be quiet.

True seekers of God always pass through the rooms of silence in order to get to the regions that bring us close to the divine habitations. The Grande Chartreuse is one of these rooms. Last night, during the Office in the monastery church, I was profoundly impressed by the silence. While the entire choir was plunged into darkness and was singing without the least bit of light, I thought that darkness was an extraordinary invention of God. It simplifies and unifies everything, concealing the differentiations, distinctions, rough spots, and accidental qualities that make the monks different from each other, submerging all distractions in the night. In that darkness where the only light shining filtered from the sanctuary, the symbol of the Real Presence, I became like the Carthusians, and nothing distinguished me from them. Only the eye of God perceived an unworthy black spot in the midst of those pure souls clothed in white. We felt as we do on the night of the Easter Vigil. But is not the whole Office a genuine Easter Vigil?

Night envelops us during the whole Office; it hears us sing the psalms and the canticles of the three young men: "Bless the Lord, nights and days ..., Bless the Lord, light and darkness ..., Bless the Lord, ice and cold ..., Bless the Lord, frosts and snows ..., Bless the Lord, mountains and hills ..., Bless the Lord, you springs" (Dan 3:47–55). In the dark silence, we sang the hymn of thanksgiving for the light that will be sent to us. And behold, Christ is here. He has come. He dwells among us. His silent Presence shines at the back of the Church through the sanctuary lamp, that burning bush that burns without being consumed by love for us. He descends into the depth of the night, gathering around him the poor, those who seek God, but also our Fathers in faith, the patriarchs and prophets, with the angels and all "who have come out of the great tribulation; they have washed their robes and made them white in the blood of the Lamb.

Therefore are they before the throne of God, and serve him day and night within his temple" (Rev 7:14–15).

Night is maternal, delightful, and cleansing. Darkness is like a fountain from which the monks emerge washed and enlightened, no longer separated but united in the Risen Christ.

Dysmas de Lassus: You say that night is cleansing; I would say also that it is revealing. At night we are more aware of the noise in which we live, the thoughts that elude us and lead us in all directions. It is no different during the day, but we notice it less. Being silent with our lips is not difficult, it is enough to will it; being silent in our thoughts is another matter.

We like to sing in darkness, despite the risks involved of making mistakes. Why? This is not easy to put into words. When the lights are lit, the books, the faces, everything is present and near, like a reality that can be grasped immediately. When the lights are extinguished and only the tabernacle lamp remains, our voices are there and, therefore, the One to whom they are addressed, yet he remains hidden. The night manifests the mystery. Night and mystery are blood brothers.

For us the mystery is an intensely positive reality. We are like children who watch the ocean for the first time. Fascinated by what they see, they nevertheless guess that what is found beyond it far surpasses their gaze and even their imagination. They can simultaneously say that they have seen the ocean, that they know it, and that they have still to discover everything. When we are talking about that ocean without a shore, God's infinitude, the mystery offers an endless overture to him whom we will never finish discovering. There are few words to describe such a fascinating reality ...

Robert Sarah: We must humbly acknowledge that it is difficult to speak about God. The [French] hymn for the Office of Readings on Wednesday of Week I says: "O You, who are beyond All, is that not all that we can sing about You? What hymn, what language can express You? No word expresses You.... You have all names, and how shall I name You, the only One who cannot be named?"

Nevertheless, the psalmist is right when, tormented by the enemy and the difficulties of life, he cries out with all his strength:

To you, O LORD, I call;
my rock, be not deaf to me,
lest, if you be silent to me,
I become like those who go down to the Pit. (Ps 28:1)

You have seen, O LORD; be not silent!
O Lord, be not far from me!
Bestir your-self, and awake for my right,
for my cause, my God and my Lord! (Ps 35:22–23)

O God, do not keep silence;
do not hold your peace or be still, O God!
For behold, your enemies are in tumult;
those who hate you have raised their heads. (Ps 83:1–2)

My God, my God, why have you forsaken me?
Why are you so far from helping me, from the words of
  my groaning?
O my God, I cry by day, but you do not answer;
and by night, but find no rest. (Ps 22:1–2)

Rouse yourself! Why do you sleep, O Lord?
Awake! Do not cast us off for ever!
Why do you hide your face?
Why do you forget our affliction and oppression?
  (Ps 44:23–24)

In fact, God seems silent, but he reveals himself and speaks to us
through the marvels of creation. It is enough to pay attention like a
child to the splendors of nature. For nature speaks to us about God.
Saint Augustine's long search also passes by way of his look at the
work of creation, as this passage from the *Confessions* testifies:

I asked the earth and it answered, "I am not He"; and all things that
are in the earth made the same confession. I asked the sea and the
deeps and the creeping things, and they answered, "We are not your
God, seek higher." I asked the winds that blow, and the whole air
with all that is in it answered, "Anaximenes was wrong; I am not

God." I asked the heavens, the sun, the moon, the stars, and they answered, "Neither are we God whom you seek." And I said to all the things that throng about the gateways of the senses: "Tell me of my God, since you are not He. Tell me something of Him." And they cried out in a great voice: "He made us." My question was my gazing upon them, and their answer was their beauty.

At the Grande Chartreuse, how can anyone not admire these beautiful tall mountains covered with snow! Look at their majestic beauty! They are a Word of God.

Man himself is like the face of God, because he was created in the image of the Father. Psalm 8 says: "You have made him little less than the angels," or, in some translations, "than God", "and you have crowned him with glory and honor. You have given him dominion over the works of your hands" (Ps 8:5–6). Man is a silent, incarnate word of God. The moon, the stars, the sun, the sea, the firmament are the visible proof of the existence and omnipotence of God, who created them out of sheer love. These creatures are the powerful, mysterious voice of God. This new discovery of God through creation awakens an immense love in Saint Augustine.

I know that no one has ever seen or heard God, except the One who comes in the name of God: he has seen the Father (cf. Jn 6:46). But I also know that he speaks to me every day in my inmost depths, and I hear him in the silence that gives rise to mutual listening, the desire for communion and love. God is a light that illumines and radiates noiselessly. His flame blazes, but its brilliance is silent. God shines and blazes like a sun. He burns like a furnace, but he is inaudible. This is why I think that it is important to allow ourselves to be inundated by God's silence, which is a voiceless word.

DYSMAS DE LASSUS: Everything in our relation to God is a paradox. The realities that are opposed in man are combined in him. Presence and absence overlap, as the poet Rainer Maria Rilke described it in a lovely stanza:

> One must be happy to find God
> For those who invent him out of grief
> Move too fast and search too little
> For the intimacy of his ardent absence.

Voiceless speech or silent communion: these expressions under-score the ever-mysterious reality of the encounter with God. How could it be otherwise? When the infinite meets the finite, this meet-ing does not fit into our usual frameworks.

In a charterhouse [Carthusian monastery], we seek, not silence, but, rather, intimacy with God by means of silence. It is the privi-leged space that will allow for communion; it is on the order of lan-guage, but a different language.

Thus the *Statutes* of the Order begin with this foundational sen-tence: "To the praise of the glory of God, Christ, the Father's Word, has through the Holy Spirit, from the beginning chosen certain men, whom he willed to lead into solitude and unite to himself in intimate love. In obedience to such a call, Master Bruno and six companions entered the desert of Chartreuse in the year of our Lord 1084 and settled there" (*Statutes* I.1).

We must ceaselessly return to the mystery of Jesus himself. Two thousand years ago, God spoke in the world with human speech just like ours. Christ lived for thirty-three years on our earth, and during thirty years his speech did not go beyond the setting of a village with a few hundred inhabitants. This is God's silence. He is on earth, and he remains hidden. Can we speak about a silent God? I would rather speak about a hidden God. These are two nuances of one and the same reality, which convey the same contrast: God is silent, and this is his way of speaking. He is silent when he speaks. When the Word is made flesh, he shows himself to our eyes, but by that very fact he veils his divinity. When that divinity speaks with our man-made words, the divine Word is audible to our ears and hidden; most peo-ple hear only human words and do not pay attention. The paradox is impressive: God stoops to speak our language, and that makes us deaf to the divine inflections of this all-too-earthly voice.

During his life, Jesus spoke with words, and once he even spoke with cords. But in the presence of the Sanhedrin, Herod, and Pilate, he is quiet. He would explain to the high priest: "I have spoken openly to the world; I have always taught in synagogues and in the temple, where all Jews come together; I have said nothing secretly. Why do you ask me? Ask those who have heard me, what I said to them; they know what I said" (Jn 18:20–21). This response would earn him a slap; is this not precisely the current situation? Jesus spoke the word that the Father wanted to address to the world. He carried out his mission to the end. If we want to know what he is saying to us, we must ask those who are his witnesses or those whom he has accredited, in other words, his Church. But this answer is not popular ... God's silence is not so much a matter of him not speaking as it is the manner in which he expresses himself and our reluctance to listen to him.

The spiritual life goes through alternating phases in which God successively shows and hides himself, makes himself heard and is quiet. Prayer teaches us the subtleties of divine speech. Is God being silent, or are we not hearing him because our interior ear and our intellect are not accustomed to his language? The fruit of silence is learning to discern his voice, even though it always keeps its mystery.

In prayer, the divine voice is powerful in that it is capable of touching us in our inmost depths, but it manifests itself in an extremely discreet way. The paths of the spiritual life are quite varied, and some may pass through a desert that seems endless. There are persons for whom God's silence in their life is almost palpable. This may take mystical forms, as shown by the very painful experience of Mother Teresa of Calcutta; after years of profound intimacy with the Lord, the saint saw everything gradually fade. During the last two years of her life, Thérèse of the Child Jesus also experienced this sort of abandonment. However, that is not the general rule, and the contemplative soul that has learned the language of the divine Bridegroom, although it never hears it as one hears human speech, still learns gradually to notice its traces everywhere. This soul then resembles a loving woman who knows that she is deeply loved, waiting to meet in the evening the man whom she loves. Now throughout the day she sees everywhere signs of his presence without ever encountering him. Here is a love note that is unsigned, but she knows the handwriting too well to have any doubt that it comes from him. There is a bouquet of flowers, with no explanation, yet from certain details she recognizes that he is the one who put it there for her. Later, while walking in the country, she hears the music of a flute; she does not know exactly where it comes from, but she knows that it is he and that he is playing for her, while the person with whom she is walking suspects nothing. And so it is the whole day. She senses him everywhere; she sees everywhere signs not only of his presence but of his attention to her, and for

her he speaks unceasingly even though she does not see him anywhere. He secretly prepares her for the evening meeting when they
will finally be able to speak. He is there like a perfume, elusive and
yet quite perceptible, present everywhere although one cannot tell
where it comes from.

I think that God speaks in silence. I am always struck by his discretion, by his very tactful manners with their boundless respect for our
freedom. We are as fragile as glass, and so God tempers his power and
his speech so as to adapt them to our weakness.

Love does not impose itself; it cannot impose itself. And because
God is infinite love, his respect and his tact disconcert us. Precisely
because he is present everywhere, he hides himself all the more carefully so as not to impose himself. There is a commandment of God
that asks us to love him, but this is only an initial level; a Carthusian
brother explained it delightfully in a note: "My God, it is extraordinary that you should ask us to love you. Given what you are and
what we are, you ought to forbid us to do so. But if you forbade us
to love you, I would love you secretly."

ROBERT SARAH: Man does not seek silence for the sake of silence.
The desire for silence for its own sake would be a sterile venture, a
particularly exhausting aesthetic experience. In the depths of his soul,
man wants the presence and company of God, in the same way that
Christ sought his Father in the desert, far from the cries and passions
of the crowd. If we really desire him and if we are in his Presence,
words are no longer necessary. This silent intimacy with God is the
only speech, dialogue, and communion.

At the Grande Chartreuse, I have the sense that silence is a ladder
that is set up on the earth and whose top reaches heaven. If Jacob
had been able to spend the night here, I am certain he would have
exclaimed: "How awesome is this place! This is none other than a
house of God and the gate of heaven" (cf. Gen 28:17).

NICOLAS DIAT: *Is the reason why Carthusians subject themselves to such a
silent asceticism because silence is the privileged means of finding God?*

DYSMAS DE LASSUS: Silence for us is a form of asceticism and a desire.
Asceticism because you have to understand that silence demands an

effort, but, more than that, it attracts us and we need it. Simple things are always difficult to explain. A person who is trying to hear a bird-song will be quite irritated if an airplane flies over; his space for perception is then reduced, and he can no longer hear the bird. Make no mistake: silence is not sought for its own sake but, rather, for the space it makes. Silence allows us to perceive better and to hear better; it opens our inner space.

NICOLAS DIAT: *It is not sought for its own sake, but it is present at every moment . . .*

DYSMAS DE LASSUS: That is our dearest wish, but do we attain this ideal? Let us be realistic, noise dwells in Carthusians, too; we know that all too well. Paradoxically, exterior silence and solitude, which have the objective of promoting interior silence, begin by revealing all the noise that dwells within us.

If you have in your pocket a radio that is turned on, you might not realize it in the hubbub of a city or of a street because the noise that it makes blends in with the environment. But if you enter a church, you suddenly understand that incessant chatter is coming from your pocket; the first thing you will do is try to turn it off. Alas, there is no switch to reduce the chattering of our imagination . . . The first step consists of becoming aware of this, even though it is not very pleasant.

The silence that reigns in the monastery is not enough. Attaining communion in silence requires long work that is started over and over again indefinitely. We must be patient, and the efforts to be made are difficult; when our imagination finally agrees to cooperate and to quiet down, the moments of profound intimacy with God amply repay the efforts that were necessary to make room for him.

But we can never create intimacy with God; it always comes from above, and our responsibility is to build the setting in which the encounter can take place.

Well, solitude helps us. Interior silence is much easier to attain when we are alone. Before the night Office in church, I have always loved the time of solitary prayer in the cell. We have just got up, in the middle of the night, and this time is something unique. We must not idealize it; I am not saying that peace of heart is always present then, but generally the silent communion blossoms much more naturally. I would like to make this recollection last during the recitation of the Office in choir that follows immediately, but I can rarely regain the same quality of communion because the communal dimension of the liturgy sets thoughts in motion.

As long as there are lovers on earth, they will seek to see each other alone, and silence will have a part in their encounter. This is perhaps the simplest way to explain our choice of life. Silence and solitude in a charterhouse have their meaning in this great desire for intimacy with God. For the sons of Saint Bruno, silence and solitude are the perfect place for a heart-to-heart conversation.

ROBERT SARAH: I am completely in agreement with Dom Dysmas. Solitude is indispensable in creating a space of silence. There is no need for particular speech in order to be with God. We have only to be quiet and to contemplate his love. In the silence, we look at God and let him look at us.

God sees us at every moment, but when we surrender to him, his look is more penetrating; we perceive the kindness of his eyes and his Presence illumines us, calms us, and divinizes us.

The Gospels urge people to seek, not silence, but the desert so as to find communion with God. In the New Testament there is no instance where Christ seeks silence. In the desert, he wishes to bring together better conditions for his intimacy with the Father so as to allow himself to be penetrated by his will.

DYSMAS DE LASSUS: In speaking about prayer, Saint John of the Cross says that it resembles "a person who opens his eyes with loving attention" (*Living Flame* 3, 33). Automatically, this look is silent and amazed. The peasant from Ars, a parishioner of Saint John Vianney, said so poetically: "I look at him and he looks at me." An exchange of looks—what could be more eloquent when this comes from the heart and goes to the heart?

ROBERT SARAH: The peasant expresses himself very little. He fathoms with his frank, pure look this silent Presence of Jesus, who burns with love for us. God is silent. But his look crosses ours and fills the human heart with its strength and its merciful tenderness.

DYSMAS DE LASSUS: Yes, we do not hear God with our ears because he speaks in another way. In his book *Paths to Contemplation*, the Jesuit Yves Raguin says: "That which comes from God may appear to us as coming from the depths of the unconscious, but in a light that has come from farther away, we know that it comes from him." It is useless to try to separate the human element from the divine; one is within the other. Retreatants who aspire to enter the Grande Chartreuse have often asked me how they could be sure that God was calling them to the desert. I always told them I had no idea ... God manifests himself in many ways, and I cannot guess, nor can they, which way he will take for them. But heaven always ends up manifesting itself.

With time, we end up knowing God's language, a language that is different for each person. I know well the language that he uses for me, with its unique way of blending human and divine elements, and I can testify that it is marvelously well adapted. More than just words, it is a love that awakens, and I know that it comes from elsewhere because its source is not in me.

Divine intimacy ... It is not always granted to us, and the desert can be arid. When it is manifested, its melody resounds much more deeply than the well-being of simple silence with God.

In one passage of the *Confessions*, Saint Augustine uses the language of interior senses to express the fact that this intimacy with God is both familiar, close, and very concrete and, at the same time, imperceptible to our ordinary senses:

> It is with no doubtful knowledge, Lord, but with utter certainty that I love You.... But what is it that I love when I love You? Not the beauty of any bodily thing, nor the order of seasons, not the brightness of light that rejoices the eye, nor the sweet melodies of all songs, nor the sweet fragrance of flowers and ointments and spices; not manna nor honey, not the limbs that carnal love embraces. None of these things do I love in loving my God. Yet in a sense I do love light and melody and fragrance and food and embrace when I love my God— the light and the voice and the fragrance and the food and embrace in the soul, when that light shines upon my soul which no place can contain, that voice sounds which no time can take from me, I breathe that fragrance which no wind scatters, I eat the food which is not lessened by eating, and I lie in the embrace which satiety never comes to sunder. This it is that I love, when I love my God. (X, 6, 8)

NICOLAS DIAT: Your Eminence, you often speak about silence as God in us. Dom Dysmas, do you agree with this concept?

DYSMAS DE LASSUS: Yes, certainly, since we are speaking about a silence of communion. I would put these two complementary dimensions together: God in us, and we in God, since Jesus uses this expression: "You [are] in me, and I in you" (Jn 14:20); "You, Father, are in me, and I in you" (Jn 17:21). These are two facets of one and the same reality. We may be more sensitive to one or the other, but I do not think it is possible to separate them entirely.

By baptism, the Trinity itself comes to make its dwelling in us. According to Saint Paul, we are temples of the Holy Spirit. This same baptism makes us children of God. If only we could really understand these few words! An unfathomable mystery is born in the extreme simplicity of the sacrament: water and the word are there to signify an unimaginable reality. I am thinking of the remark of a Byzantine poet who alluded to the theophany on Mount Sinai: "Thunder, lightning, the earth quakes. But when you descended into the womb of a virgin, your step made no noise."

If God's entrance among us occurred in silence, it is quite normal that communion with him should be marked by the same seal. Our *Statutes* (13.15) quote Basil of Ancyra (*De Virginitate*, PG 30, 765): "In solitude, then, let the monk's soul be like a tranquil lake, whose waters well up from the purest sources of the spirit and, untroubled by news coming from outside, like a clear mirror reflect one image only, that of Christ."

God in us! However much these words may lead us to dream, it is a reality. Jesus says: "If a man loves me, he will keep my word, and my Father will love him, and we will come to him and make our home with him" (Jn 14:23).

This truth of the faith opens us *hic et nunc* [here and now] to the most profound intimacy with God. It is the lighthouse of our life. I am deeply convinced that if Christians were more conscious of this reality, their lives would be transformed, and the world, too.

It seems to me important to maintain an equilibrium between the closeness and the transcendence of God. In the *Confessions*, Saint Augustine famously formulated the problem: "*Intimior intimo meo et superior summo meo.*" ["More inward than the most inward place of my heart and loftier than the highest."] To hold one without the other can lead to spiritual disorders. On the one hand, a sort of excessive familiarity with a God who is too much on our own scale, who is no longer really God, and, on the other hand, an uneasy, almost Jansenist distance.

The mystery is none other than the divine "filiation" or sonship that is offered to us. If only we could understand! If only we could experience it more! Nothing could trouble us then. The difficulties of life would not be changed, but they could no longer affect the heart of our life. Saint Paul tells us: "He who did not spare his own Son but gave him up for us all, will he not also give us all things with him?" (Rom 8:32). If I know that I have received everything, I can lack nothing. We speak about silence: the profound peace of the soul that knows that it is loved beyond its wildest dreams, the unchangeable calm that dwells within it—is that not interior silence? A living, expressive, inhabited silence. Trembling expectation in the hope of the day of the great face-to-face encounter.

It is fundamentally important to remain in the intimacy of God and of his extraordinary simplicity, I would even say "familiarity" toward us, yet also to understand the meaning of transcendence, the immensity that surpasses us and calls us in one and the same movement. Only this balance can lend to our relation with God its full depth, because the ineffable miracle of divine intimacy comes precisely from his transcendence. How can what is infinite not only come to meet us but also form an intimate relation with what is finite, its creature?

ROBERT SARAH: God is great. God is beyond contingencies, God is immense. It is true that I would never automatically use the word "familiarity" in speaking about God. When you are familiar with someone, you take almost every sort of liberty, and you are less careful about your gestures and words. It is not possible to allow oneself to behave that way with God, even though he is our Father. God is silence, God is love. We approach love as something sacred, with dignity, respect, and adoration. To me it seems strange to try to create tangible relations with the divine that are devoid of reverence.

The silence that brings us close to God is always a respectful silence, a silence of adoration, a silence of filial love. It is never a trivial silence.

God in us, and we in God; only love can carry out that plan infallibly. Jesus, on several occasions, confirms that God is a burning presence in the depths of our soul, a real presence, the presence apart from which we cannot encounter anyone: "He who eats my flesh and drinks my blood abides in me, and I in him" (Jn 6:56).

Saint Paul offers us his own interior experience, which seems to convey this grace given to mankind: "I have been crucified with Christ; it is no longer I who live, but Christ who lives in me; and the life I now live in the flesh I live by faith in the Son of God, who loved me and gave himself for me. I do not nullify the grace of God" (Gal 2:20–21).

After his conversion, Saint Augustine, too, would discover this Presence of God hidden in the inmost depths of every man. In his *Confessions*, he writes these magnificent lines: "Late have I loved Thee, O Beauty so ancient and so new; late have I loved Thee! For behold Thou wert within me, and I outside; and I sought Thee outside and in my unloveliness fell upon those lovely things that Thou hast made. Thou wert with me and I was not with Thee. I was kept from Thee by those things, yet had they not been in Thee, they would not have been at all."

In a great, thoroughly erudite book, *Saint Grégoire le Grand: Culture et expérience chrétiennes*, Bishop Claude Dagens writes:

And so in converting, Saint Augustine made a twofold discovery. First of all, he understood why he had lived until then in sin: his error had consisted in letting himself be distracted from himself, drawn by carnal lusts, dominated by exteriority. This way could not lead to God because—and this is the second discovery, which complements the first—God is a reality that is profoundly interior to man, and, consequently, man can find him only by not going out of himself, by not giving in to the fascination of exteriority, and by converting to interiority. Of course, Saint Gregory the Great had no experience of sin or conversion comparable to Saint Augustine's. It is all the more significant to observe how close his concept of sin is to that of the author of the *Confessions*: for both writers, the soul lives in sin when it goes out of itself and becomes the prey of the seductions of the external world, of this wicked, adulterous generation. The path that leads to God is the path of interiority.

The silent apostasy of which Saint John Paul II spoke has turned into a militant apostasy. In our relativistic societies, no one acknowledges any more that he is a sinner. Sin and repentance have become traumatizing states of soul from which one must be liberated so as to be able to enjoy good spiritual health. We consider ourselves victims of our heredity, of our environment, or of circumstances. Men no longer want to see themselves as anything but fragile, wounded persons. The impression is given that sin no longer exists; adultery, divorce, cohabitation are no longer to be considered serious sins. They are failures or stages along the way to a distant ideal. Who worries about the invasion of hedonism and moral laxism, of barbaric disdain for women, who are exploited as sex objects by pornography and prostitution? Nevertheless, "If we say we have no sin, we deceive ourselves, and the truth is not in us. If we confess our sins, he is faithful and just, and will forgive our sins and cleanse us from all unrighteousness. If we say we have not sinned, we make him a liar, and his word is not in us" (1 Jn 1:8–10). Why is the posthumanist world no longer willing to acknowledge sin? Sin is not an abstract reality or a stain on a garment. It is the rejection of God's law, opposition to God. Sin is a breach of an alliance, the deterioration of our personal relationship with God. Sin is self-destructive, comparable to a person who ruins himself by drug abuse or taking poison. Nevertheless, God does not want us to destroy something important in ourselves or in others; sin displeases him and painfully offends him. God calls us to conversion and to a radical rejection of sin. If we experience a genuine conversion of heart, after the example of Saint Paul and Saint Augustine, we will really be able to touch the silent presence of God in our life. In the *Confessions*, Saint Augustine calls this Presence the Life of his life: "When once I shall be united to Thee with all my being, there shall be no more grief and toil, and my life will be alive, filled wholly with Thee."

How could we live without God? His Presence in us is terrifying, unsettling, but life-giving, sweet, and calming at the same time. It is distant, because of our sins, and close because of God's infinite mercy. It is frightening, because it burns and consumes us like a charring fire, but it embraces us tenderly like a Father.

NICOLAS DIAT: *In a charterhouse, how do the monks learn to tame silence, to get past their failures when silence becomes impossible, and simply not to fear silence?*

DYSMAS DE LASSUS: I will start with the last part of your question; I would say that someone who fears silence will not remain with us.

The uneasiness does not come from the silence itself but about what it reveals. A retreatant comes to a charterhouse in order to encounter God, and he begins by encountering an unexpected person: himself. The surprise is not particularly pleasant.

Let us suppose you have a rather gloomy room and that you are not a specialist in orderliness or sweeping. Since you do not consider it a big deal, it does not bother you too much. But now a guest has the unfortunate idea of turning on a very powerful floodlight. The spectacle becomes embarrassing ... When a candidate comes to make a retreat with us, many memories rise again to the surface. They have been in him for a long time, covered up by the noises of life. When the commotion stops, he can no longer escape, and he understands that the silence and solitude of the cell that he perceived as a place of rest are also a place of trial where he will have to face the most difficult combat: the battle with himself.

It is a matter of taming the menagerie that lives inside us if we want the wild animals to be able to leave us in silence some day. Exterior silence, the silence of the house itself and the silence of the lips, is part of the itinerary. It is prescribed in our *Statutes*. The simple experience of constantly being quiet strikes an invisible chord within us. In the act of being quiet together, there is a very rich dimension, the tangible expression of our common quest to maintain a dialogue with God. It is a matter of respecting the other's silence. The apprenticeship of this external level is completed with time. We learn to give meaning to silence.

But the more difficult task is interior silence. In the cell, or during prayer, the big noises of the soul can be unleashed. Mental games, thoughts, and emotions are happy to come distract us from our prayer. In the etymological sense, it is a noise that comes to tear us apart and separate us from one another. What are these distractions? If we look closely, we observe that it is always an imaginary dialogue. We speak to persons about this or that subject ...

The silence of the lips requires a bit of willpower; interior attention, in silence, to what is dwelling within us, requires long work—a genuine taming process, to repeat the word that you used.

The apprenticeship of silence requires that we rest in the Lord's presence. It is a matter, not of struggling against our interior thoughts, but rather of unceasingly returning to God. Distractions are formidable because we do not see them coming and before we realize it they have led us away! The movement of returning to God, as soon as we notice that we have strayed, shows that our intention has not changed: to be with him. Really there is one aspect of the work, which has to be started over again and again indefinitely, that consists of letting oneself be drawn. But the essential thing is contributed by the Lord. We work in one part of the garden, but the true germination is God's gift. The saying by Isaac of Nineveh is correct: "God led his servant into the desert to speak to his heart; but only the one who keeps listening there in the silence perceives the breath and the light breeze in which the Lord manifests himself. At the beginning it takes an effort in order to be quiet, but if we are faithful, little by little, something is born of our silence that attracts us to more silence." We know that this "something", whose contours I could not define, is in reality "Someone" who draws us more and more into his mystery.

When the monk enters into the depths of solitude, and his desire to be with God is sufficiently strong, silence really becomes a privileged way.

ROBERT SARAH: Authentic silence, in other words, exterior and interior silence, the absolute silence of the imagination, memory, and will, plunges us into a divine milieu. Then our whole being belongs to God.

It is necessary, however, to acknowledge that silence is difficult. It scares us. It gives us a greater awareness of our helplessness and awakens a certain fear of our isolation in the presence of the invisible God. Silence awakens the anxiety of confronting the bare realities that are at the bottom of our soul. Our interior temple is often so ugly that we prefer to live on the outside of ourselves in order to hide in worldly devices and noises. But the moments of silence lead infallibly to profound decisions, wordless decisions, a gift of my inmost "self". Conversions take place silently and not in spectacular gestures. Returning to God, burying oneself in him, this total gift, these moments of intimacy with God are always mysterious and secret. They involve an absolute silence, a formidable discretion. I think that it is really necessary to practice silence.

In my life, I was initiated into silence during my years at seminary. There were obligatory times of silence. But it is necessary to consent joyfully, to welcome them as precious, privileged moments for building up our interior life. Indeed, the priest's vocation and mission is to stand constantly facing a silent God, whose heart nonetheless watches, listens, and reshapes us in his likeness so that we might "be conformed to the image of his Son, in order that he might be the first-born among many brethren" (Rom 8:29). During this period of formation, I quickly realized that unless there is a very strong discipline that consists of desiring to encounter God, silence is difficult and nothing urges you to seek it diligently. In fact, silence is an elevator that allows us to encounter God, on one level after another.

Monasteries, charterhouses in particular, are special silent ways of gaining access to God. But silence must also shape the souls of seminarians and priests.

NICOLAS DIAT: Could we then speak about a spiral of silence?

DYSMAS DE LASSUS: Man can notice these spirals in any loving relationship that goes a certain distance. At the beginning, speech rules; there is so much to discover about the other person. With time, silent presence becomes increasingly prevalent. It is enough to be together because a look expresses more than words do. The same trend is found in our relationship with God. Like any relationship, it has a history, it develops. Isaac of Nineveh, in the text I just quoted, expressed it as follows: "Little by little, something attracts us to more silence", which implies, in fact, a new mode of relationship. It all happens as with a book: in order to uncover a new page, you have to turn—and therefore hide and, in a way, abandon—the preceding one.

With God, this movement has no end, since he is infinite. The divine intimacy that overwhelmed us gives way little by little to a kind of dissatisfaction; we hear something like a call to go farther but without knowing in what direction. Everything happens as though the Lord stopped showing up at our appointment with him; or, more precisely, we are the ones who no longer show up. We stayed at the same place, while the Lord walked farther on. At this stage, it is necessary to give something up in order to listen for the signs that he is giving, like a child lost in the forest who listens in the utmost silence so as to have a chance to hear a voice that would give him some indication of what direction to take.

In a beautiful passage about the prayer of the heart, Dom André Poisson relates how, before entering a charterhouse, he had found "a little spring that established between my heart and God an infinitely profound, true bond". And then one day, much later, he had a doubt and realized that this little spring was not God, whereas he thirsted for him alone. Dom André understood that he had to abandon his dear spring in order to "find the means, the attitude of heart, by which I would open the door directly to him who had been knocking in vain for so long, because in my prayer I was primarily concerned with myself." The little spring of Dom André was certainly good and precious, but only for a time, and he was not to stop there. Like a hiker who discovers some marvelous scenery; he will stop so as to enjoy it for a long time. But the moment comes when he must get back on the road again for other even more beautiful surprises.

This is the reason for these alternations that seem to be a spiral. In order to discover a new relationship, a new language, the one we know must be quiet. It takes a lot of silence and attention to discover the new music to which we are not accustomed.

The major obstacle, generally, comes from our tendency to stand still as long as we have a system that works. Our heart, accustomed to a certain relationship with God, is reluctant to change in order to enter into a new relationship; nevertheless, the Lord is impatient to make progress. Then he goes on ahead in order to oblige us to set out again on the road.

NICOLAS DIAT: *The Christian God is a hidden God. This is one of the great mysteries of Providence as it governs the world. It is also one of the aspects of life here on earth that prevents people from believing: this famous* Deus absconditus . . .

DYSMAS DE LASSUS: It is important to quote the statement by Saint Paul: "The creation waits with eager longing for the revealing of the sons of God" (Rom 8:19). We do not yet know what we are and what we will be.

In the day-by-day course of the world, God's silence is a very impressive phenomenon. How are we to understand the meaning of this absence? It is certainly easier to comprehend in our personal life.

Man, as a creature, is marked by an ontological selfishness. An infant who is born has consciousness only of himself. Initially he perceives his mother as an extension of his own person. We all started by being solipsists! Gradually, through frustration, the baby ends up understanding that his mother is another person. Several stages and some years later, he will arrive at a love that is at first prompted by self-interest but finally gratuitous.

In a parallel way, in the spiritual life we must travel an immense distance. It is necessary to go from total selfishness to sacrificial love that is no longer focused at all on self, in the image of God's own great love. This is the progress of the smallest creature toward the infinity of heaven ... Such an evolution would normally take an extremely long time. But everything happens as though God were in a hurry. Therefore, we should not be surprised if this accelerated course is rather rough. Life is too short to complete such an important journey! If you look at it from the perspective of eternity, our life is only a brief instant. But that does not prevent us from feeling that it is long, especially if one is suffering. Let us keep this difference in mind; it will help us to understand. When we have gone over to God's side, we will see things just as he does. Jesus explained this: A woman who is giving birth is in pain because her hour has come. But when the infant is born, she no longer remembers her suffering, because she is happy that a child is born into the world (Jn 16:21).

On this earth we have the unique opportunity to love God while he is hidden from our eyes and ears. Faith is not granted in the light because that dazzling splendor is reserved for eternity. But when the time comes for him to reveal himself fully, our joy will be eternal for having loved him thus without seeing him. Jesus had said to his disciples: "You are those who have continued with me in my trials; as my Father appointed a kingdom for me, so do I appoint for you that you may eat and drink at my table in my kingdom, and sit on thrones judging the twelve tribes of Israel" (Lk 22:28–30). And as for him: "Was it not necessary that the Christ should suffer these things and enter into his glory?" (Lk 24:26). It is the same with those who are invited to follow him by taking up their cross.

It may be heavy and terrifying, but Saint Paul reminds us that "God is faithful, and he will not let you be tempted beyond your strength" (1 Cor 10:13).

Let us remain humble when we speak about someone else's suffering. Only the one who has truly suffered has the right to speak. In *Le Heurtoir* [The door knocker], Paul Claudel wrote: "God did not come to do away with suffering; he did not even come to explain it. He came to fill it with his presence." I would add: he came to share in it, and this mystery, which is engraved on the risen body of Jesus, will always remain a source of joy and wonder. Psalm 116 says: "What shall I render to the LORD for all his bounty to me?"

ROBERT SARAH: I agree with Dom Dysmas' insight. True love is not necessarily visible. God is true love. He is a consuming fire that cannot be extinguished, so passionately does he love us through the mystery of the Cross. He is *Deus absconditus*, the invisible, hidden God. But at the same time he made himself visible in his Son, "through whom he created the ages. He reflects the glory of God and bears the very stamp of his nature, upholding the universe by his word of power" (Heb 1:2–3). He is therefore close to us. In our materialistic societies, we always think that what is true has to be tangible and immediate. But God's love is veiled in silence, suffering, death, in the tortured, ruined flesh of Jesus who is dying on the Cross.

The prophet Elijah would have loved to see the face of God. This is also the desire and the religious anxiety most deeply anchored in the heart of every person. But one cannot see God without dying of fright, astonishment, and wonder. Nevertheless, God could not leave us alone without satisfying such a profound human desire. According to the Letter to the Hebrews, when the time was fulfilled, God hid himself behind the face of a little infant. Majesty chose vulnerability. The Infinite accepted the Cross and the greatest humiliation, because self-emptying is the expression of love.

Man would like to possess an immediate comprehension of God. But the Father is hidden behind a veil, and we will not be able to remove the mystery completely until after our death.

By his silence, God wants to give us an opportunity to go beyond merely human love so as to understand divine love.

NICOLAS DIAT: *How can a Carthusian understand the unfathomable mystery of God's silence, given the atrocities that are committed every day right before our eyes? In Iraq and Syria, children are mutilated, violated, sold, reduced to slavery, crucified, and God does not say a word? The Islamic State's policy of extermination is unleashed against the Christians of the Near East, and the God of love seems absent?*

DYSMAS DE LASSUS: May I first broaden the question? The current genocide of babies with Down Syndrome in the West is no less tragic, and I am not sure that it is less barbaric; it is only less visible. In these circumstances, which affect both East and West, I think that we must meditate on the Book of Job. In his certainty that he has the right to do so, Job goes so far as to provoke God to judgment. What is God's response? God simply tells Job that he cannot understand, but he takes part in his revolt and says that he is right. At the end of the book he addresses Job's friends as follows: "You have not spoken of me what is right, as my servant Job has" (Job 42:8).

But Job cannot understand God's designs because the essential key, eternal life, has not yet been granted. The worst things have an end when we have gone over to the side of the kingdom of God. Look at the migrants: they are ready to face extreme dangers in the faint hope of finding a better life in Europe for a few years. But God our Father is preparing us for an infinitely better life without limits. What man lacks is the ability to imagine eternity, unending fullness granted through total communion with God, the land where the justice that the prophets attempted to describe will take shape.

God's silence cannot be understood without the perspective of eternal life. God's time is different from ours; for him, "a thousand years [are] as one day" (2 Pet 3:8). He lets us experience trials for a little while before saving us for a whole lifetime. Who would dare to complain about a surgeon who, in the two hours of a painful operation, cured a sick person for the rest of his life? His office would be swamped with calls! Before entering Carmel, Saint Thérèse of the Child Jesus had read Father Arminjon's conferences on eternal life. One remark had struck her; the priest said that when the soul had departed from this life, the Lord would say to her: "My turn now!" This means: "During your earthly life, you gave me all you could by way of love, and now it is my turn to give, infinitely and for all eternity." Jesus had said: "Truly, I say to you, there is no one who has left house or brothers or sisters or mother or father or children or lands, for my sake and for the gospel, who will not receive a hundredfold now in this time, houses and brothers and sisters and mothers and children and lands, with persecutions, and in the age to come eternal life" (Mk 10:29–30).

We must understand in the same way God's silence, which has no definitive meaning. He keeps quiet for a few hours while leaving the world in our hands. But the day will come when he will "make all things new" (Rev 21:5).

God can draw the greatest good from evil itself. Everything God permits has a meaning. To the mystic Julian of Norwich, who liked to talk about God's courtesy, affability, simplicity, and modesty and who one night had fifteen visions on which she meditated for the rest of her life, Jesus had "showed me that Adam's sin was the greatest harm that ever was done, or ever shall be, until the end of the world". He then added this extraordinary remark: "Since I have turned the greatest possible harm into good, it is my will that you should know from this that I shall turn all lesser evil into good." In order to console her, he told her: "I shall make well all that is not well and you shall see it." The recluse concluded: "[It was] as if [our Lord] said: 'Pay attention to this now, faithfully and confidently, and at the end of time you will truly see it in the fullness of joy.'"

Finally, we are a little like Job. We know now that eternal life exists, but we have no experience of it. So we continue to stumble over the evil of this earth. With Pascal, we must place a bet on eternity. Jesus did not say very much that allows us to imagine eternal life, but we can be certain about one thing: "Whatever is true, whatever is honorable, whatever is just, whatever is pure, whatever is lovely, whatever is gracious, if there is any excellence, if there is anything worthy of praise" (Phil 4:8); and also whatever is beautiful: nothing of that will be destroyed; on the contrary, all will be accomplished so as to attain it fullness.

ROBERT SARAH: We are often revolted by unbearable events. God seems to sleep and not to defend his weakest children. He has his way of caring for the poor that we cannot understand. God wants this suffering to contribute to the salvation of the world like the death of Christ himself. In reality, a world without God is a very cruel world that sheds rivers of blood; its barbarity is repeated under all skies and in every historical era.

Let us remember Auschwitz. Inside the concentration camp, there was a horrible prison, the famous starvation bunker designed for a slow, cynical death. There, in an underground cell, Saint Maximilian Kolbe died after a long and terrible agony. All around him there was nothing but torture, barbarity, suffering, and misery. Outside there was a yard where some twenty thousand men were assassinated; beside it, the "hospital" where they conducted vivisection on human beings and, at the end of an avenue, the crematorium. However, in Father Maximilian Kolbe's heart, joy reigned, along with the peace that Christ had promised to give to his disciples and to those who follow his example in dying on the Cross, like him, so that others might live. In similar circumstances, Saint Thomas More, who was imprisoned and then executed, prayed in the Tower of London for the grace "of worldly substance, friends, liberty, life and all, to set the loss at naught, for the winning of Christ."

I could look the same way at the murder of the seven monks in Tibhirine, Algeria, in 1996. Their sole vocation was prayer and the service of God and of their brothers. All these deaths participate in the death of Christ for the salvation of the world.

There are many today who are enduring a non-bloody martyrdom while trying to live out their faith in a world that is increasingly atheistic, hedonistic, and indifferent or even hostile to God. We must not fear the world's opposition; this growing hatred should instead gladden us. This is what Jesus had promised: "Remember the word that I said to you, 'A servant is not greater than his master.' If they persecuted me, they will persecute you; if they kept my word, they will keep yours also. But all this they will do to you on my account, because they do not know him who sent me" (Jn 15:20–21). When the Christian faith is persecuted, it becomes stronger.

Certainly, we will always be surprised by God's choices. Man cannot immediately grasp the good that God intends for him while he is going through the most horrible trial.

Only a faith perspective can enable us to continue to advance toward God. Who knows whether God might give, at the moment of his choosing, a magnificent springtime to the Christians of the Near East? Our human eyes are too feeble and sick to understand heaven's economy.

DYSMAS DE LASSUS: I would simply like to recall a story. One issue of the magazine *Cahiers sur l'Oraison* [Notebooks on prayer] reports that before leaving for the gas chamber, a Jew wrote on a slip of paper: "Lord, remember also the men of ill will, but do not remember then their cruelties. Remember the fruits that we have borne because of what they did. And grant, Lord, that the fruits that we have borne may one day be their redemption."

We should meditate on the grandeur of this message, which shows that the Holy Spirit was at work in the horror of the concentration camps. In the Book of Daniel, God does not prevent the three young men from being thrown into the furnace, but he protects them because the angel of the Lord goes down into it with them. This story is symbolic. God does not spare us the trial, but as he tells us in Psalm 91:15–16: "I will be with him in trouble, I will rescue him and honor him. With long life I will satisfy him, and show him my salvation."

ROBERT SARAH: It is urgent for the modern world to regain a faith perspective. Otherwise mankind is headed for its destruction. The Church cannot confine herself to a merely social vision. Charity has a spiritual meaning. Charity is closely related to God's silence.

God has a plan of salvation for the whole world, and men must always seek to understand his perspective better. We must be willing to join him in his silence.

NICOLAS DIAT: Reverend Father, as we were preparing our interview, you said to me: "As with all the great questions, the more we reflect on silence, the less we understand. Who has ever understood love?" Your Eminence, do you subscribe to this difficult yet hope-filled remark?

ROBERT SARAH: Who can understand God? Who can enter into his silence so as to comprehend its mystery and fruitfulness? We can reflect on silence so as to draw closer to God, but there comes a time when our thinking can make no more progress. As with all questions connected with God, there is a stage when the search can go no farther. The only thing to do is to raise our eyes, to stretch out our hands toward God, and to pray in silence while awaiting the dawn.

Silence is part of these inquiries that show us that there is a mystery in the presence of mystery.

Silence is the prerequisite for being open to the great answers that will be given to us after death. We would like God to speak right now while we are passing through this world. But for the moment, we live in the night, praying in silence. One day we will understand everything. Until then, it is necessary to seek without making noise. I know well that God's silence constantly runs into man's impatience. Nowadays, moreover, man fosters a kind of compulsive relationship with time.

DYSMAS DE LASSUS: When I was in the novitiate, the Novice Master assigned me to read *The Mysteries of Christianity* by Matthias Joseph Scheeben. At the end of each chapter, the theologian took care to emphasize that we had understood little and that most of it still eluded us. He was right: the more we study a mystery, the more we understand that we do not understand, and this causes our wonder to grow.

It is fortunate that so many problems elude us; an infinite number of them remain to be discovered. The most familiar realities are full of mystery. For example, the more science advances, the less it understands matter. Only someone who has not reflected on it thinks that he knows what time is. How can we imagine that we could solve the problem of the meaning of God's action in this world?

Contemplation is nourished more by what we do not understand. In meditation, a man seeks to grasp something of the mystery. In contemplation, he marvels and abandons himself to God's love, which surpasses us.

"If you understood him, it would not be God", Saint Augustine wrote (*Sermon* 117). In faith, lack of understanding is essential, and it is not a form of frustration; it enables us to dream. A yawning space has opened, and our silence comes to slip into this expectation.

NICOLAS DIAT: *Why is silence so important for the Church?*

ROBERT SARAH: If man seeks God and wants to find him, if he desires a life of the most intimate union with him, silence is the most direct path and the surest means of attaining it. Silence is of capital importance because it enables the Church to walk in the footsteps of Jesus, imitating his thirty silent years in Nazareth, his forty days and forty nights of fasting and intimate dialogue with the Father in the solitude and silence of the desert. Like Jesus, confronted with the demands of his Father's will, the Church must seek silence in order to enter ever more deeply into the mystery of Christ. The Church must be the reflection of the light that pours out from Christ. And the light of Christ gleams, radiates, and illumines in silence and cannot be stopped by the deafening night of sin, which prompts Saint John to say: "The light shines in the darkness, and the darkness has not overcome it" (Jn 1:5).

Light makes no noise. If we want to approach this luminous source, we must assume an attitude of contemplation and silence.

In order to reflect the brilliant light of Christ, Christians must resemble the Son of God. This outpouring of light is always discreet.

The true nature of the Church is not found in what she does but in what she testifies. Wherever deep, mysterious things are, there is silence. Christ asked us to be a light. He ordered us, not to conquer the world, but to show men the way, the truth, and the life. He asked us to be silent but convincing witnesses of his love.

Silence is the place where we welcome mysteries. Why is Holy Week celebrated in silence? The answer is simple: We must enter into the Passion in order to be conformed to Christ, to be in communion with his sufferings, to become like him in his death, so as to arrive at the resurrection from the dead (cf. Phil 3:10). The profound silence of Holy Saturday is not a day of sadness but a moment of our being placed into the tomb with Christ and of contemplating the mystery that reason cannot fathom without the help of him who reads the secrets of hearts and knows what is the desire of the Spirit (cf. Rom 8:27). Led by the Holy Spirit, the Church has a mission to educate the faithful in silence because there is no life in silence without a life totally led by the Spirit.

How could I forget the Holy Spirit missionaries whom I saw praying for long hours in the silence of the church in my village of Ourous? They were absolutely faithful to Christ's teachings. These priests withdrew to the interior desert of their heart to be with God. I was very fortunate to have such men as a model.

Children should be introduced to silence. Youngsters who are about to receive the Body of Christ for the first time should get ready by setting the world aside for a few days, leaving for a deserted place where they can prepare themselves in silence to encounter God.

Without silence, the Church does not live up to her calling. I fear that the reform of the liturgy, especially in Africa, is often the occasion for noisy, purely human celebrations that are hardly in keeping with the will of the Son of God as expressed during the Last Supper. It is not a matter of rejecting the joy of the faithful, but there is a time for everything. The liturgy is the place, not for human rejoicing, passions, a profusion of discordant words, but for pure adoration.

Today, noise invades so many aspects of people's lives. The Church would make a serious mistake by adding noise to the noise. Love does not need words.

DYSMAS DE LASSUS: My humble experience as a Carthusian leads me to say that the Church must not lose the sense of the sacred. If we abandon the mystery, we lose the Infinite One. As Qoheleth said, there is "a time to keep silence, and a time to speak" (Eccles 3:7). The Church has the burning obligation to bring the mystery of God to mankind. The word that will bring this message must first have penetrated the individual who speaks it so that it becomes totally his. *Lectio divina*, listening to the Word of God, which has always been at the heart of monastic life, is the time of the word, the time of the heart that listens, receives, and allows itself to be impregnated. It is also the time of silence that will meditate at length so as to let the Word penetrate the very depths of our being and to become truly ours. If we move along too quickly, the imprint will remain superficial or will be erased. Carthusians do not have the mission to preach, and therefore I have no experience in that area, but no one can doubt that a word that comes from the heart and has been experienced in depth by the person who brings it will make a deeper impression on the one who listens to it.

In a famous document, the "Ladder of Monks", Guigo II, the twelfth prior of the Grande Chartreuse, illustrated the stages of this penetration. It begins with reading and continues with meditation. The latter leads to the heart-to-heart conversation with God and will blossom into contemplation. When we are face to face with a God who has become man, how can we not remain silent? Reading, study, and reflection, these initial stages finally lead to silence; there, instead of working ourselves, it is important to let the Holy Spirit work in us, to explain the mystery that our intellect cannot understand. The Spirit has the power to capture us to the very depths of our soul by the love that he awakens in us.

The silence of the Church's life, it seems to me, is connected to the mystery and gentleness of the divine voice. In order to hear it, you have to turn your ear because the Holy Spirit does not speak loudly, nor do Jesus and his Father. When the Word became man and came to live in Nazareth, for thirty years the Nazarenes saw nothing! It takes time and silence, therefore, to discern the voices of heaven, which are discreet and infinitely respectful.

ROBERT SARAH: Mystery is the Infinite who comes to encounter the finite. When we look at the life of Jesus, his discretion and silence are striking. The Church must follow the message and the manner of Jesus. She must give witness by her life and be sober in her words.

If we only brood over our own thoughts, we distance ourselves from the mystery; the Church runs the risk of being founded no longer on a faith but on changing, relative opinions.

The great saints hardly spoke, and yet they are the best messengers of the Church. When the martyrs were attacked, they did not defend themselves, they kept quiet. They now live a life hidden with Christ in God (cf. Col 3:3). Success, praises, persecutions, or death have no importance. Along these lines, Saint Bruno is a perfect example.

Of course, when the barbarians doggedly persist and use the most refined methods to destroy morality, the family, and the mystery, it is necessary to speak forcefully. As children of God, we must know how to choose the right time, the right words, and the weapons of faith and charity. Those who fight the good fight hate vulgarity and useless chattering. A few sentences are enough to tell the truth. Today the crisis of the modern world, with its sinister repercussions on the Church and her hierarchical leaders, does not prevent Christian life from developing or the faith from being consolidated, strengthened, and propagated. The Church continues to evangelize the peoples despite the powers that strive ever more perversely, with so many financial and technological means at their disposal, to demolish religion, morality, the family, marriage, and fundamental human, spiritual, and ethical values. The Church today is going through unprecedented exterior and interior trials. Something like an earthquake is seeking to demolish her doctrinal foundations and her centuries-old moral teaching.

Mankind itself has always imposed demanding ethical rules, pro-hibitions, and essential laws to prevent man from giving in to momentary impulses and to help him to ensure a greater quality of personal and social life. This is the result of efforts that are necessarily long and often demanding and difficult. The Church is being shaken violently by a general apostasy in formerly Christian countries. She is suffering from the infidelity of traitors who abandon and prostitute her. But this universal weakening, which affects the world, the faith, and believers, must be a special opportunity for the Church to take a stand for God (cf. Mt 10:32–33) with clarity, vigor, and determi-nation by proclaiming the Gospel of Jesus Christ. It is necessary to reinforce in every faithful Christian the love of God; it is necessary to revive staunch adherence to the Catholic faith, it is necessary to proclaim the consistency of the Church at the heart of a world that is in complete upheaval and threatened with collapse.

NICOLAS DIAT: *What is the connection between silence and humility?*

DYSMAS DE LASSUS: As soon as we talk about God, mystery is every-where. Man himself is a mystery because he is in the image of God. Creation is a mystery since God is all and nothing can exist apart from him. We can affirm the creation of the world by God, according to the first verse of the Bible, but we cannot explain it.

Facing the mystery, facing what is too large and too beautiful for us to be able to grasp, we can remain in an astonished silence. In his book *Face à Dieu: La prière selon un chartreux* [Facing God: Prayer according to a Carthusian], Augustin Guillerand correctly wrote: "In order to find humility, it is better to look at him than to look at oneself."

I can find no more fitting answer to your question.

ROBERT SARAH: In the presence of God, we can only be humble and silent. He is, in fact, the great mystery on which to meditate. In the presence of God, we are like well-diggers. We dig ceaselessly, trying to find water. As we go down toward the divine source, we will find the wellsprings from which flow our dignity and our own mystery. But we will be able to penetrate the secret of our con-sciences only in a state of radical perfection. Saint Augustine had this magnificent experience. Maurice Zundel quotes Augustine as saying: "We ourselves are outside, strangers to ourselves, and we can reach ourselves only in total openness to God." We must deepen our quest for silence by following the paths of humility. Thus Saint Peter exhorts us, saying: "Clothe yourselves, all of you, with humility toward one another, for God opposes the proud but gives grace to the humble. Humble yourselves therefore under the mighty hand of God" (1 Pet 5:5–6).

The humility of Carthusians shows that silence is a school of meekness, wisdom, and self-surrender. They remain humble and confident in God's hands. The sons of Saint Bruno are an exceptional model. "If you seek [wisdom] like silver, and search for it as for hidden treasures" (Prov 2:4), then clothe yourself in humility and silence, like the well-digger who climbs down into his well and like the miners who descend into the mine in work clothes. We find ourselves only by returning humbly to the *humus*, the soil of our origins. This is also the meaning of our profound prostration when, casting down to earth the crowns of our pride and pretentions, we fall on our knees before the throne of the Lamb to adore him (Rev 4:1–11; 5:6–14; 7:9–17; 8:1–5; 11:15–18; 14:1–5; 19:1–4).

NICOLAS DIAT: What place can silence have in the liturgy?

DYSMAS DE LASSUS: Adoration must be the heart of the liturgy. This attitude of the heart is scarcely expressed by words, but rather by our posture, gestures, or silence. A genuflection speaks for itself if it is well done. If you take away all the signs that express adoration, the attitude itself will disappear, and then the sense of the sacred. Kneeling down, kissing the ground, as we do in the charterhouse at the Angelus, bringing the chalice at the offertory with the humeral veil—which is a distinctive characteristic of our liturgy—all these gestures bear within themselves their meaning.

In our monasteries we have a beautiful sign in prostration. Before Mass, the priest prostrates himself in the sanctuary; he stretches out on the ground, slightly bent over his elbows. After the consecration, the whole community does the same. Finally, during the thanksgiving, which lasts for several minutes in silence, we are free to prostrate ourselves or to remain seated. Carthusians thus show the complete submission of their beings in the presence of the holy mysteries.

Prostration is worth all the rhetoric in the world to express faith in the mystery of the Real Presence of Jesus, the Eternal Word, in the Eucharist.

ROBERT SARAH: If I may say so, it seems to me to be fundamentally important for the Carthusians to keep this magnificent gesture of submission to God and of docility, humility, and silent adoration. The liturgy today exhibits a sort of secularization that aims to ban the liturgical sign par excellence: silence. Some seek to eliminate by all possible means the gestures of prostration or genuflection before the divine Majesty; nevertheless, these are Christian gestures of adoration, of holy fear of God, of veneration and respectful love. These are the gestures of the heavenly liturgy: "And all the angels stood round the throne and round the elders and the four living creatures, and they fell on their faces before the throne and worshiped God" (Rev 7:11); "Let us go to his dwelling place; let us worship at his footstool!" (Ps 132:7); "O come, let us worship and bow down, let us kneel before the LORD, our Maker! For he is our God" (Ps 95:6–7).

I find it regrettable that some bishops' conferences or priests decide, for reasons of inculturation, to eliminate these heavenly gestures so as to replace them with courteous gestures or cultural habits. Why do we always resist God's intentions and ways so as to cling to our customs?

I am an African. Allow me to say it clearly: the liturgy is not the place to promote my culture. Rather, it is the place where my culture is baptized, where my culture is raised to the height of the divine. Through the Church's liturgy (which the missionaries brought everywhere in the world), God speaks to us, he changes us and grants us a share in his divine life. When someone becomes a Christian, when someone returns to full communion with the Catholic Church, he receives something more, something that changes him. Certainly, the cultures and the new Christians bring riches into the Church: the liturgy of the Ordinariates for Anglicans who are now in full communion with the Catholic Church is a fine example of this. But they bring these riches with humility, and the Church, in her maternal wisdom, utilizes them if she deems it appropriate.

But it seems to me timely to specify what we mean by inculturation. If we really understand the meaning of the term "knowledge" as penetration of the Mystery of Jesus Christ, we then possess the key to inculturation, which is not to be presented as a quest or a claim for the legitimacy of an Africanization or Latin-Americanization or Asianization of Christianity instead of a Westernization. Inculturation is not the canonization of a local culture or the decision to settle in that culture at the risk of absolutizing it. Inculturation is an epiphany of the Lord, who breaks into the most intimate recesses of our being. And this irruption of the Lord into a life causes in man a destabilization that wrenches him away from what is familiar with a view to journeying according to new landmarks that create a new culture that bears Good News for man and his dignity as a child of God. When the Gospel enters a life, it destabilizes it and transforms it. It gives it a new orientation, new moral and ethical points of reference. It turns the person's heart toward God and toward neighbor to love and serve them absolutely, without selfish calculation. When Jesus comes into a life, he transfigures it, divinizes it by the blazing light of his face, just as Saint Paul was transfigured on the road to Damascus (cf. Acts 9:5–6). Inculturation is truly a silent kenosis, a kind of destitution, an obedient, humble submission to the will of the Father and to the Holy Christian mysteries that we celebrate through Jesus Christ, with him and in him.

Indeed, just as through the Incarnation the Word of God became just like men, except for sin (cf. Heb 4:15), so too the Gospel takes up all human and cultural values, but refuses to take shape in the structures of sin. This means that the more abundant individual and collective sin is in a human or an ecclesial community, the less room there is in it for inculturation. Conversely, the more a Christian community shines with sanctity and radiates Gospel values, the more opportunities it has to inculturate the Christian message successfully. The inculturation of the faith is therefore a challenge to holiness. It allows us to determine the degree of sanctity and the level of the penetration of the Gospel and of faith in Jesus Christ in a Christian community. Inculturation is therefore not a type of religious folklore.

It is not essentially accomplished by the utilization of local languages, Latin American instruments and music, African dances or African or Asian rites and symbols in the liturgy and the sacraments. Inculturation is God descending and entering into the life, the moral conduct, the cultures and customs of men so as to free them from sin and to introduce them into the Trinitarian life. Certainly the faith needs a culture in order to be communicated. That is why Saint John Paul II affirmed that a faith that does not become a culture is a dying faith. "Properly applied, inculturation must be guided by two principles: compatibility with the Gospel and communion with the universal Church" (encyclical *Redemptoris missio*, December 7, 1990, no. 54).

DYSMAS DE LASSUS: We have preserved silence during the Eucharistic Prayer because it was in keeping with our life. Silence is a liturgical sign. Independently of Carthusian life, the consecration is the great moment of mystery, and the Roman Missal emphasizes this by asking that the faithful kneel at this precise moment. In a charterhouse, the long silence that surrounds the consecration invites us to enter into adoration, the strongest expression of which will be prostration. Silence is for us the best way of touching the ineffable.

I agree with Your Eminence when you say that mystery expresses the center of human life and of the Christian faith: the encounter of the Infinite and the finite that alone can fill our heart and fascinates our mind. "See what love the Father has given us, that we should be called children of God; and so we are" (1 Jn 3:1). In these words, "and so we are", there is an astonishment that will never end.

I cannot help thinking that this astonishment has faded terribly. Several times I have asked retreatants this question: Have you ever heard about the four last things and eternal life discussed in a homily? The answer was always: "Never." If I had added, "What about divine filiation?" I probably would have received the same answer. Why do preachers never speak about the object of our hope? Moreover, if we look more closely, we understand that this hope is inscribed on the heart of every person: hope for a boundless love that will never end.

May the Church ceaselessly recall, therefore, the importance of the mystery of divine filiation. May priests not hesitate to speak about the last things and about eternal life. Then adoration will appear to modern man, not as a humiliation, but as the natural attitude of someone who discovers that he has received everything. Along with adoration, silence will regain its natural place.

NICOLAS DIAT: How would you characterize what I could call the illnesses that come from noise? To what sort of problem does an excess of noise lead?

DYSMAS DE LASSUS: My experience of the charterhouse necessarily influences the way in which I will respond to your question. Since I am rarely exposed to outside noise, particularly in the city, and possess neither mobile phone nor television nor radio—the latter two have always been excluded from our monasteries—my comments will be a bit outdated.

If there is an illness that comes from noise, we would have to call it the suffocation syndrome. I notice it through the experience of candidates who come on retreat. Memories, desires, hurts, and fears of which they are unaware and that lie at the bottom of their souls resurface. In their everyday routine, the constant influx of news, meetings, and various activities have ceaselessly covered up these voices in the depths of their being and allowed them no opportunity to reemerge into consciousness. Silence and solitude reveal them. Since the discovery is not always pleasant, and the one concerned is rather at a loss, he tries to keep them outside the field of consciousness by maintaining the permanent noise that prevents them from becoming manifest.

In this area, modern man has never had to confront so many and such strong temptations.

The proliferation of information on demand, of sounds and images in the last century or so is stupefying. Man's sonic and visual landscape no longer has anything in common with that of our grandparents. I imagine that it must take a certain spiritual fortitude to protect oneself from this invasion, not by a wholesale rejection, but by a proper asceticism. Solzhenitsyn rightly remarked that although there is a right to information, there is also a right not to be informed.

As Prior of the Grande Chartreuse, I am responsible for transmitting to the community important news concerning the life of the Church, of France, and of the world, and therefore I must read the newspaper. How many interesting but useless things, and what a risk of letting them occupy the imagination and provide it with weapons against interior silence! A sort of triage becomes necessary, especially since journalists emphasize above all the exceptional events. They talk about an airplane that crashed; no one will write an article saying that all the airplanes landed today without incident or that mothers of families are caring for their children. And yet, is that less important?

One final aspect deserves to be emphasized: I am not responsible for the war in Syria, and I have nothing to contribute to resolve that tragedy. In contrast, I am responsible for my neighbor down the hall if I learn that he is sick or alone. But because the first tragedy is bigger than the second, there is a danger that it will obscure my view of it.

The temptations have multiplied; discernment and renunciation have become more necessary than ever. We have chosen to dedicate our life to the search for God in silence and solitude. Both things must be defended by clear choices, otherwise soon not much of either will be left. Our vocation is very uncommon, but does not every person need a bit of silence and solitude if he wants to be able to stay in contact with his heart? We have a cloister and a Rule that protect us. Someone who lives in the world must find his own cloister and his own rule; this is not something obvious!

Finally, I wonder whether the voice that the modern world seeks to stifle with incessant noise and movement might not be the one that tells us: "Remember that you are dust and that you will return to dust." It is a well-known fact that our society characteristically ignores death. It is understandable: Without God, without eternal life, without Christ, and without redemption, how can anyone bear the thought of death? Let us eat and drink because tomorrow we will die. The memory of our precarious state is only too insistent; therefore we seek to silence it.

What are the remedies for illnesses that come from noise? They follow from what I just said. The major remedy, as always, will be the discovery of God's love, of his call to eternal life, of Christ's victory over death, which makes the latter a friend, the door that opens onto Life. And the Divine Mercy that heals the fear of the evil that we find in ourselves. In a word: hope.

ROBERT SARAH: For someone who is far from God, silence is a difficult confrontation with his own self and with the rather dismal realities that are at the bottom of our soul. Hence, man enters a mentality that resembles a denial of reality. He gets drunk on all sorts of noises so as to forget who he is. Postmodern man seeks to anesthetize his own atheism.

Noises are screens that betray a fear of the divine, a fear of real life and of death. But "what man can live and never see death? Who can deliver his soul from the power of Sheol?" (Ps 89:48). The Western world ends up disguising death so as to make it acceptable and joyful. The moment of demise becomes a noisy moment in which true silence is lost in weak, useless words expressing compassion.

This anxious response to something that makes no noise is a telling trait of fluid societies that have developed neurotic fears of silence.

A Christian cannot fear silence because he is never alone. He is with God. He is in God. He is for God. In the silence, God gives me his eyes so as to contemplate him better. Christian hope is the foundation of the true silent search of the believer. Silence is not frightening; on the contrary, it is the assurance of meeting God.

The children of God are called to live eternally with the Father. Through silence they must become accustomed to being with God. Here below, the silent prayer of the citizens of the earth is an apprenticeship in what the citizens of heaven will experience eternally. In the silence of the church in Ars, the peasant was already participating in the heavenly liturgy: "I look at him, and he looks at me!" Seated silently at the feet of Jesus, we learn to pray without ceasing and to become fearless witnesses to the Gospel.

We must beware of the racket of contemporary life. This noise imposed on us is an insidious danger for the soul. The difficulties encountered today in finding silence are more formidable than ever. This is a diabolical situation. But Christ himself had to tear himself away from the crowd so as to go off into the desert. In those immense spaces, he experienced the most intimate, the most sublime face-to-face conversations!

This reminds me of the strong words of Saint John Paul II in his encyclical *Redemptoris missio*:

> The renewed impulse to the mission *ad gentes* demands holy missionaries. It is not enough to update pastoral techniques, organize and coordinate ecclesial resources, or delve more deeply into the biblical and theological foundations of faith. What is needed is the encouragement of a new "ardor for holiness" among missionaries and throughout the

Christian community, especially among those who work most closely with missionaries.

John Paul II concluded:

The missionary must be a "contemplative in action".... My contact with representatives of the non-Christian spiritual traditions, particularly those of Asia, has confirmed me in the view that the future of mission depends to a great extent on contemplation. Unless the missionary is a contemplative he cannot proclaim Christ in a credible way. He is a witness to the experience of God, and must be able to say with the apostles: "that which we have looked upon ... concerning the word of life, ... we proclaim also to you" (1 Jn 1:1–3).

Today the Church has one central mission. It consists of offering silence to the priests and to the faithful. The world rejects solitude with God repeatedly and violently. Well, then, let the world keep quiet, and let silence return ...

NICOLAS DIAT: *What might be the connection between silence and continual prayer?*

DYSMAS DE LASSUS: The expression "continual prayer" should not mislead us: it does mean saying prayers without stopping. Actually, this expression refers to a way of being with God ceaselessly, of letting him dwell within us, of consciously experiencing this *indwelling*. A woman who was acquainted with this experience testifies: "My superficial self 'sees' my interior self in adoration. And although the 'surface' wants to get involved and join in the deep adoration through a spoken prayer, that stops everything. I can join in with this interior self only through silence, 'looking' at the adoration in me and keeping quiet" (*Cahiers sur l'oraison*, no. 211, January–February 1987). This woman lives in the world, which means that this experience is not reserved to consecrated religious.

Can we consider silence to be a way to continual prayer, or, rather, continual prayer to be a way to silence? Framed in this way, the question would be too simplistic, because both are true. I would prefer to combine two aspects that I have already mentioned: the more one enters into the mystery, the more one enters into silence. Similarly, the more one enters into intimacy with a person, the more room is taken up by silence and a simple look. Continual prayer contains both: a habitual intimacy with God that makes his mystery more fascinating than ever. The monk then receives what Saint Bruno mentioned: "A peace that the world does not know and joy in the Holy Spirit". The joy of intimate union does not need a lot of words. Silence does not demand more efforts at this stage; rather, it would take an effort to emerge from it.

Such a state is not habitual. A Carthusian brother who has experienced continual prayer told me: "We are not the master." This means that the choice belongs to the interior guest, to the Holy Spirit, who draws the soul into a world where you can hardly do anything but keep quiet, as when you are seized by an intense emotion. In everyday life, prayer will take the form mentioned a moment ago: the ordinary activity continues, but something inside remains silently united to the one whom we love and who loves us, a loving presence that is enough to fill the heart. When we no longer live "with" but rather one in the other, since the person praying is not in control of the work that God is doing in him, he simply unites himself to this mystery without needing to know the contours of it. He does not ask for explanations. "I am my beloved's and my beloved is mine", says the Song of Songs (6:3).

ROBERT SARAH: If our heart succeeds in escaping from the world and its seductions so as to be with the Lord, we will have the grace of silence. All the most degrading or most vulgar noises will never be able to cover up a soul that has chosen Christ. A person who truly loves God can be in a continual relationship with the Transcendent. A person who lives in silence with God will be able to help draw souls toward the contemplation of the Creator of the world.

Saint Augustine was strongly attracted by monastic life. In *De moribus ecclesiae catholicae* [*On the Morals of the Catholic Church*], he writes:

> Who can but admire and commend those who, slighting and discarding the pleasures of this world, living together in a most chaste and holy society, unite in passing their time in prayers, in readings, in discussions, without any swelling of pride, or noise of contention, or sullenness of envy; but quiet, modest, peaceful, their life is one of perfect harmony and devotion to God, an offering most acceptable to

Him from whom the power to do those things is obtained? No one possesses anything of his own; no one is a burden to another. They work with their hands in such occupations as may feed their bodies without distracting their minds from God.

Plotinus himself had clearly seen the conditions essential for contemplation. So he was able to reflect in the *Enneads* that "in order to be elevated to contemplate the Universal Soul, the soul must be worthy by its nobility, free of error and detached from the things that bewitch common souls; it must be immersed in quietude. Let not only the agitation of the enveloping body and the turmoil of the sensations be stilled, but all that lies around: earth at peace, and sea at peace, and air and the very heavens."

DYSMAS DE LASSUS: Let everything be quiet so that God can make himself heard. And as you like to say, he makes himself heard in silence. Is this the reason why monks have always loved nocturnal prayer? Saint Antony spent whole nights in prayer. The night office is a central time in Carthusian life that we will never abandon.

In the middle of sleep, this time is completely devoted to prayer, which gives it a special dimension: the night office is a gratuitous gift for God alone. As watchers in the night, we offer our poverty, which we know well, and at the same time the poverty of the world. These beautiful words from our *Statutes* make more sense than ever: "Apart from all, to all we are united, so that it is in the name of all that we stand before the living God" (*Statues*, chapter 34.2). I have always loved this statement from the chapter entitled "The Function of Our Order in the Life of the Church". While the world sleeps, we choose to rise to unite our praise and intercession to Christ's, so that the prayer of mankind, this vital bond between heaven and earth, may not cease. Then, when we go to bed, others, Benedictines or Cistercians, will take up the relay.

NICOLAS DIAT: *The night office is the soul of the Carthusian Order, is it not? The prayer that runs through its entire history?*

DYSMAS DE LASSUS: I hesitate to answer yes, in the sense that the Eucharist, through the mystery that is accomplished in it, naturally remains the center of our days. And yet no one doubts that the night office has a very special place in our life. Because of its duration, two to three hours every night; because of this very special moment, between two periods of sleep, nocturnal prayer will always remain an irreplaceable time. Whether we are distracted or recollected, this moment shapes us. It is a prayer of the body as much as of the mind, because of the chant, but also simply because we are there.

Our forefathers insisted so much on nocturnal prayer that until the French Revolution they used to chant from memory the whole psalmody of the night office in complete darkness. This has a particular dynamic. We are together, and we are alone. The equilibrium of our life, made up of solitude and communal life, is brought about at the heart of our prayer, in a profound unity; singing in choir is a collective work in which we need one another. But at night, the invisible choir leaves us alone in an atmosphere of intimacy that facilitates the heart-to-heart conversation with God. His mystery seems closer and more incomprehensible.

We unite our prayer with Christ's according to the beautiful remark of Saint Augustine: "When we speak to God in prayer ..., [Christ] prays for us, as our Priest; He prays in us, as our Head.... Let us therefore recognize in Him our words, and His words in us" (*In Ps 85*, PL 37, 1081). Only the light of Christ burns intensely in the church.

The Eucharist still has the first place; it unites us to the whole Church. The night office is rather a mark of our particularity, distinguishing us from our brethren who are present at the Divine Office but generally do not sing, praying in silence in the darkest part of the church. The balances that characterize Carthusian life are thus present: solitary life and common work, silent prayer and prayer in choir, lay monks and cloistered monks, and, I must add, monks and nuns.

This is a little-known fact, but almost since the origin, the Carthusian vocation has been lived out by men and by women. The Carthusian nuns were born only fifty years after the death of Saint Bruno, and they are still very much alive today, discreet and self-effacing, but no less essential to the fullness of the charism of Saint Bruno. They, too, pray as we do in the middle of the night.

The soul of the order is the thirst for God. We bear within us the expectation of mankind that, without knowing it, thirsts for God when it aspires to peace, justice, and love.

We would like to respond to God, who desires so much a loving relationship with men. "I thirst", Jesus said on the Cross.

In the silence of the night, that of the cell and the one in the hearts of Carthusians, we present to him the unquenchable thirst of men, and to mankind we present the thirst of God, thus participating in the work of Jesus in whom these two urges met, forever.

This has been, for two millennia, the great and humble ambition of the Grande Chartreuse and of all the children of Saint Bruno.

CONCLUSION

How does one conclude a discourse on God and silence? I must humbly acknowledge that I have been stammering in the presence of a great mystery. Who can really speak about silence, and above all about God, in an adequate way? It is a steep, smooth rock. It is impossible for us to climb it. It slips through our hands, and our intellect, in focusing on it, is overcome by vertigo. Indeed, "Who shall ascend the hill of the LORD? And who shall stand in his holy place? He who has clean hands and a pure heart, who does not lift up his soul to what is false" (Ps 24:3–4). God is incomprehensible, inaccessible, invisible. How can we dare to speak about a person whom we have not met or touched when our hearts are impure?

Before the mystery of God, I experience the same feelings as Saint Gregory of Nyssa when he writes in his Homily on the Beatitudes:

> Consider the feelings of a man who looks down into the depths of the sea from the top of a mountain. This is similar what my mind experiences, when from the heights of the Word of the Lord, as from a mountaintop, it peers into unfathomable depths of the divine counsels. Along the seacoast, you may often see mountains facing the sea ... with a sheer drop from top to bottom. At the top a projection forms a ledge overhanging the depths below.... My soul grows dizzy when it hears the great voice of the Lord saying: *Blessed are the clean of heart, for they shall see God.* The vision of God is offered to those who have purified their hearts. Yet, *no man has seen God at any time.* These are the words of the great Saint John and they are confirmed by Saint Paul's lofty thought, in the words: God is *he whom no one has seen or can see.*

Nevertheless, we can attempt to speak about God based on our own experience of silence. For God drapes himself in silence and reveals himself in the interior silence of our heart.

In this book I have tried to show that silence is one of the chief means that enable us to enter into the spirit of prayer; silence disposes us to establish vital, ongoing relations with God. It is difficult to find a pious person who, at the same time, talks a lot. On the contrary, those who possess the spirit of prayer love silence.

Since time immemorial, silence has been considered the rampart of innocence, the shield against temptations, and the fertile source of recollection. Silence fosters prayer because it awakens good thoughts in our heart. According to Saint Bernard, it enables the soul to think better about God and about the realities of heaven. For this simple reason, all the saints have ardently loved silence.

God's first language is silence. In her book, *In the Heart of the World*, Saint Teresa of Calcutta declares that:

> We need to find God, and he cannot be found in noises and restlessness. God is the friend of silence.... The more we receive in silent prayer, the more we can give in active life. We need silence to be able to touch souls. The essential thing is not what we say, but what God says to us and through us. Jesus is always waiting for us in silence. In this silence he listens to us and speaks to our souls. And there, we will hear his voice.... In this silence we find a new energy and a real unity. God's energy becomes ours, allowing us to perform things well. There is unity of our thoughts with his thoughts, of our prayers with his prayers, of our actions with his actions, of our life with his life.

In these pages, in answering the fine questions from Nicolas Diat, I hope to have succeeded in showing that silence and prayer are inseparable and mutually fructifying.

Excessive, presumptuous, slanderous, and immoderate chatter often has disastrous consequences. Silence fosters recollection; it is always compromised by facile words and demagoguery. A person can recollect himself, but if he is not capable of holding his tongue, his meditation will not help him to enter into the mystery of God or to prostrate himself silently at the foot of his throne.

If you open the door of a furnace, the heat will escape from it. "Beware of gossip," says Saint Dorotheus, "because it causes pious thoughts and meditation on God to flee." It is certain that a person who speaks incessantly to creatures will have difficulty speaking with God, and, for his part, God will speak little to him. Thus says the

Lord: "I will ... bring her into the wilderness, and speak tenderly to her" (Hos 2:14). The Book of Proverbs says: "When words are many, transgression is not lacking, but he who restrains his lips is prudent" (Prov 10:19). Saint James is unequivocal: "The tongue is an unrighteous world" (Jas 3:6).

"Interior noise makes it impossible to welcome anyone or anything", Pope Francis recalls wisely and authoritatively in the Apostolic Constitution *Vultum Dei quaerere* [On Women's Contemplative Life].

Yes, a multitude of sins are due to chattering or listening complacently to the chatter of others. How many souls will be lost on the day of the Last Judgment because they did not keep watch over their tongue? The Psalmist says that the gossip wanders without a guide (cf. Ps 140), and that is why he goes down a thousand and one paths without hope of return. "He who guards his mouth preserves his life; he who opens wide his lips comes to ruin" (Prov 13:3). And Saint James writes: "If any one makes no mistakes in what he says he is a perfect man" (Jas 3:2). Someone who keeps silence for the love of God will take to meditation, spiritual reading, and prayer before the Blessed Sacrament. Saint Mary Magdalene de Pazzi thinks that someone who does not love silence cannot appreciate the things of God; very quickly he will throw himself into the great furnace of the pleasures of the world.

The virtue of silence does not mean that we must never speak. It invites us to remain mute when there are no good reasons to speak up. Ecclesiastes says: "There is ... a time to keep silence, and a time to speak" (Eccles 3:7). Referring to these words, Saint Gregory of Nyssa remarks: "The time to keep silence is mentioned first, because by silence we learn the art of speaking well." When, therefore, should a Christian who desires to become holy be silent, and when should he speak? He should be silent when it is not necessary to speak, and he should speak when necessity or charity requires it. Saint Chrysostom gives the following rule: "Speak only when it is more useful to speak than to be silent."

Saint Arsenius acknowledges that he often regretted having spoken, but never regretted having kept silence. Saint Ephrem says: "Speak much with God but little with men."

I encourage everybody not to forget these few bits of advice. If, in your presence, someone uses inappropriate, sinful language, leave that gathering, if possible. If circumstances oblige you to stay, at least lower your eyes and remain silent or seek to direct the conversation toward another subject. That way your silence becomes a protest against sickening chatter. When you are obliged to speak, weigh well what you intend to say. "Make balances and scales for your words", says the Book of Sirach (28:25). As for Saint Francis de Sales, he colorfully remarks: "In order to avoid faults in speech, we should have our lips buttoned, so that while unbuttoning them we may think of what we are going to say."

It is time to revolt against the dictatorship of noise that seeks to break our hearts and our intellects. A noisy society is like sorry-looking cardboard stage scenery, a world without substance, an immature flight. A noisy Church would become vain, unfaithful, and dangerous.

In *Vultum Dei quaerere*, Pope Francis reflects that we must seek "liberation from 'worldliness'. Asceticism fosters a life in accordance with the interior logic of the Gospel, which is that of gift, especially the gift of self as the natural response to the first and only love of your life." These forceful words of the pontiff resound like a warning.

In order to learn to keep silence and to nourish it with the presence of God, we should develop the practice of *lectio divina*, which is a moment of silent listening, contemplation, and profound recollection in the light of the Spirit. *Lectio divina* is a great river that carries all the riches accumulated over the course of Church history by the fervent readers of God's Word.

Lectio divina is never solely our own reading. It feeds on the interpretation of those who have preceded us. The monk, the priest, and the deacon are accustomed to it by the Divine Office itself [in the Office of Readings], which has them listen to the Holy Book and then afterward to the commentaries by the Fathers of the Church. These commentaries are sometimes very different. They can seem austere, disconcerting, and strange to our contemporary mentalities. But if we persevere in *lectio divina* and silent listening to what the Spirit is saying to the Churches, our effort will be rewarded by unheard-of jewels and riches.

Thus Isaac of Stella marvels at the inexhaustible resources of the sacred text. "Wisdom is aptly described as 'a fountain bordered with gardens, a well of running water' (Sg 4:15). It is a fountain because it never ceases to flow; its unfathomable depth makes it a well, a well of running water of ever-fresh bubbling up insights" (Sermon 16, 1). With this same hermeneutical agility, he finds in the text itself authorization for ever new commentaries: "The child of the promise not only kept the wells his Father had, but opened fresh ones (Gn 26:18ff.)" (Sermon 16, 5).

Like a living presence, the Word does not let go of us, and we do not let go of it, either. We commemorate it all day long. Our memory ruminates, and our heart meditates on it. It becomes a source of water that flows continually within us. Is this not what Jesus said to the Samaritan woman: "Whoever drinks of the water that I shall give him will never thirst; the water that I shall give him will become in him a spring of water welling up to eternal life" (Jn 4:14)? The Word read in silence accompanies us, enlightens us, and feeds us. "Oh, how I love your law [O Lord]! It is my meditation all the day" (Ps 119:97). This Word is loved, revisited regularly, sought out, because it is the Presence of the One who loves us eternally.

Through it, he who seeks my soul is there. He meets me, and I meet him. He reveals himself to me, and he reveals me to myself.

Then prayer can be lost in silence; not the silence of the absence of the other or of myself, which occurs also at times, but the silence that comes above and beyond the Word when it has affected us.

In a word, God or nothing. Because God is enough for us.

Robert Cardinal Sarah

AFTERWORD

by Pope Emeritus Benedict XVI

Ever since I first read the Letters of Saint Ignatius of Antioch in the 1950s, one passage from his Letter to the Ephesians has particularly affected me: "It is better to keep silence and be than to talk and not to be. Teaching is an excellent thing, provided the speaker practices what he teaches. Now, there is one Teacher who spoke and it came to pass. And even what He did silently is worthy of the Father. He who has truly made the words of Jesus his own is able also to hear His silence, so that he may be perfect: so that he may act through his speech and be known through his silence" (15, 1f.). What does that mean: to hear Jesus' silence and to know him through his silence? We know from the Gospels that Jesus frequently spent nights alone "on the mountain" in prayer, in conversation with his Father. We know that his speech, his word, comes from silence and could mature only there. So it stands to reason that his word can be correctly understood only if we, too, enter into his silence, if we learn to hear it from his silence.

Certainly, in order to interpret Jesus' words, historical knowledge is necessary, which teaches us to understand the time and the language at that time. But that alone is not enough if we are really to comprehend the Lord's message in depth. Anyone today who reads the ever-thicker commentaries on the Gospels remains disappointed in the end. He learns a lot that is useful about those days and a lot of hypotheses that ultimately contribute nothing at all to an understanding of the text. In the end you feel that in all the excess of words, something essential is lacking: entrance into Jesus' silence, from which his word is born. If we cannot enter into this silence, we will always hear the word only on its surface and thus not really understand it.

As I was reading the new book by Robert Cardinal Sarah, all these thoughts went through my soul again. Sarah teaches us silence—being silent with Jesus, true inner stillness, and in just this way he helps us to grasp the word of the Lord anew. Of course he speaks hardly at all about himself, but now and then he does give us a glimpse into his interior life. In answer to Nicolas Diat's question, "At times in your life have you thought that words were becoming too cumbersome, too heavy, too noisy?", he answers: "In my prayer and in my interior life, I have always felt the need for a deeper, more complete silence.... The days of solitude, silence, and absolute fasting have been a great support. They have been an unprecedented grace, a slow purification, and a personal encounter with ... God.... Days of solitude, silence, and fasting, nourished by the Word of God alone, allow man to base his life on what is essential" (no. 134, p. 76). These lines make visible the source from which the cardinal lives, which gives his word its inner depth. From this vantage point, he can then see the dangers that continually threaten the spiritual life, of priests and bishops also, and thus endanger the Church herself, too, in which it is not uncommon for the word to be replaced by a verbosity that dilutes the greatness of the word. I would like to quote just one sentence that can become an examination of conscience for every bishop: "It can happen that a good, pious priest, once he is raised to the episcopal dignity, quickly falls into mediocrity and a concern for worldly success. Overwhelmed by the weight of the duties that are incumbent on him, worried about his power, his authority, and the material needs of his office, he gradually runs out of steam" (no. 15, pp. 28–29).

Cardinal Sarah is a spiritual teacher, who speaks out of the depths of silence with the Lord, out of his interior union with him, and thus really has something to say to each one of us.

We should be grateful to Pope Francis for appointing such a spiritual teacher as head of the congregation that is responsible for the celebration of the liturgy in the Church. With the liturgy, too, as with the interpretation of Sacred Scripture, it is true that specialized knowledge is necessary. But it is also true of the liturgy that specialization ultimately can talk right past the essential thing unless it is grounded in a deep, interior union with the praying Church, which over and over again learns anew from the Lord himself what adoration is. With Cardinal Sarah, a master of silence and of interior prayer, the liturgy is in good hands.

Vatican City State, Octave of Easter 2017

Benedict XVI, Pope Emeritus

BIBLIOGRAPHY

Accart, Xavier. *Comprendre et vivre la liturgie*. Revised edition. Paris: Plon, 2015.

Ambrose of Milan (Saint). *On the Mysteries*. Translated by H. de Romestin. In vol. 10 of *Nicene and Post-Nicene Fathers*, second series, edited by Philip Schaff and Henry Wace. Peabody, Mass.: Hendrickson, 1994.

Augustine (Saint). *City of God*. Translated by Marcus Dods. In vol. 2 of *Nicene and Post-Nicene Fathers*, first series, edited by Philip Schaff. Peabody, Mass.: Hendrickson, 2009.

———. *Confessions*. Translated by F.J. Sheed. Second edition. Indianapolis and Cambridge: Hackett, 2006.

———. *Expositions on the Book of Psalms*. Translated by A. Cleveland Coxe. In vol. 8 of *Nicene and Post-Nicene Fathers*, first series, edited by Philip Schaff. Peabody, Mass.: Hendrickson, 1995.

———. *Of the Morals of the Catholic Church*. Translated by Richard Stothert. In vol. 4 of *Nicene and Post-Nicene Fathers*, first series, edited by Philip Schaff. Peabody, Mass.: Hendrickson, 1995.

———. *St. Augustine on the Psalms*. Translated and annotated by Scholastica Hebgin and Felicita Corrigan. 2 vols. Westminster, Md.: Newman Press, 1960–1961.

Bernanos, Georges. *Dialogue des carmélites*. Paris: Éditions du Seuil, 1995.

———. *Diary of a Country Priest*. Translated by Pamela Morris. 2nd ed. New York: Carroll & Graf, 2002.

Bérulle, Pierre de. *Œuvres de piété*. Paris: Éditions du Cerf, 1996.

Bux, Nicola. *Benedict XVI's Reform: The Liturgy between Innovation and Tradition*. Translated by Joseph Trabbic. San Francisco: Ignatius Press, 2012.

Camus, Albert. *The Rebel: An Essay on Man in Revolt*. Translated by Anthony Bower. Revised edition. New York: Vintage, 1992.

Comastri, Angelo. *Quand le ciel s'ouvre: Récits de conversions au XXe siècle*. Nouan-le-Fuzelier, Éditions des Béatitudes, 2010.

———, and Saverio Gaetta. *Dio scrive dritto*. Cinisello Balsamo (Milan): San Paolo, 2012.

Cyprian of Carthage (Saint). *The Epistles of Carthage*. In vol. 5 of *Ante-Nicene Fathers*, edited by Alexander Roberts and James Donaldson. Peabody, Mass.: Hendrickson, 1995.

Dagens, Claude. *Saint Grégoire le Grand: Culture et expérience chrétiennes*. Paris: Éditions du Cerf, 2014.

Dillard, Victor. *Au Dieu inconnu*. Paris: Beauchesne, 1938.

Dionysius the Areopagite (Saint). *The Mystical Theology and The Divine Names*. Translated by C. E. Rolt. Mineola, N.Y.: Dover, 2004.

Eckhart, Meister. *The Essential Sermons, Commentaries, Treatises and Defense*. Translated by Edmund Colledge and Bernard McGinn. Revised edition. Classics of Western Spirituality. New York: Paulist Press, 1981.

Green, Julian. *The Green Paradise*. Volume 1 (1900–1916). Translated by Anne and Julian Green. New York and London: Marion Boyars, 1993.

———. *To Leave before Dawn*. Translated by Anne Green. New York: Harcourt, Brace & World, 1967.

Gregory of Nyssa. Homily on the Beatitudes. In *The Liturgy of the Hours*, 3:403–4. New York: Catholic Book Publishing, 1975.

Gregory the Great (Saint). *The Book of Pastoral Rule*. Translated by James Barmby. In vol. 12 of *Nicene and Post-Nicene Fathers*, second series, edited by Philip Schaff and Henry Wace. Peabody, Mass.: Hendrickson, 1995.

———. Letter 1.5. In *The Letters of Gregory the Great: Books 1–4*, translated by John R. C. Martyn. Toronto: Pontifical Institute of Mediaeval Studies, 2004.

Grumett, David. *Teilhard de Chardin: Theology, Humanity, and Cosmos*. Studies in Philosophical Theology 29. Leuven, Paris, and Dudley, Mass.: Peeters, 2005.

Guardini, Romano. *Der Herr*. Würzburg: Werkbund, 1950. Translated by Elinor Castendyk Briefs as *The Lord* (1954; Washington, D.C.: Gateway, 2014).

Guillerand, Augustin. *Face à Dieu: La prière selon un chartreux*. Les Plans-sur-Bex: Éditions Parole et silence, 1999.

———. *Silence cartusien*. Paris: Desclée de Brouwer, 1976.

———. *They Speak by Silences*. Translated from *Silence cartusien* and *Voix cartusienne* by a monk of Parkminster. Leominster, Herefordshire: Gracewing, 2006.

———. *Voix cartusienne*. Les Plans-sur-Bex: Éditions Parole et silence, 2001.

Guitton, Jean. *Paul VI secret*. Paris: Desclée de Brouwer, 1986.

Ignatius of Antioch (Saint). "Ignatius to the Ephesians". In *The Epistles of St. Clement of Rome and St. Ignatius of Antioch*. Translated by James A. Kleist, S.J. Ancient Christian Writers. New York: Paulist Press, 1946.

Ignatius of Loyola (Saint). *The Spiritual Exercises of Saint Ignatius.* Edited by Louis J. Puhl, S.J. Chicago: Loyola Press, 1951.

Irenaeus (Saint). *Against Heresies.* In vol. 1 of *Ante-Nicene Fathers*, edited by Alexander Roberts and James Donaldson. Peabody, Mass.: Hendrickson, 1995.

Isaac of Stella. *Selected Works: A Cistercian Voice from the Twelfth Century.* Aldershot, England, and Burlington, Vt.: Ashgate, 2007.

Isaac the Syrian. *The Ascetical Homilies of Saint Isaac the Syrian.* Revised second edition. Boston, Mass.: Holy Transfiguration Monastery, 2011.

Jankélévitch, Vladimir. *Penser la mort?* Paris: Liana Levi, 2007.

Jérôme (Father). *Écrits monastiques.* Montrouge: Sarment, 2002.

———. *OEuvres spirituelles.* Paris: Ad Solem, 2014.

John Chrysostom (Saint). *Homilies on the Gospel of Saint Matthew.* In vol. 10 of *Nicene and Post-Nicene Fathers*, first series, edited by Philip Schaff. Peabody, Mass.: Hendrickson, 1995.

——— "Sur le cimetière et la Croix". In *Œuvres complètes.* Mouzeuil-Saint-Martin: Bes éditions, 2010.

John of the Cross (Saint). *Maxims and Counsels.* In *The Collected Works of St. John of the Cross*, translated by Kieran Kavanaugh, O.C.D., and Otilio Rodriguez, O.C.D. Washington, D.C.: ICS Publications, Institute of Carmelite Studies, 1979.

———. *The Spiritual Canticle.* In *The Collected Works of St. John of the Cross*, translated by Kieran Kavanaugh, O.C.D., and Otilio Rodriguez, O.C.D. Washington, D.C.: ICS Publications, Institute of Carmelite Studies, 1979.

John Paul II (Saint). Apostolic Letter *Orientale Lumen* (May 2, 1995).

Jonas, Hans. "The Concept of God after Auschwitz". In *Wrestling with God: Jewish Theological Responses during and after the Holocaust*, edited by Steven T. Katz, Shlomo Biderman, and Gershon Greenberg. New York: Oxford University Press, 2007.

Julian of Norwich. *Revelations of Divine Love.* Translated by Elizabeth Spearings. London: Penguin, 1999.

Kierkegaard, Søren. *For Self-Examination.* In vol. 21 of *Kierkegaard's Writings*, edited and translated by Howard V. Hong and Edna H. Hong. Princeton: Princeton Univ. Press, 1990.

La Palma, Luis de. *The Sacred Passion.* Translated by Mary Gottschalk. New York: Scepter, 2004.

Leo the Great. *Letters and Sermons.* Translated by Charles Lett Feltoe. In vol. 12 of *Nicene and Post-Nicene Fathers*, second series, edited by Philip Schaff and Henry Wace. Peabody, Mass.: Hendrickson, 1995.

Marie-Eugène, O.C.D. (Father). *Au souffle de l'Esprit.* Chouzé-sur-Loire: Saint-Léger, 2014.

————. *Je veux voir Dieu*. Toulouse: Éditions du Carmel, 2014. Translated by Sister M. Verda Clare, C.S.C, as *I Want to See God: A Practical Synthesis of Carmelite Spirituality* (1953; Westminster, Md.: Christian Classics, 1978).

Marini, Guido. *La Liturgie: Gloire de Dieu, sanctification de l'homme*. Perpignan: Artège, 2013.

Merton, Thomas. *The Sign of Jonas*. New York: Harcourt, Brace, 1953.

Messori, Vittorio, and Joseph Cardinal Ratzinger. *The Ratzinger Report*. Translated by Salvator Attanasio and Graham Harrison. San Francisco: Ignatius Press, 1985.

Nabert, Nathalie. *La Grande Chartreuse, au-delà du silence*. Grenoble: Glénat, 2002.

Nouwen, Henri J.M. *The Way of the Heart: Connecting with God through Prayer, Wisdom, and Silence*. New York: HarperCollins, 2003.

Pascal, Blaise. *Pensées; The Provincial Letters*. Translated by W.F. Trotter and Thomas McCrie. New York: Modern Library, 1941.

Paul VI. Address at Nazareth, January 6, 1964. In *The Liturgy of the Hours*, 1:426–28. New York: Catholic Book Publishing, 1975.

Plotinus. *Ennéades*. Paris: Éditions des Belles Lettres, 1964. Translated by Stephen Mackenna and B.S. Page as *The Six Enneads* (New York: Pantheon Books, 1969).

Porion, Jean-Baptiste. *Amour et silence*. Paris: Ad Solem, 2010. Translated by a Monk of Parkminster as *The Prayer of Love and Silence* (Leominster, Herefordshire: Gracewing, 2006).

Raguin, Yves. *Paths to Contemplation*. Translated by Paul Barrett. Religious Experience Series, vol. 6. St. Meinrad, Ind.: Abbey Press, 1974.

Rassam, Joseph. *Le Silence comme introduction à la métaphysique*. Toulouse: Éditions universitaires du Sud, 1989.

Ratzinger, Joseph Cardinal. *A New Song for the Lord: Faith in Christ and Liturgy Today*. Translated by Martha M. Matesich. New York: Crossroad, 1997.

————. "The Regensburg Tradition and the Reform of the Liturgy". In *Theology of the Liturgy: The Sacramental Foundation of Christian Existence*. *Collected Works*, vol. 11, edited by Michael J. Miller, translated by John Saward et al. (San Francisco: Ignatius Press, 2014).

————. *The Spirit of the Liturgy*. Translated by John Saward. San Francisco: Ignatius Press, 2000.

Rilke, Rainer Maria. *The Complete French Poems of Rainer Maria Rilke*. Translated by A. Poulin, Jr. New edition. St. Paul, Minn.: Graywolf Press, 2002.

Rueg, Jean Gabriel (de l'Enfant-Jésus). *Le Son du silence au saint désert*. Toulouse: Éditions du Carmel, 2010.

Saint-Thierry, Guillaume de. *Lettre aux frères du Mont-Dieu*. Paris: Éditions du Cerf, 2004.

Samuel (Father). *Qui cherchait Théophane*. Turnhout: Brepols, 1992.

Scheeben, Matthias-Joseph. *Les Mystères du christianisme*. Paris: Desclée de Brouwer, 1947.

Sesboüé, Bernard. *Croire: Invitation à la foi catholique pour les femmes et les hommes du XXIe siècle*. Paris: Droguet et Ardant, 1999.

Tauler, Johannes. *The Sermons and Conferences of John Tauler, of the Order of Preachers*. Translated by Walter Elliott. Washington, D.C.: Apostolic Mission House, 110.

Teresa of Avila (Saint). *The Interior Castle*. In vol. 2 of *The Collected Works of St. Teresa of Avila*, translated by Kieran Kavanaugh, O.C.D., and Otilio Rodriguez, O.C.D. Washington, D.C.: ICS Publications, Institute of Carmelite Studies, 1980.

Teresa of Calcutta (Saint). *In the Heart of the World: Thoughts, Stories & Prayers*. Edited by Becky Benenate. Novato, Calif.: New World Library, 2010.

———. *No Greater Love*. Commemorative edition edited by Becky Benenate and Joseph Durepos. Novato, Calif.: New World Library, 2016.

Thérèse of Lisieux (Saint). *Her Last Conversations*. Translated by John Clarke, O.C.D. Washington, D.C.: ICS Publications, Institute of Carmelite Studies, 1977.

———. Letter from Thérèse to Céline. In *General Correspondence*, vol. 2, 1890–1897, translated by John Clarke, O.C.D. Washington, D.C.: Institute of Carmelilte Studies, 1988.

———. *Story of a Soul: The Autobiography of Saint Thérèse of Lisieux*. Translated by John Clarke, O.C.D. Third edition. Washington, D.C.: ICS Publications, 1996.

Thomas à Kempis. *The Imitation of Christ*. Translated by Ronald Knox and Michael Oakley. New York: Sheed & Ward, 1959.

Thomas Aquinas (Saint). *Commentary on the Gospel of St. John*. Translated by Fabian R. Larcher, O.P. Albany, N.Y.: Magi Books, 1998.

Valéry, Paul. *Tel quel*. Paris: Gallimard, 1996.

The Wound of Love: A Carthusian Miscellany. 1994; Leominster, Herefordshire: Gracewing, 2006.

Zundel, Maurice. *Un autre regard sur l'homme*. Montrouge: Éditions du Jubilé, 2006.

———. *L'Humble Présence*. Montrouge: Sarment, 2008.

———. *Ton visage, mon Lumière*. Paris: Mame, 2011.